The chefs of Belgium

The chefs of Belgium

Willem Asaert &
Marc Declercq

photography
Kris Vlegels &
Andrew Verschetze

Trendsetters in Belgian cuisine

 | LANNOO

CONTENTS

HERE THEY ARE: THE MOST INFLUENTIAL BELGIAN CHEFS OF THE PRESENT DAY!

In this book you will make the acquaintance of more than thirty chefs who together give shape and form to contemporary cuisine in Belgium. Through a series of open-hearted interviews, recipes and question-and-answer lists, we let them have their say about Belgian cooking at the start of the 21st century. You will learn about their ideas and you will learn about their dishes. Even better, you can try them out for yourself!

It is remarkable just how many exceptionally good chefs are currently at work in Belgium. This is unique in the world. Not even France comes anywhere close. As a result, the selection of the chefs for inclusion in this book was no easy matter. The culinary offerings in Belgium are immensely rich and varied. Our country has exponents of every different type of cuisine, often preparing food to the very highest standard. For this reason, we had to set clearly defined limits to our self-imposed culinary 'mission'. For example, because we wanted to focus the Franco-Belgian culinary tradition, we have not included chefs schooled in the Italian and Japanese traditions. This has resulted in a more modest – but nonetheless fascinating – assessment of the current state of affairs in the world of Belgian cooking.

In making our choice, we have also focused on chefs who have made a name for themselves since 1990. The majority are active as restaurant chefs, but we have also found room for chefs who can legitimately be regarded as trendsetting professionals outside the classic culinary framework. To set our choice in a broader perspective, we also spoke to two 'retired' chefs: Pierre Wynants and Roger Souvereyns. They can quite rightly be seen as the 'godfathers' of modern Belgian cooking. Their extraordinary natural talent and exceptional powers of taste have influenced a whole generation of modern chefs. Both men are now at the end of their seventies, but both are still very active. Even more than their words, their culinary inspired activities demonstrate their continuing passion for 'our cuisine'. This is a passion that they share with the younger chefs who have been included in The Chefs of Belgium. In this sense, our book also wishes to pay tribute to their incontestable cultural and culinary legacy.

A land of milk and honey

Whoever, like us, has the good fortune to visit the many excellent restaurants of our country on an almost daily basis, is in the privileged position of being able to describe the culinary skills of the leading Belgian chefs of the modern era. Or to put it another way, we know what we are talking about! Moreover, our regular trips abroad provide us with a framework within which we can make culinary comparisons. In addition, the comments which we pick up from our European colleagues about Belgian cooking further sharpen our focus. During their visits to our country, they are often pleasantly surprised by things that we take for granted. For example, many of them are full of praise for the high number of quality-driven restaurants, brasseries and eating houses which they find in such a small geographical area. They are equally impressed – if not more so – by the huge availability of products of the very highest quality. What we regard as normal, they regard as exceptional.

This great culinary richness is not easy to explain. Of course, there is the wide range of available ingredients, stimulated by a mild climate with rapidly changing seasons. We also have a number of products which are unique to our cultural tradition, such as grey shrimps, hop shoots and endives. Perhaps just as importantly, Belgium is located at a geographical and cultural crossroads, where new products and new ideas from all around the world come together and influence each other. At the same time our country also has its own rich gastronomic history, with numerous dishes dating back to medieval times which are still popular today. Contemporary chefs are always happy to make use of these traditional dishes, and to give them a new twist which helps to strengthen their identity. Last but not least, there is the essentially 'Burgundian' nature of the Belgian way of life. The Belgians are bon-vivants, who simply enjoy eating and drinking. And in recent decades, economic progress has meant that more people have more money to spend on eating out – and that is precisely what they do. It is this golden triangle – talented chefs, fresh and varied products and an enthusiastic and relatively wealthy public – that forms the indispensable basis for a specific and broadly based restaurant culture. A culture that, when viewed from a European perspective, sadly forms the exception rather than the rule.

Trendsetters with an identity of their own

The chefs and restaurants mentioned in our book reflect this unique culture. Each and every one of them is a trendsetter in his own right, with an exceptional passion and talent for creating fine food. They work with quality products from their own region and, in a growing number of cases, even from their own gardens. And what they cannot find at home, they buy from the very best suppliers abroad: not only in neighbouring countries, but sometimes from the other side of the world. This wide range of products and the interest for new and defining flavours from around the globe is largely determined by the curiosity of the end user. The thirst of the Belgian consumer for new tastes, new textures and new experiences has helped in no small measure to shape the identity of these chefs.

This desire for knowledge and innovation also means that the Belgian chefs not only keep up to date with the most recent cooking techniques, but also help to further develop and improve those techniques. They have a varied arsenal of equipment on which they can draw to create intensely flavoured, light, textured and visually attractive dishes. Their cuisine tastes, smells, feels and looks contemporary. Their respect for the quality and qualities of the product forms the basis for their cooking philosophy; as does their desire to fashion food which gives a clear culinary added value through the use of tastes, aromas and texture that give their creations greater relief and a more personal profile. In the very best instances, these master craftsmen – for that is what they are – not only appeal to all five of our senses, but seek to take matters a stage further. They aim to provide us with nothing less than a total experience, full of emotions and memories. In so doing, these Chefs of Belgium go far beyond their role as mere culinary trendsetters, and instead become something much more unique and distinctive. So read this book; get to know the most influential Belgian chefs of the present day. You will be hearing about them for many years to come.

Willem Asaert & Marc Declercq

THE GODFATHERS OF BELGIAN GASTRONOMY

Pierre Wynants

Pierre Wynants has won many honours and titles throughout the years, but perhaps the most important of these is his honorary title as an ambassador of Belgian cuisine. With his Restaurant 'Comme Chez Soi', he almost single-handedly put Belgium on the world map of cooking. And as a staunch defender of regional Belgian products, he has helped to ensure the preservation of our nation's culinary heritage. These are all matters about which he still feels passionately.

'Comme Chez Soi'

We meet Pierre Wynants in the salon at 'Comme Chez Soi', the restaurant which he ran so successfully for forty-five years. In 2006 he handed over the running of the kitchen to his son-in-law, Lionel Rigolet, and in 2009 he withdrew from the running of the business altogether. Pierre Wynants was the third generation of his family to lead 'Comme Chez Soi' but the first with professional cooking training. "My grandfather was a maître d'hotel and my father was a butcher by profession. I did a few years at hotel school, but school as such never really interested me and they soon showed me the door. However, I was fascinated by the practical side of cooking, and so I went to work for three and a half years in the 'Savoy', which at that time was one of the two great eating houses in Brussels, along with the 'Carlton'. That, and with my parents, was where I learnt my trade."

When Wynants finally went to work in the family business in 'Comme Chez Soi', he introduced classic French cuisine, but also kept the good plain cooking on which the reputation of his grandfather and father had been built. "There was much more variety in classic cooking back in those days than there is now," says Pierre Wynants. "There were also more specialities. A lot of that has disappeared. There aren't many lef of the great houses of those days With the

closure of "'t Oud Konijntje', 'Clos St.-Denis' and 'Grandes tables du Monde' there are only four remaining 'Relais et Châteaux' in Belgium. The family aspect has also more or less disappeared from top restaurants. In the old days, if you went to a French three-star restaurant, you knew that you would be in the hands of someone who would look after you with great care. The chef and his family were visibly present and personally made sure that everything ran with smoothness and precision. Now you are just a number. In many of today's top restaurants the chef has become an 'entrepreneur', often hiding behind his kitchen team. The charm and ambiance of yesteryear is almost totally lacking. I won't deny it: I am very much of the old school. And I know that each generation brings its own changes, for good or ill. The secret is to only adopt the things that interest you or can help you. When I was starting out, there was only plain 'bourgeois' cooking and classic 'gastronomic' cooking. A major evolution came at the beginning of the 1970s and the 1980s, with the arrival of nouvelle cuisine and its focus on lighter sauces and more vegetables. This also inspired me to modify some of my own recipes. We gradually began to serve a mix of traditional and modern dishes, a mix that still forms the strength of our restaurant's cuisine. Nouvelle cuisine certainly led to some excesses, but you still have that today. I don't want to go to a restaurant to eat twenty-eight different mini-courses. Three or four substantial dishes, properly made, are more than enough. I get the impression that today's public is primarily interested in visiting trendy restaurants. People are less concerned with the food and more concerned with the

experience. I have to admit that I am not that familiar any more with many of these new restaurants. When they took away my third Michelin star, I lost interest. I don't follow the sector so closely nowadays. I used to know all the three-star restaurants, but not any more. But I am not bitter. I know that my kitchen is in excellent hands. I am very happy with what Lionel is doing. He is giving a little twist to the dishes with his new techniques, but he has kept the taste and the flavours – and that is what counts. What's more, his plates are presented elegantly and have much more 'class' than mine ever used to have!"

Flavour, consistency, staff and ambiance

If you ask Pierre Wynants to sum up the strengths of a good chef, he answers with just five words: flavour, consistency, staff, ambiance and simplicity. He goes on to explain: "Flavour is the basis of your food's attractiveness – and for this you need super-fresh products of top quality. Consistency of cooking is also very important, since your customer will expect the same high standard every time he comes to eat. We have always cooked with great precision. Everything that has ever been served in 'Comme Chez Soi'

There was much more variety in classic cooking back in those days. There were also more specialities.

is noted on a filing card. All the ingredients are detailed to the gram, so that every member of staff can make the dish as it should be. Choosing your staff carefully also stimulates confidence in a kitchen and increases consistency. And you create ambiance by encouraging a warm family atmosphere, which is something my wife always did so well. My daughter Laurence and Lionel

are doing much the same. The real weakness of Belgian cooking at the present time is a lack of discipline and consistency. This is largely the result of a change in mentality. It is so much harder to find good staff nowadays and those that you do find seem to change jobs much more frequently than in the past. We are also struggling with an image problem. French cuisine is already famous throughout the world and is relatively easy to sell. Belgian cuisine is every bit as good, but does not yet have the same international reputation, because our cooking lacks a clear identity. If we want to create this identity, we must bring our own products into sharper focus. If you compare the relative surface areas of Belgium and France, we have many more quality products and specialities as they do. I have an idea to organise a competition for teams of foreign chefs cooking with Belgian ingredients. For example, we would give them the three main ingredients of a classic Belgian recipe and ask them to create a new dish. This would not only put our traditional products and specialities firmly in the spotlight, but the input of these foreign chefs would actually help to create a new Belgian cuisine. A cuisine based on simple dishes that people at home would be able to copy and make. With the wonderful home-grown products that we all know and love."

Roger Souvereyns

How many chefs have had such an influence on Belgian cuisine and such vision that they deserve the proverbial statue? Roger Souvereyns would certainly be on any shortlist. His fine and remarkable features, like his name, have something proud, almost imperial; a dream for every artist or sculptor. But how will the contribution of this legendary chef be remembered? What is his true heritage?

Once a chef, always a chef

"Me? The godfather of Belgian gastronomy?" Roger Souvereyns laughs at the idea when we confront him with the history of cooking in Belgium during the past half century. But when we remind him of how many top Belgian and Dutch chefs have completed their training in his restaurant, he grudgingly agrees with our conclusion. We talk with Souvereyns at an impeccably laid table – where else? The chef offer us his left hand in greeting: the right is recovering from the effects of a minor operation – a small accident when cutting a pineapple, from which he was planning to make some jam. These things happen. Even to the very best and most experienced professional. Souvereyns began his impressive career as a chef in 1953 – a year in which very few of the present generation of Belgian top chefs were even born. He still hasn't

decided when he plans to call it a day. "Why should I? Preparing good food is my job, my life. It's in my genes. Why should I give it up? How can you expect me to stop? As long as my health is good, I will keep on going. I have never been bored in the kitchen – this is as true today as it was sixty years ago." Souvereyns stopped with restaurant work some time back, but he still occasionally does special commissions for specific occasions, either at home or elsewhere – and still of the same superlative quality. He has lost none of his dedication and passion, and still keeps in touch with what is happening in the world of cooking. He always has and he always will do – as long as he can. He knows most of the world's great chefs personally. Some of them he refers to carelessly by their first names; for others he uses the family name. Sometimes he forgets their names altogether. "My memory is not what it once was!" he admits with a smile. But if we ask him to describe some of his signature dishes in detail, he soon knows exactly what we mean. His huge depth of experience and vast knowledge of the international culinary scene make him the ideal person to assess the current state of gastronomy in Belgium.

Curiosity and a willingness to learn

"Few cuisines have such a wide range of products, styles, atmospheres and concepts as Belgian cuisine. I know of no other European land where the chefs are so interested in their products. Our chefs are curious and willing to learn. The range of possible ingredients in our country, some local, some imported from all over the world, is immense. But we have a market for this variety. Our chefs, and the public they cook for, are interested

> ## *People can only enjoy themselves to the full if all their senses are engaged. Flavours and aromas are obviously important, but it doesn't stop there.*

in trying anything new – as long as it is of quality. And this is not only true of ingredients: it is equally true of new techniques and new forms of presentation. If I compare our situation with the situation in France, then I see that the French chefs are much more inclined to fall back on French products and French knowledge. In our country there is a much greater willingness to listen to what others have to say. This is hugely enriching for our culinary culture. For years, we offered the same classic dishes presented in the same classic style. Even the so-called 'nouvelle cuisine' could do little to change this in the long run. The major switch to a lighter style of cooking, in my opinion, occurred in the middle of the 1990s under the influence of the Catalan model.

This generated a creative momentum whose effects are still being felt."

A total experience

"Alongside the new wave, you can also see a certain type of more refined classical cuisine that has been able to survive and prosper, thanks to a greater emphasis on lighter accents. My own style of cuisine falls within this group, and the same is true for several other chefs who have worked with me in the past. I can still remember how at the end of the 1980s and the beginning of the 1990s a number of then unknown Spanish chefs, including Ferran Adrià, paid a visit to our Restaurant 'Scholteshof'. They were interested

in our approach. My cooking was not trend-setting, but I always had a passion for depth of taste and relief. I always considered this to be the most natural thing in the world." Souvereyns' Restaurant 'Scholteshof' enjoyed widespread international acclaim from the 1980s onwards. His integral approach, with an emphasis on produce from his own farm and fields, was far ahead of its time. His presentation on the plate was also original. He was the first Belgian chef to embrace the concept of the 'total experience', with an eye for unusual accents and nuances of flavour that found expression in new novelties, such as the use of bite-size appetisers on spoons. "I always devoted considerable attention to good shape and content. You can't have one without the other. A person can only enjoy themselves to the full if all their senses are engaged. Flavours and aromas are obviously important, but it doesn't stop there. Many of the younger chefs seem to understand this better than in the old days. But at the end of the day, the most important thing is still the quality and taste of the things on the plate. In this respect, a good sense of taste is crucial. I think that I was better at tasting than cooking. We never tested dishes in my kitchen. What I tasted in my head was what we made and served to the customers. In addition to product knowledge and technical ability, young chefs also need to concentrate on their tasting skills. Some people have this as a natural talent, but it is also a talent that can be learnt, if you are willing to make the effort. It is a talent that makes you more critical – and self-criticism is a quality that any good chef needs, if he wants to make it to the top."

Warm

As a timeless culinary legend, Roger Souvereyns has the following advice for anyone who is thinking of following a career in gastronomy. "Our cuisine is amongst the best in the world. But let us remember to serve our warm dishes warm! The temperature of a dish is a vital factor if you want to extract its full taste and do full justice to its authenticity. Some professional chefs (and gifted amateurs as well) are too concerned with decorative elements. While they are busying

themselves with the presentation of the plate – which requires considerable time and effort – their food is actually going cold! This sounds like common sense, but you would be surprised how often it happens. It is certainly true that knowledge of products, technical skill, determination to succeed and will-power form the basis of a good chef. But a warm, varied and intense taste palate determines to a large extent the identity of a great chef. It is so much more than mere technical mastery."

Felix Alen

♪ Hof te Rhode ♫

Thanks in no small measure to his more than twenty cooking books and his participation in television and radio programmes, Felix Alen has become the most well-known organiser of festive events in Flanders. Yet behind the scenes he has also been responsible for considerable innovation in the sector. It was he who first pioneered vacuum cooking back in the 1980s, which is now a generally accepted technique.

A real party-builder

Most of Felix Alen's life revolves around the organisation of parties and festive events. In fact, it always has. Sixty years ago his parents were active as a kind of mobile catering service. With just an old motorbike for transport and loaded with pots and pan, they rode deep into the Limburg, to cook in other people's homes for their festive occasions. Later, his father became a cook in the officers' mess at the Leopoldsberg army camp. Occasionally, young Felix was allowed to attend the bigger events and it was there that he developed his boyhood dream: to become a famous restaurant cook. All these holiday jobs and his later training pointed in this same direction. The first time he cooked for a large group was during his national service in the navy. When his ship docked in a strange port, it was the custom to invite crew members from other Belgian ships to dine. Sometimes guest cooks would even come aboard. From them Felix learned about the standard dishes of international cuisine and he was bursting to put all this theory into cooking practice. After his national service, he was taken on by the Royal Palace in Laken. Here real 'bourgeois' cooking was the order of the day. "It was an excellent training ground. There was no compromise. Everything was based on classic practice. You weren't allowed to use ready-made gelatine squares; you had to extract fresh gelatine from bones. To make a mousseline farce of filleted pike, the pike was first hand-mashed with a mortar and pestle, following which it was passed three times through a fine sieve; the mousse was set on ice, after which the cream was slowly added. It was almost like a ritual. There were even standard sizes for things like spaghetti and chips: we had to measure them with a ruler, before cutting them to the required length! Everything that came on the table had to be of the finest quality, but it was not really sophisticated. I helped at a number of major state banquets and was always impressed by the attention to detail and the professionalism of both the kitchen staff and the serving staff. This was what finally pushed me in the direction of my future career: I no longer wanted to be a top restaurant chef; I wanted to be a chef for festive occasions, a real party-builder."

Cooking in bags

By preparing cold buffets, cooking in people's homes and organising small domestic events, he finally managed to scrape together enough money to buy a dilapidated old villa. This half-ruin was transformed to become 'Hof te Rhode', where Felix further built on his professional career. He soon began to experiment with new techniques for keeping his dishes as fresh as possible, so that he could provide constant quality on the plate. He was one of the first Belgian chefs to explore vacuum cooking, which was still in its infancy. "I helped to refine the whole process, and it was quite a job! Vacuum cooking requires great precision and hygiene. I toured the whole country giving demonstrations. It took considerable effort and even more conviction. The technique was sneeringly called 'cooking in bags'. Nowadays, the description has become a little more complimentary – cooking at low temperature in a roner – and the technique has become widely adopted, particularly by younger chefs. For a party cook like myself, it is a perfect method. I can plan accurately, since it allows me to prepare the meals in advance. I only need to warm them up and plate them immediately prior to serving. And I can do this for hundreds of people at the same time."

Recognisable but refined

"My cuisine is obviously banquet cuisine. My dishes all pay due respect to the classical tradition. You will find many of the flavours that you have been used to tasting for decades. They are the flavours that most of us grew up with at home and this is important in terms of recognition. My customers are mainly families who ask us to share in the most important moments of their lives. And each family is a heterogeneous group. Some family members simply want to eat until they burst, whereas other might be regular restaurant goers who look more critically at the food we serve. I also cater for many business events, such as seminars and presentations, where quality and value for money are high on the agenda. These different target groups mean that I need to think commercially. The ingredients in my dishes need to be recognisable, the portions need to be large enough and the presentation needs to be refined. At the same time, I need to show my customers in a subtle

In a nutshell

→ **Who or what influenced your choice of profession?**
I was spoon-fed it as a child. My father was head chef in the officers' mess at Leopoldsberg army camp.

→ **What was your first culinary experience or memory?**
When my father took me along to help prepare a prestigious buffet in the camp at the age of fourteen.

→ **What can really make you mad in the kitchen?**
When people do not do as they are asked or are dishonest (stealing or deception).

→ **What is your most important personal quality?**
Too hot-tempered in the heat of the moment and too soft afterwards. Fortunately, these cancel each other out.

→ **What would you like to have more time for?**
To be able to ride my motorbike more often and to enjoy my wonderful family.

→ **What are you best at in the kitchen?**
Preparing game dishes and anything to do with the grill.

→ **What do you most enjoy doing in the kitchen?**
Outdoor cooking, even if that means a winter barbecue.

→ **What is your favourite vegetable?**
Chiconettes (mini-endives) and young spinach.

→ **What is your favourite type or cut of meat?**
Entrecôte from a Duke of Berkshire pig, preferably with a nice thick layer of fat.

→ **What type(s) of fish do you like to work with?**
With line-caught sea bass from Zeeland.

→ **What are your preferred herbs for fish and meat dishes?**
We make our own herb mixes and mingle them with Mycryo (cacao powder in butter form). Fennel seeds are the basis of our fish mix and sweet marjoram for our meat mix.

→ **What are you favourite aromas and smells in the kitchen?**
The young shoots of panicum grass or sage in the spring.

→ **Which small object could you not do without in the kitchen?**
My Windmill knife.

→ **Which chef has inspired you the most?**
The late Julien Vermeersch, the great chef of the Brussels Carlton and the godfather of many other classically trained chefs. Also the kitchen team at the Royal Palace in Laken: chef Mullot, Paul and Liesette Druyts, who gave me the drive and inspiration to become a festivities chef.

→ **What type of cuisine do you not like?**
The 'copycat' cuisine of people who then think that they can really cook.

→ **What was the last celebrated restaurant that you visited and what was your opinion?**
'Pastorale' in Reet. It took a little while to get used to the interior, but the dishes we were served were all jewels of contemporary gastronomy. We dined there with my head chef Roland and his wife. We have been working together for thirty years and that deserved to be celebrated in style – and it was.

→ **Who is your perfect table companion?**
Friends and other people who are dear to me.

→ **What do you most enjoy eating on your day off?**
My wife Conny is also a wizard in the kitchen. She helps me in my constant battle against being overweight. Her daily cooking is about as good as it gets.

→ **What are your favourite book and your favourite cooking book?**
Europa aan tafel by Leo Moulin, a reference work about our eating and table culture. And the famous little red book *Le Répertoire de la Cuisine*.

manner that my business is up-to-speed with the latest contemporary trends and techniques. It is a question of finding the right balance." Felix Alen has always been a great patron of Belgian cuisine. He was one of the original sponsors of 'Flavour Week' and misses no opportunity to passionately defend good Belgian – and particularly good regional – cooking. "Even so, we need to acknowledge our debt to French cuisine. Their cooking still has the best flavour combinations. All the great Belgian chefs were trained in France. The new generation of Spanish and Scandinavian chefs also learnt much from the French masters, although they have given what they learnt some interesting twists; often with their own regional cuisine as a basis for creating new dishes in a new style. Likewise, my own style of cooking is also based on the French model, but with the addition of strong regional elements. I believe firmly in the taste heritage passed down to us by popular cuisine through the ages. These tastes have been in our blood for centuries and therefore must also have a role of merit to play in modern gastronomy. What is true Belgian cuisine? It is what you experience in a restaurant or on a market square or in a village or in a town. It is what ordinary people like to eat. And I can assure you: wherever you go in Belgium, you will eat well. There are not many countries in the world that can make the same boast."

What is true Belgian cuisine? It is what ordinary people like to eat. And I can assure you: wherever you go in Belgium, you will eat well.

Hof te Rhode
Rodestraat 7, 3290 Schaffen (Diest)
013/33 36 09
www.hofterhode.be

Fillet of eel in abbey beer with a terrine of green garden vegetables and herbs, semolina and a beer mousseline

For 4 people

pepper and salt
400 g filleted river eel
1/2 finely chopped onion
1 dl blond Leffe beer

For the semolina:
1 tablespoon olive oil
1 carrot, cut into blocks
1 clove of pressed garlic
1 stick of green celery, cut into blocks
2 dl fish stock
100 g semolina (couscous)
1 tablespoon of finely chopped parsley
pepper and salt

For the herb jelly:
1 teaspoon agaragar
2 dl fish stock
1 dl white wine
100 g peas, cooked
100 g courgette, cut into blocks and cooked
100 g green herbs in season, finely chopped (mint, chervil, tarragon, coriander, parsley, marjoram, etc.)
zest and juice of 1/2 lime

For the sauce:
2 egg yolks
juice of 1/2 lemon
eel stock (from the preparation)
100 g butter, melted and clarified
pepper and salt
1 dl lightly-whipped cream

For the garniture:
50 g Ganda ham, cut into blocks
2 small potatoes (Nicola), cut into shape and boiled
1 stick of young leek, cut into pieces and boiled
¼ fennel, cut into blocks and boiled
4 green asparagus tips, boiled and cut lengthwise
1 tomato, peeled and cut into blocks
a few stalks of fennel
a few stalks of garden herbs in season
8 thyme flowers
16 stalks of young calicornia

› Season the eel fillet with the pepper and salt and pack them with the chopped onion and the beer in a vacuum bag. Cook for 25 minutes in a bain-marie or steam oven at 70 °C. Open the bag, remove the fish and pass the cooking juice through a sieve. Keep the resulting juice for the sauce.
› Put half the olive oil in a pot and add the chopped onion (from the vacuum bag), carrot, garlic and celery. Simmer lightly and then add the fish stock. Allow to cook for a further two minutes and pour the mixture over the semolina, to which you have first added the rest of the olive oil. Add further warm fish stock, if the semolina is not properly cooked through. Also add the parsley and season with pepper and salt.
› Stir the agaragar into the fish stock and white wine, and allow to gradually come to the boil. Add the peas, courgette, herbs and the zest and juice of the lime. Season with pepper and salt, and allow to cool. When stiff, cut the resulting jelly into slices 1 cm thick.
› Make an emulsion sauce by beating the egg yolks with the lemon juice and the cooking juices from the eel. Drizzle in the melted and clarified butter and season with pepper and salt. At the last minute, stir some of the lightly-whipped cream into the sauce.
› Gently warm the semolina, the jelly (you can warm this kind of jelly without it melting) and the eel. Pile the different ingredients neatly on top of each other. Lightly warm the ham, potato, leek, fennel, asparagus and tomato. Arrange this elegantly (and as creatively as possible) on the plate with the herbs, thyme flowers and the calicornia. Spoon the sauce around the composition.

The preparation in 1, 2, 3

1

Fillet the eel.

2

Cut the vacuum-cooked eel into smaller pieces.

3

Spoon the semolina onto a tray and press firmly into place.

4

Place a portion of semolina on the plate.

Cut the cooled jelly into slices of the same thickness as the semolina.

Place a slice of jelly on the semolina.

Place the pieces of eel on top of the jelly. The three layers can be gently warmed.

As a basis for the sauce, beat up a classic Hollandaise.

Add calicornia stalks as a garnish.

You can also add a sprig of mint, a herb that also goes beautifully well with 'eel in the green'.

Detail of the garnishing.

Finish by spooning the sauce around the completed dish.

Carpaccio of Meritus beef with asparagus, stuffed potato and Pas de Bleu

For 4 persons

400 g of beef (Meritus)

For the sauce:
1 tablespoon mustard
1 tablespoon mayonnaise
2 tablespoons yoghurt
1 pinch of ginger powder
1 pinch of cayenne pepper
zest and juice of ½ lemon
pepper and salt

For the parsnips in black olive powder:
3 young parsnips
2 dl herb vinegar
100 g black olives (without stones)

For the stuffed potatoes:
6 small potatoes (Nicola or Charlotte), boiled
1 tablespoon of finely chopped onion
100 g grated celeriac
1 stalk of blanching celery
1 tomato, peeled and with the seeds removed

For the garniture:
fleur de sel and pepper
100 g Pas de Bleu (or some other blue-veined cheese)
6 white asparagus, boiled
6 green asparagus, boiled
pieces of lemon
stalks of garden herbs
some lemon thyme flowers (or other thyme flowers)
lemon
olive oil
white balsamic vinegar
warm toast

› With the help of some cellophane and aluminium foil, make small roulades from the beef and put them for a few hours in the freezer. The meat must stiffen, which occurs at a temperature around 0 °C.
› Mix all the ingredients for the sauce and check the taste.
› Peel the young parsnips and cut out a number of balls, using a parisienne scoop. Drench the balls liberally with a boiling, well-spiced wine vinegar, then allow to cool.
› Cut the black olives into small pieces and dry them in a drying cabinet or oven at 80 °C. Grind them to a fine powder. Dry the parsnip balls on some kitchen paper and cover them with the olive powder.
› Hollow out the boiled potatoes and chop the extracted potato into chunks. Mix these chunks with the finely chopped onion, celeriac, blanching celery and tomato blocks, adding a couple of spoonfuls of sauce. Mix well and fill the hollowed potatoes.
› Cut the meat into fine slices and arrange them on cold plates. Season with fleur de sel and pepper.
› Arrange the stuffed potatoes, the parsnip balls and the other garnishing as creatively as possible on the plate.
› Drizzle some fine quality olive oil and white balsamic vinegar over the dish. Serve the sauce separately, together with some warm toast.

Leg of guinea fowl marinated in cherry beer with a Hageland garnish

For 4 people

4 guinea fowl legs
100 g bacon chunks

For the marinade and the sauce:
2 dl cherry beer
50 g honey
0.35 dl red wine vinegar
5 cl oil
250 g mirepoix of vegetables (celery, carrot, onion)
2 cloves of garlic
10 elderberries
1 bouquet of herbs
pepper and salt
2 dl chicken stock

For the potato dish:
250 g potatoes
salt
1 chopped shallot
50 g small bacon blocks
50 g butter
2 finely chopped lettuce
50 g crushed hazelnuts
pepper
nutmeg

For the red beetroot:
2 red beetroot, cooked in the skin
100 g chopped onion
50 g butter
25 g sugar
1 tablespoon of vinegar

pepper and salt
1 tablespoon chopped mint
50 g diced pistachio nuts

For the garniture:
1 apple, peeled and cut into segments
butter
100 g cherries
lemon verbena
marjoram
celery leaves, deep-fried

› Place the guinea fowl legs and the bacon blocks for 24 hours in a marinade consisting of the cherry beer, honey, wine vinegar, oil, garlic, elderberries, vegetable mirepoix and the bouquet of herbs. Remove the meat and pass the marinade through a sieve.
› Fry the marinated vegetables with the herbs, bacon blocks and garlic in a pan with a little olive oil. Remove and spread on a baking tray. Fry the guinea fowl legs in the same pan and place them on top of the fried vegetables. Pour over half the marinade and put the baking tray into an oven at 220 °C for twenty minutes. Turn the meat occasionally.
› Reduce the remaining half of the marinade until it forms a syrup. Remove the meat from the baking tray, place it in another oven dish and cover it with the reduced marinade. Pour the chicken stock over the marinated vegetables and allow to simmer for 15 minutes. Pass through a sieve, remove any fat and reduce further, until a thick sauce is formed.
› Boil and drain the potatoes. Fry the chopped shallot and the bacon blocks in butter, and add the chopped lettuce. Cook until the mixture has boiled dry, then add the potatoes and the nuts. Mash thoroughly and season with pepper, salt and nutmeg.
› Cut the red beetroot into two cubes and hollow them out with a parisienne scoop (saving the balls for the garnish). Dice the remaining beetroot and fry it with the chopped onion in a little butter. Add the sugar and allow the mixture to caramelise. Dilute with the vinegar and season with pepper and salt. Add the mint at the last moment. Fill the cubes with the mixture, stir in the pistachio nuts and place a beetroot ball on top. Keep warm.
› Fry the apple segments in a little butter and warm the cherries in the same pan. Add a small amount of the reduced cherry syrup. Arrange all the ingredients on a plate and decorate with sprigs of lemon verbena, marjoram and the fried celery leaves. Dress with the sauce and serve with the left-overs of the beetroot filling, the potatoes and the apple (separately on the table).

Luc Broutard

∫ La Table du Boucher ∿

Armed with an apprentice's contract, Luc Broutard began working in a kitchen at the age of fifteen. As he grew up in a family of cattle breeders and farmers, he had been more or less spoon-fed meat from birth! He quickly learnt that a good tasting product requires little embellishment. Perhaps for this reason, Luc Broutard has become the standard bearer for all those chefs whose main concern is to find quality ingredients, with the aim of presenting them to their customers in all simplicity and purity.

Fascinated by meat

Luc Broutard has been fascinated by meat for more than thirty years. From stable to star restaurant. From production to kitchen. And his interest continues to increase. "The more I learn, the more interested I become," says the French chef who has been active in our country for the past two decades. "It is an extremely complex and enthralling subject and you need plenty of knowledge and experience before you can understand it fully." For this reason, Luc thought that it was not a bad idea to create a themed brasserie around his passion. The name of his restaurant in Mons says it all: 'La Table du Boucher' – the Butcher's Table. In the same city he also opened 'La Madeleine' in an old fishmonger's shop, where only marine products are served.

'Terroir': territoriality in the broadest sense of the word

His menu – or rather his blackboard – in 'La Table du Boucher' is unusual both in terms of its diversity and the information it provides. "My preference is for different types of beef from different origins. My customers are all meat-lovers and/or experts. This is why I always give details of the origin. They always want to know exactly what they are eating. My personal favourites are breeds such

as Limousin or Aubrac, which come from the areas of the same name. They taste better if they are born, bred and slaughtered there. Meat is like wine, or perhaps more like the grapes from which a wine is made. You can find chardonnay grapes just about everywhere, but the best results always come from the chardonnay grapes grown in the Bourgogne. I believe strongly in a territorial concept which is more than just soil and climate, but also includes local traditions, the local methods of working, and the 'spirit' which typifies the region. You can see the same with Limousin cattle. Today they are bred in more than seventy different countries, but the meat from around Limoges always has that little bit of extra flavour and authenticity. And just as the winemaker has a crucial role in making good wine, so the breeder and the chef have crucial roles in determining the quality of the meat that ends up on the plate. The breeder/farmer ensures the best possible living conditions and feeding for the cattle; the chef ensures that the meat is properly matured at the right temperature and humidity. The chef is also responsible for the correct method of cooking, so that optimal taste, texture and juiciness can be served to the end customer. It all sounds simple, and the perfect execution of those 'simple' things forms the basis of my cuisine."

> **My preference is for different types of beef from different origins. This is why I always give details of the origin.**

A master of simplicity

'Simple': it is a key word. Luc Broutard stands as a symbol for all the chefs in our country who like to keep their food as natural and as honest as possible. And who, above all, seek to create added value through the choice of the right product and its perfect preparation. "The Belgians are critical eaters, but their expertise allows them to appreciate simple things. I see this every day in my restaurant and it never ceases to give me pleasure. It goes without saying that 'La Table du Boucher' largely attracts carnivores. They come from every corner of the country, because they expect to be served something special here." This 'something special' might be a plate of 'Americain' (steak tartar), made with meat specially selected by Luc Broutard for its flavour and fibrous structure. Customers with a healthy appetite can order a portion with their aperitif, so that they have something to nibble on while they peruse the delicacies on his blackboard. The unusual cuts of meat that you will seldom find in other restaurants make the choice extra difficult. Luc also has a good selection of offal dishes, which only complicates matters further! His personal preference is for proven quality breeds such as Limousin and Angus, but he also offers interesting alternatives, such as the near extinct Parthenaise breed. Providing they are

> *The breeder/farmer ensures the best possible living conditions and feeding for the cattle; the chef ensures that the meat is properly matured at the right temperature and humidity.*

available, of course. "I am dependent on the meat available on the market at any given time. I go to the slaughterhouse myself to select my products on the spot. But it is getting harder to find good carcasses. Only one or two animals per hundred are able to meet my standards. I always choose female animals that are at least four years old. They have the necessary basis for good meat. The feeding they were given obviously plays an important role. For example, the quality of the barley used during the final fattening period can have a determining effect on both taste and fat content. Good fat acquisition ensures a rich and intense flavour. These are all factors that you need to take into account before making your purchase. The animals at the local slaughterhouse are not always able to convince me. For this reason, I prefer to work with specialists who hunt down the best animals for me in France, Ireland or America. They can deliver every week. I pay a bit more this way, but you can't put a price on top quality. My super-critical suppliers know my standards and know how I work. In fact, most of them eat regularly at the restaurant. They can be sure that my meat is perfectly matured, which can sometimes take up to sixty days, depending on the breed. A top product of this kind deserves the limelight to itself. As a result my preparations are essentially simple: the meat is fried in the pan or roasted on the grill, and served with salted farmyard butter and chips deep fried in beef dripping." And for those who are interested, you can also get a fresh green salad...

La Table du Boucher
Rue d'Havré, 7000 Mons
065/31 68 38
www.monmagazine.be/latabledouboucher

In a nutshell

➜ **Who or what influenced your choice of profession?**
My mother, who is an excellent cook.

➜ **What can really make you mad in the kitchen?**
I never lose my temper; there is a solution for every problem.

➜ **What is your most important personal quality?**
Determination.

➜ **What would you like to have more time for?**
To be with my wife and children.

➜ **What other job would you like to do?**
None!

➜ **For you, what is the epitome of luxury?**
Being happy.

➜ **What are you best at in the kitchen?**
Organising.

➜ **What do you most enjoy doing in the kitchen?**
Making stews and casseroles.

➜ **What is your favourite vegetable?**
Asparagus.

➜ **What is your favourite type or cut of meat?**
Onglet (top skirt).

➜ **What type(s) of fish do you like to work with?**
Cod.

➜ **What are your preferred herbs for fish and meat dishes?**
Saffron for fish and black pepper for meat.

➜ **What are you favourite aromas and smells in the kitchen?**
The smell of veal stock.

➜ **What is your favourite dish?**
Parmentier (hash) of oxtail with truffles.

➜ **Which small object could you not do without in the kitchen?**
My kitchen knife.

➜ **Which chef has inspired you the most?**
Older chefs such as Jean Ducloux, Paul Bocuse and Jacques Lameloise.

➜ **What type of cuisine do you not like?**
Bad cuisine.

➜ **What was the last celebrated restaurant that you visited and what was your opinion?**
Restaurant 'L'Eau Vive'; an exceptional experience.

➜ **Who is your perfect table companion?**
Customers who enjoy my food and want to discover new dishes.

➜ **What is your favourite aperitif?**
Champagne.

➜ **What do you most enjoy eating on your day off?**
Endive gratin.

➜ **What are your favourite book and your favourite cooking book?**
All the great classic books about French cuisine, as well as the *Gault Millau Magazine* and *Ambiance Culinaire*.

'Parmentier' of oxtail with truffles

For 4 people

For the oxtail parmentier:
1 oxtail, cut into pieces
5 cl oil
4 carrots
3 onions
1 leek white
1 stick celery
6 cloves garlic
1 tablespoon tomato concentrate
100 g flour
thyme
laurel
salt and pepper
10 cl white wine
water

For the puree:
1 kg potatoes, peeled
12 cl milk
50 g butter
salt and pepper
nutmeg

50 g truffles

› Cook the oxtail pieces in a cast-iron pot in a little oil. Degrease and add the carrots, onions, leek, celery and garlic. Sauté the vegetables with the oxtail. Add the tomato concentrate, then the flour, thyme, laurel, salt and pepper. Put into the oven for 15 minutes. Add the wine and dilute with water until the meat is just covered. Allow this mixture to cook slowly for 3 hours at 150 °C.
› Cook the potatoes and mash them into a puree. Add milk, butter, salt, pepper and nutmeg, stirring well. Keep the puree warm.
› Remove the oxtail from the oven. Cut the meat away from the bone. Pass the sauce through a pointed sieve and add finely diced truffle to the liquid.
› Place a stainless steel kitchen ring on the plate. Fill the ring with the puree, and put pieces of oxtail on top. Coat with the truffle sauce.

Carpaccio of prime beef with rucola and parmesan

For 4 people

500 g prime beef (for example, flank
steak), thinly sliced
fleur de sel
pepper from the mill
12 basil leaves
80 g parmesan flakes
some rucola leaves
fine olive oil

› Ask the butcher to cut the meat in very fine slices. Place a number of slices on a plate, so that the surface is well covered. Season with fleur de sel and pepper from the mill. Sprinkle with finely chopped basil leaves and the parmesan flakes. Decorate with the rucola leaves and finish with a stripe of fine olive oil.

Veal cutlets with morel mushrooms and 'vin jaune'

For 4 people

4 veal cutlets
100 g butter
50 g shallot
400 g morel mushrooms
25 cl 'vin jaune' ('yellow' wine from
the Jura)
35 cl fresh cream
pepper and salt
fleur de sel

› Lightly fry the veal cutlets in a little butter. When they are half cooked, put them in a warm oven.
› Remove the excess fat from the pan. Add the shallot and the morel mushrooms. Cook for 10 minutes. Add the 'vin jaune' and flambé the sauce. Finally, add some cream and allow the resulting liquid to reduce. Season with pepper and salt. Take the cutlets out of the oven. Pour some sauce onto a plate and place a cutlet in the middle of the sauce. Finish with fleur de sel.

The preparation in 1, 2, 3

› Half-cook the veal cutlets in foaming butter.
› Place the half-cooked cutlets into a warm oven.
› Fry the finely chopped shallot in a degreased pan.
› Add the morel mushrooms.
› Add the 'vin jaune'.
› Flambé the sauce.
› Add the cream.
› Allow the sauce to reduce.
› Pour some sauce onto a plate and place a cutlet in the middle of the sauce. Finish with fleur de sel.

Wout Bru

∫ *Chez Bru* ∿

Cooking is a hard business. Just ask Wout Bru: he knows all about it. He took a beating during his training, once had to carry on working with two burned hands and has even been threatened by jealous villagers! But you can't keep a good man down, and nowadays Wout's face is never out of the public gaze for long: in television programmes, advertisements, popular magazines, in a pop-up restaurant in Antwerp, etc. Yet for all these sidelines, he is still best known as the chef in his own restaurant, 'Chez Bru' in the Provence.

"If I wasn't a cook, I would probably have learnt one of the old craft skills, like carpentry or furniture making," says Wout Bru. "There was a saw-mill in my mother's side of the family. After each family get-together, I used to load up the boot of my dad's car with old planks and other bits of wood. When we got home, I used them to make a tree house and camps in the garden. I have always liked doing things with my hands. That's why I have such a great admiration of people who do things with great passion and dedication, like craftsmen, artists and musicians. I am also someone who needs to be constantly on the go. I need action. I still do. I initially followed a sport-based secondary education programme in Turnhout. But in my last year but one I failed... for French! (laughs) Now I can speak French as good as my own language! I was just sixteen at the time. My dad suggested that hotel school might be a good idea.

Wout had a choice between the hotel schools in Koksijde and Bruges. "I chose Bruges because it was a bigger city, with more going on. I did my first training course in a two-star restaurant in Brittany. My mother thought that this was a good idea, so that I could learn to speak French. It was the first time that I had come into contact with the proper world of cooking and it was a very hard baptism of fire! The chef was an animal. He called me an 'idiot' and a 'tourist', and wasn't afraid to give me a good thump every now and then. I worked as a kitchen help, 18 hours a day. My job was to collect and empty the serving plates. And it happened quite often that he threw a full plate at my head! I slept in a dingy old garret, on a mattress on the floor. When I phoned home in tears, begging them to come and get me, my dad said that I had to stick it out. The chef was unlikely to kill me (or so my dad thought), so he would only come and collect me when my training period was over! Yet when all is said and done, I had the time of my life in Brittany. I slept on the beach, visited Brest, Quiberon, and Carnac, and hung around with the 'locals'."

In the restaurant, he began to acquire the first layer of the thick skin that every professional cook needs. "If the chef started balling me out in French, I did the same to him in Dutch. That really made him go bananas! When I had finished hotel school, my dad was not prepared to sponsor me further. 'Just ask for a job anywhere you can. Only board and lodgings to begin with, until you have learnt your trade. And just make sure,' he added, 'that you are the best in everything you do.' I started work at a restaurant in Provence. Here the chef was equally hard, but at least he was fair. In the meantime, I had already met Suzy. She had followed hotel school at Spermalie and had done an extra year in hotel management. She came down to Provence and worked in the grape harvest, so that we could be together. One day, I went to eat with my future father-in-law at 'L'Ousteau de Baumanière' in Les Baux de Provence. It had three stars and was one of the best restaurants in the entire region. 'You should come and work here,' he said, 'and I will be willing to pay whatever it takes.'

> ## *If I wasn't a cook, I would probably have learnt one of the old craft skills, like carpentry or furniture making*

In those days there were huge waiting lists. Getting a place in a three-star restaurant was a bit like winning the lottery. Suzy and I both wrote a letter of application and at the end of the year we heard that we could start on the payroll, her in the dining area and me in the kitchens. The chef was very clear, right from the start: 'It is very simple. It is make or break. I will give you just one week.' I stayed there for three years. It was damned hard work: 18 hours a day, most of it in total silence. We did 120 covers a day, without order bons. We were expected to remember it all in our heads. The chef was a bit of a tyrant. If you said or did something he didn't like, you had to do 'special duties' for a whole week in your free time. This might involve turning crates full of artichokes, cleaning the extractor fan, scrubbing out the ovens. I remember having quite a lot of special duties. Once I slipped during the lunchtime service, and to prevent myself from falling I grabbed hold of a red-hot stove. My hands had second degree burns, but the chef told me to stop whinging and get on with my job. But after three years, we were the best of pals. I had won his confidence. He saw that he wasn't going to break me, and that I could take anything he had to throw at me."

If the chef started balling me out in French, I did the same to him in Dutch. That really made him go bananas!

Get out of here!

It was time for something else. Wout and Suzy moved to the St. James Court Hotel in London. The hotel had 450 rooms and four restaurants. When the head chef left without warning, Wout took over. "I was only 23 years old. I had nine people working under me, who were all older than I was. I had to show what I was made of: once again it was a question of sink or swim. I needed to make some really big orders and I had two telephones, so that I could play the suppliers one against the other. It was a very competitive atmosphere. But I learnt a huge amount. After two years, we were fed up with the noise and bad weather in London. We decided it was time to move back to sunny Provence. We had the chance to start again at 'L'Ousteau de Baumanière', this time with me as gourmet chef. Then my father-in-law asked if I had ever thought about opening my own business. Our gardener advised me to go and take a look at Eygalières, a typical Provence village with 1,200 inhabitants but no decent place to eat. The local grocer's shop had stood empty for four years but would make a good restaurant. We went to twenty different French banks to try and get a loan, but most of them just laughed in our faces. Our salaries were just too low. In the end, my father-in-law loaned us 12 million francs for the business. Slowly we transformed the old grocer's shop into our bistro 'Chez Bru', doing most of the work ourselves. I had built up a good reputation at 'L'Ousteau de Baumanière' and that helped with the opening. Caroline of Monaco and Calvin Klein were amongst our first customers. The villagers had thought that we would soon go 'belly up', but 'Chez Bru' was a great success. That is when the criticism started. Supposedly, I was earning money on the backs of the villagers. We even had threatening

telephone calls: 'Get out of here, you dirty foreigner.' 'We'll set fire to your restaurant.' Even the mayor would have preferred to see us go, but of course he had to listen to what his voters were saying. But my training had made me hard - and determined. We focused instead on the positive comments of our customers, and a year and a half later we were awarded our first Michelin star. I was 26, the youngest chef from the Benelux with a star - and a foreigner as well! But still the criticism kept coming. We didn't have a fixed menu; we simply bought what was available at the market in the morning. And we were probably the only bistro with a star where the customers could eat on the pavement outside and where the atmosphere was so relaxed. Okay, we were different from other star-rated restaurants - but we weren't prepared to compromise. We stuck to our vision. If things were going well, why should we change? And that's still how it is today. We are a simple bistro. Nothing fancy, no cinema. We want the people who come here to visit us to feel free and at ease. It needs to be fun. And we treat everyone the same - including 'regulars' like Rod Stewart and Jean-Paul Belmondo.

Back to basics

In the meantime, Wout and Suzy had plans for a new venture in Eygallières: in 2007 they bought a dilapidated motel and transformed it into a luxury hotel. "I wanted to have a hotel to fall back on when I get a little bit older. Because one day the moment will come when I no longer have the physical ability and the mental energy to carry on with the very hard work that top cooking actually involves. The hotel gives me a good alternative. I will only need to cook for us and for a handful of hotel guests, something nice and simple: a succulent piece of fish with a good bottle of rosé under an olive tree... Then perhaps - but I emphasise perhaps - we really will feel 'like God in France', as the old Belgian saying puts it. Why 'perhaps'? Because since we opened the hotel, the economic crisis has simply gotten worse. Even Wout Bru has to fight hard to make ends meet. Things are really bad in the catering business, also in France. And not just because of the crisis. The taxes and the administration are strangling the business. So we will have to find a different way to work. Not because we want to, but because we have to. Staff cost money, and we can simply no longer afford it. We will need to make cuts and concessions. Not by buying cheap products, but by continuing to invest in good products that we then cook and present in a simple manner without too many frills. Back to basics: that is the message for the future. But without betraying our roots in classic cooking. This can only work to the benefit of Belgian cooks. We are probably the only country in Europe where you can find such a large variety of top quality products. In France, the range

> *Back to basics: that is the message for the future. But without betraying our roots in classic cooking.*

of products is limited by comparison, and very regionally based. To get to the nearest wholesalers, I need to drive for more than an hour. That's not how it is in Belgium. Yet in spite of this excellent range of products, Belgian cuisine still lacks its own identity. We have plenty of home-grown talent and we make some truly great dishes that are beautifully presented, but our best young chefs still feel the need to go to Spain or Denmark, so that they can copy their styles. Why, for goodness sake? In France, they just carry on doing their own thing, refining things further, learning how to make their recipes more attractive, but they are not really helping to push out the boundaries of culinary excellence. Every chef has his own speciality, which he can make perfectly thousands of times over. But surely these chefs are just getting stuck in the same old rut? They are not really moving forward. True, some of them do manage to develop an own style and create innovatively. So why can't our young Belgian cooks learn to do the same thing? It is not because people are happy to eat grass and moss in Scandinavia that we should copy them. It is not because the Catalonians are mad about plates full of mousses, foams and jellies that we should follow them. We have the products, we have the skills and we have the opportunities: we should just be more creative about how we use them."

Chez Bru
Route d'Orgon
13810 Eygalières
(33) 4 90 90 60 34
www.chezbru.com

In a nutshell

➜ **Who or what influenced your choice of profession?**
My father.

➜ **What was your first culinary experience or memory?**
The 'Oude Hesp' in Turnhout. I went there often with my parents and also did a training course there. We ate steak and chips with stroganoff sauce and sole meunière. The meat and the fish were cut at the table. It's a shame it no longer exists.

➜ **What can really make you mad in the kitchen?**
If I need to say the same thing three times. Then I can get a bit irritated.

➜ **What is your most important personal quality?**
Tasting, tasting, tasting, all day long.

➜ **What would you like to have more time for?**
To be with my children.

➜ **What other job would you like to do?**
Carpenter. I am a big fan of people who work with wood.

➜ **For you, what is the epitome of luxury?**
Getting up in the morning and being able to do what I want, with no obligations.

➜ **What are you best at doing in the kitchen?**
Telling people what to do.

➜ **What do you most like doing in the kitchen?**
Organizing, coordinating, delegating.

➜ **What do you least like doing in the kitchen?**
The monotonous jobs, like turning ten crates of artichokes or cutting twenty crates of tomatoes. I did too much of that kind of thing in the past.

➜ **What is your favourite vegetable?**
I like all vegetables, but for me asparagus is still the tastiest.

➜ **What is your favourite type or cut of meat?**
Plumaiberico, but it has to be nicely veined with fat.

➜ **What is type(s) of fish do you like to work with?**
Sea bass and redfish

➜ **What are your preferred herbs for fish and meat dishes?**
I love Jamaican pepper and the really distinctive flavour of vadouvan.

➜ **What are your favourite aromas and smells in the kitchen?**
Vanilla

➜ **What is your favourite dish?**
Flemish meat stew and chips; they have absolutely no idea here in France what that is!

➜ **What small object could you not do without in the kitchen?**
My Bamix.

➜ **Which chef has most inspired you?**
I have always been a big fan of Joel Robochon. A chef who not only treats his products with great respect, but also has the feeling to prepare them in a simple but super-delicious manner.

➜ **What type of cuisine do you not like?**
Techno-cuisine.

➜ **What was the last celebrated restaurant you visited and what was your opinion?**
Martin Barasategui. A chef with exceptional product knowledge, which he transforms into beautifully balanced dishes.

➜ **Who is your perfect table companion?**
My wife and children on holiday; and my good friends who don't talk about cooking; and letting my hair down with my other chef friends.

➜ **What do you like eating at home on your day off?**
When I come home from the restaurant, I cut a nice, crispy French bread in half, fill it with salami and go and enjoy it in my hammock. That is my moment of the day to philosophize about life and the world general.

➜ **What is your favourite aperitif?**
Campari orange.

➜ **What are your favourite book and your favourite cooking book?**
Le Grand Livre de la Cuisine by Ducasse; a book that has inspired me right from the very beginning of my career.

➜ **Which famous customer would you one day like to welcome, and why?**
Joel Robuchon, because he is a great chef.

Fried goose liver with beetroot and powdered gingerbread

For 4 people

3 eggs
6 dl grape seed oil
1 tablespoon mustard
3 tablespoons beetroot puree (finely
  mixed boiled beetroot)
1 dash of balsamic vinegar
2 boiled beetroots
1 dash of olive oil
1 dash of sherry vinegar
4 radishes
1 pomegranate
4 slices of gingerbread
4 pieces of goose liver (portions of
  about 80g)
pepper, sea salt
croutons

› Beetroot mayonnaise: Put one egg and two egg yolks into a measuring cup with 6 dl of grape seed oil, 1 tablespoon of mustard, 3 tablespoons of beetroot puree and a dash of balsamic vinegar. Work this with a hand-held mixture until a smooth and light mayonnaise is obtained. This is a larger quantity than you need but you can easily keep the rest in a squeeze bottle in the fridge.

› Cut one of the boiled beetroot into fine slices and cut out a number of shapes from the slices, using the cutter you prefer. Marinate these shapes in the sherry vinegar and the olive oil. Cut the radishes into fine slices and marinate them as well. Cut the pomegranate in two and knock out the seeds, using a whetting iron or the blunt edge of a kitchen knife.

› Pre-heat the oven and dry the gingerbread for 4 hours. Allow to cool and mix finely in a blender. Keep in a sealed box.

› Finishing: Fry the goose liver in a hot pan or on the plancha. Season with pepper and sea salt. Dress the board with a neatly sprayed and spread line of the beetroot mayonnaise. Place the marinated vegetables on top. Add the pieces of fried goose liver and sprinkle with the powdered gingerbread. Mix the beetroot juice with an equal amount of olive oil and a dash of balsamic vinegar and sprinkle over the plate. Add a number of croutons.

The preparation in 1, 2, 3

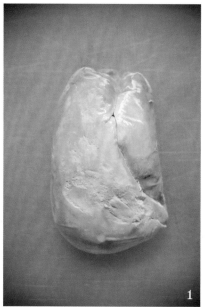

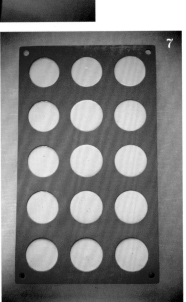

Tartar of langoustines and fried langoustines with a celery sorbet, oxtail and artichoke

For 4 people

8 langoustines
1 lime
1 gumbava
1 dash of olive oil
2 dl molasses
20 g celery leaves
5 cl lime juice
100 g cooked oxtail meat
10 g chives, finely diced
1 clove of garlic, pressed
10 g shallots, finely diced
50 g artichoke brunoise
croutons
1 teaspoon salmon eggs
some sprigs of freshly plucked
   seasonal herbs

> Tartar of langoustines: Cut 4 langoustines into a fine brunoise. Add some grated lime zest, the gumbava, a dash of olive oil, pepper and salt. Work up this mixture into a tartar and keep in the fridge.
> Celery sorbet: Mix 2 dl of molasses, 20 g of celery leaves and 5 cl of lime juice until a fine consistency is obtained. Place in a Pacojet pot and keep in the freezer.
> Oxtail: Stir together 100 g of the cooked oxtail meat, 10 g of finely-diced chives, 1 pressed clove of garlic, 10 g of finely-diced shallots and 50 g of artichoke brunoise. Finish with a dash of olive oil, and season with salt and pepper. Keep in the fridge.
> Finishing: Brush and spread a stripe of the langoustine tartar on the plate. Make the sorbet in an ice-cream machine. Fry the remaining 4 langoustines briefly on the plancha or in a non-stick pan. Arrange the oxtail mixture next to the langoustine tartar. Add a fried langoustine and, finally, a quenelle of celery sorbet. Dress with some croutons, salmon eggs and some fresh, green herbs.

Crisp-fried saddle of suckling pig with pork belly and a port sauce

For 4 people

200 g smoked pork belly
100 g breadcrumbs
100 g shallot, finely diced
olive oil
30 g sugar
5 cl port
a dash of balsamic vinegar
20 cl brown veal stock
100 g chanterelle mushrooms
4 pieces, loin of suckling pig
2 cloves of garlic, finely diced
1 sprig of rosemary
8 Paris mushrooms

> Pork belly crumble: Pre-heat the oven to 90 °C. Dry 100 g of smoked pork belly for 2 hours in the warm oven. Remove from the oven and mix the meat with 100 g of breadcrumbs. Keep at room temperature.
> Port sauce: Stew 50 g of finely diced shallots in a little olive oil, then caramelize with 30 g of sugar. Douse with the port and a dash of balsamic vinegar. Allow to reduce almost completely, before adding the brown veal stock. Allow to reduce further by half. Season with salt and pepper.
> Chanterelle tapenade: Stew 50 g of finely diced shallots in a little olive oil. Add the chanterelles and allow to stew further for about 5 minutes until they are cooked through. Blend the mixture to a fine consistency and season with salt and pepper.
> Pork belly: Cut the remaining 100 g of pork belly into slices and vacuum cook at 70 °C for 20 hours. Cool in ice-cold water. Divide into four equal portions.
> Suckling pig: Vacuum cook the loin of suckling pig with two cloves of garlic and the sprig of rosemary at 75 °C for 12 hours. Cool in ice-cold water.
> Finishing: Fry the piece of suckling pig under a weight on the plancha until one side is nice and crispy. Pre-heat the oven to 220 °C. Pour some of the port sauce over the pork belly and heat in the oven for 3 minutes.
> Cut the Paris mushrooms into four and fry them briefly in some butter. Season.
> Heat the tapenade gently.
> Dress the dish according to your preference.

Stéphane Buyens

ℐ *Hostellerie Le Fox* ⸏

The sea and the polders play an important role in the cuisine of Stéphane Buyens. Perhaps for this reason, he is also a passionate defender of regional products and the following of the seasons.

Local food-trend

Stéphane Buyens is like Obelix, the giant Gaul in the cartoon strip, who fell into a cooking pot filled with magic potion – and so acquired his great strength. In Stéphane's case, the magic potion was the gastronomic culture in which his parents and grandparents had immersed him almost since birth. At the end of the 1950s, his parents took over the brasserie 'Les Caves d'Artois' from his grandparents. In 1971 they opened 'Le Fox Grill', the first night restaurant on the Belgian coast and the first with an open kitchen. From 1972 onwards – when he was just 12 years old - Stéphane worked as a helper in the dining area during weekends and high season. At first he was interested in the serving side of the business and planned to become a maître d'hôtel, but following an accident involving his father and part of the kitchen staff, he suddenly found himself as the 'rotisseur' in 'Le Fox'. He took to it like a duck to water and quickly began refining his cooking. In 1987 he was awarded his first Michelin star. A second followed in 2005. Buyens is also chairman of the Order of the Thirty-three Masterchefs, the oldest cooks' association in Belgium.

"My cooking philosophy is easy to sum up: I offer cuisine inspired by the sea and made with local, home-grown vegetables of great taste and quality. From the sea I use grey shrimps, sole, megrim, mussels, oysters and Oosterschelde lobster. From the land I use endives, salsify, red cabbage, spinach, tomatoes, asparagus, hop shoots, apples, pears and strawberries. I cook 'first in, first out'. Everything that comes into my kitchen must be super fresh and I use it immediately. We have a great richness of products in Belgium, of which we can be rightly proud. We have a 'terroir' philosophy, but we don't take it to extremes. You find the best scallops in Brittany, not in West Flanders – and so we buy in Brittany. The evolution towards 'local food' is a trend, but it is a trend that can rebound against us. It also sounds so attractive, the idea of growing

high quality local products on a small scale. I see many chefs starting up their own vegetable gardens and nurseries. But if you are turning out between twelve and thirteen thousand couverts each year, it is impossible to do it with just your own produce. I have talked with many farmers and professional breeders, and they say that in the long run it just can't be done. In the spring I use fifteen saddles and crowns of lamb each week. This means that a breeder will need a good number of lambs just to keep me supplied, let alone anyone else! We don't need to exaggerate and say that everything must be 'terroir'. This is the problem in France, where everything has to come from their own backyard. That doesn't happen in Italy or Spain, where it is noticeable how few products are used locally. The richness of Belgian cuisine lies in the great range of products that is available to us. I recently heard Rene Redzepi of 'Noma' say that he was longing for the spring, because until then he won't have any decent products to cook with. This is a problem we never have. In this respect, we have access to an almost unlimited supply of riches, which means that we also have the finest range of dishes. We buy the best from the best – and so we make the best. But there is a reverse side of the coin. Because we have access to everything all the time, some chefs are sometimes inclined to overdo things and put too many ingredients on a single plate."

French cuisine in Belgium

The recipes of Stéphane Buyens can be described as classic, but with a contemporary twist. The French-Belgian style of cooking which his parents taught him forms the basis. But is this still appropriate in this modern day and age? "Of course it is! Good classic cooking is not the same as heavy cooking – because that is bad classic cooking. A good classic dish is subtle, light and rich in flavour. In the same way, it is bad molecular cooking that had given molecular cooking in general a bad name. We live in a country that has been strongly influenced by French cuisine. In my time and for many years afterwards all the hotel schools in Belgium organised the practical training courses for their students in France. Twenty or thirty years ago we all drove to France because you could eat better there than in Germany or the Netherlands. Even the French-speaking Walloons went across the border if they wanted to eat a decent meal – and they still do! Now that has all changed. Nowadays I always come back from France feeling that everything is ten times better here. There are too many star-restaurants in France that would never get a star in Belgium. I always say that we have 150 stars too few and the French have 250 stars too many. If you look at the top Belgian restaurants, we are the cheapest country in Europe. I recently ate in 'Pic', the three-star restaurant in Valence, and took

We have a great richness of products in Belgium, of which we can be rightly proud.

In a nutshell

- **Who or what influenced your choice of profession?**
  My parents; they had a restaurant.

- **What was your first culinary experience or memory?**
  A top banquet with the Thirty-three Masterchefs.

- **What can really make you mad in the kitchen?**
  When things don't go the way I want.

- **What is your most important personal quality?**
  Being open for dialogue.

- **What would you like to have more time for?**
  Golf.

- **What other job would you like to do?**
  Culinary adviser for both beginners and experts.

- **For you, what is the epitome of luxury?**
  Potato 'Moscow'.

- **What are you best at in the kitchen?**
  Delegating.

- **What do you most enjoy doing in the kitchen?**
  Creating.

- **What do you least enjoy doing in the kitchen?**
  Being in the soup!

- **What is your favourite vegetable?**
  All vegetables, but only in season.

- **What is your favourite type or cut of meat?**
  Saddle of lamb in the spring.

- **What type(s) of fish do you like to work with?**
  Any fish from my own pond: the North Sea.

- **What are your preferred herbs for fish and meat dishes?**
  Maldon salt.

- **What are you favourite aromas and smells in the kitchen?**
  The mingling of different stocks and bouillons.

- **What is your favourite dish?**
  I like everything!

- **Which chef has inspired you the most?**
  Cees Helder.

- **What type of cuisine do you not like?**
  Molecular kitsch.

- **Who is your perfect table companion?**
  My wife, Ellen.

- **What is your favourite aperitif?**
  Stella Artois.

- **What do you most enjoy eating on your day off?**
  Day-fresh fish from Nieuwpoort for a one-pan recipe.

- **What are your favourite book and your favourite cooking book?**
  Larousse Gastronomique.

- **Which famous customer would you one day like to welcome, and why?**
  The royal family.

- **Which famous person from the past would you like to have welcomed as a customer?**
  Winston Churchill.

as an extra entremets their famous 'gratin aux écrévisses'. I paid 104 euros for four common-or-garden crayfish. You could never try that here – but in France they can get away with asking the most ridiculous prices. In my opinion, the best French cooking is made and eaten in Belgium. The great strength of the Belgian chefs is their attention to detail. We will always try to cook even the tiniest garnish perfectly – even if it is only the third one on the right, half hidden behind the lobster! Foreign chefs are much more nonchalant about this kind of thing. We have also have the best wine cards in the world with the best wines from around the world. In France, you only find local wines on the card. This means that in the Bourgogne you can only drink cheap Bordeaux, because the locals simply aren't interested in buying the decent stuff. This is the negative side of what 'terroir' thinking can mean, if taken to extremes. This, again, is our strength. No one knows better than us the difference between a Belon oyster and a Zeeland oyster or between lamb from Pauillac and lamb from Texel. Good information is crucial in this respect. In Belgium, we are fortunate to have excellent cooking programmes on television and excellent culinary journalists who really know what they are talking about. The media abroad always seem to miss the point, and concentrate less on the cooking and more on the chef's entourage. Be that as it may, we need to do more to promote our culinary heritage and our culinary skill. There is no point in holding the Flemish Primitives (an annual event where Belgian and foreign cooks demonstrate their most recent innovations) in Ostend. You need to hold it in Copenhagen or Madrid. If you can show 5,000 Spaniards what Belgian chefs can do, then you will score. For the moment, we are focusing too much on a limited group of people in our own country."

Carte blanche

Buyens has noticed that we are returning to a more basic type of cuisine. "A Fleming is still a 'bon-vivant', a 'Burgundian' as we say here in Flanders. He likes a big chunk of meat and a classic Saint-Emilion. I have nothing against that. But the steak must be of top quality and it must be accompanied by fresh Béarnaise or Provençal sauce, or a real Blackwell. What I would really love to do is to throw my menu card through the window and cook carte blanche. Three or four fun dishes each day, based on what I find in the market that morning. This helps you to stay creative as a chef and allows you to surprise your guests – and, hopefully, to make them happy. This, after all, is where we all started: following the great revolution in classic French cuisine, it was the chef who went to the market and simply made what he found there. And if you are cooking for family and friends at home in the evening, nothing is more fun than working with the fresh ingredients you bought earlier that same day. That is the great truth behind all good eating and drinking."

Le Fox
Walckierstraat 2, 8660 De Panne
058/41 28 55
www.hotelfox.org

Emulsion of cauliflower with a salad of Nieuwpoort shrimps and a contrast of croquette

For the croquettes (+/- 20 pieces):
50 g butter
80 g flour
1 small cup shrimp juice
1 tablespoon tomato puree
35 g grated cheese
125 g shrimps
80 g cream
pepper and salt
cayenne pepper
egg
breadcrumbs

1 cauliflower
butter
1 bundle asparagus
200 g peas
300 g unpeeled grey shrimps
chives
chervil

› Make the croquettes with a roux of butter and flour. Moisten the mixture with the juice. Add the tomato puree, cheese, shrimps and cream. Let this all cook briefly and then season. Allow to cool overnight in the fridge before forming the croquettes. Dip the croquettes in the beaten egg white and then roll them in the breadcrumbs. Bake to a crispy brown in the deep fryer.
› For the emulsion, boil half a cauliflower in lightly salted water. Cut the remaining half into very fine pieces and fry briefly on a strong heat, so that the pieces form a crispy couscous. Mix the boiled cauliflower in the blender with some butter, until it forms a smooth emulsion.
› Cook the corn asparagus and peas al dente. Peel the shrimps.
› Dress and decorate the plate as shown in the photograph.

Sea bass with potato, champagne and caviar

1 sea bass (2 kg)
250 g potatoes (Bintjes)
1 crop of celery
butter
2 glasses of champagne
1 dl cream
125 g caviar

› Cut the sea bass into fillets and remove all impurities.
› Boil the potatoes in their peel. Mash the potatoes and add as much butter as there is potato. Season.
› Peel the celery and cut into fine slices. Cook lightly.
› Allow the champagne to reduce by half. Add the cream and allow to reduce to a third.
› Steam the sea bass for 15 minutes in the oven.
› Use the cooking juice from the fish to finish the sauce. Spoon this juice into the champagne cream and stir lightly with a spatula.
› Place the puree in a rectangle on the plate. Cover with the celery strips, sea bass and caviar.
› Foam up the sauce with a hand mixer and pour over part of the ingredients. Serve.

Turbot in pastry with a Nantais butter

600 g turbot in fillets
250 g flat-leaf spinach
4 tomatoes in finely chopped blocks
2 shallots
4 basil leaves
1 slice of puff pastry,
40 x 40 centimetres
2 egg yolks

For the Nantais butter
1 glass dry white wine
2 shallots, finely chopped
1 tablespoon cream
1 tablespoon balsamico
200 g butter
pepper and salt
1 bundle of chives, finely chopped

› Fillet the turbot and cut into two equal portions.
› Finely chop the spinach and cook for a few minutes in the steam oven.
› Cut the tomatoes into four segments, remove the seeds and cut the flesh into small pieces. Stew the tomatoes with the shallot and the basil leaves.
› Place a mixture of spinach, tomato, shallot and basil between the two pieces of fish.
› Take a rolled slice of puff pastry and cut it into two pieces, according to the size of the fish. Put the fish and the vegetables onto the first piece and then cover them with the second piece. Push the pastry gently around the fish, so that its shape becomes clear. Brush with a beaten egg yolk and bake for 20 minutes in a pre-heated oven at 210 °C. Remove from the oven and cut into two pieces.
› Make the Nantais butter with the white wine, shallot, cream and basil leaves. Put all the ingredients in a pot and reduce them to a quarter. Thicken with pieces of cold butter. Season with salt and pepper and add the chives.
› Cover the plate with the Nantais butter and arrange the pastry-covered fish neatly in the middle.

The preparation in **1, 2, 3**

Fillet the turbot and cut into two equal pieces.

Cut the puff pastry into two equal pieces.

Place one piece of the turbot on one of the pastry pieces.

Stew the finely chopped tomato with the shallot and the basil leaves.

5

6

Cover the turbot with the mixture.

7

Place the second piece of turbot on top.

Add the steamed spinach.

8

Cover with the second piece of puff pastry.

9

Press the pastry into the shape of a fish.

10

Brush the pastry with beaten egg yolk and bake in the oven.

Filip Claeys

ʃ De Jonkman ₹

Filip Claeys worked for six years in 'De Karmeliet' and five years for Sergio Herman. In his own restaurant, he has attempted to create a synthesis between the styles of these two master-chefs, but with a very clear identity of his own: product-oriented, fresh and powerful, and with plenty of depth.

Freshness first

Filip Claeys belongs to the younger generation of Belgian chefs who have come to the fore in recent years. When he started 'De Jonkman' in 2006, he had just completed five years in the kitchen of Sergio Herman. Sergio's dynamism and creativity were also reflected in Filip's own dishes. Perhaps a little excessive, perhaps too many details, but always the right balance in the end. His cuisine is characterised by attention to detail, finely accentuated flavours, purity and great depth. During the past few years, his interest in local products has also increased. "In 2008 I followed a cooking course in Tokyo. I was amazed, overwhelmed almost, by the way the Japanese push their own products. In fact, they are so chauvinistic that they want to keep all the best products for themselves. I saw super-fresh tuna of a superior quality. The tuna that I used in my restaurant – which came from Rungis – bears no comparison. This is when I decided to change tack. I decided that I was mad to buy inferior tuna from France, when we all fail to make full use of the quality products that are available here in Belgium. For this reason, I decided to join the Local Food project organised by Kobe Desramaults of 'In De Wulf' and Rik Delhaye. Together with a number of other colleagues, I also set up the Foundation for Sustainable Fisheries Development (SDVO), which allows us to offer day-fresh fish of top quality, provided by day-fishers on the North Sea. Both of these initiatives have created valuable extra work for our farmers and our fishermen. In addition, I have a separate agreement with another fisherman, who guarantees me the quality of his catch. If I see during preparation that a fish has been damaged, I can return it to him without charge. But I am careful not to take this 'local' thing too far. Like many other chefs, I buy my milk lamb from the Pyrenees, simply because it is the best quality you can find. Even so, something like eighty percent of my products are of Belgian origin. This is part of the strength of my cuisine.

For example, mine is the only restaurant that buys live North Sea shrimps at the coast. This was a project that I started with Rudi Van Beylen of 'Hof ten Damme' in Kallo. The shrimps are provided by a fisherman, who keeps the last drag of his nets especially for us. He delivers them in polystyrene trays and they can be kept alive for up to three weeks in a special tank with running sea water – a homarium. This has the advantage that our shrimps are always à la minute – which guarantees our customers a super-fresh quality that they can find nowhere else. The quality of shrimps deteriorates rapidly after they have been cooked. There is already a huge difference in flavour between day-old and two-day-old shrimp. Moreover, by cooking my shrimps myself, straight from the tank, I can season the cooking medium as required, so that the taste best matches the composition of the dish. In the future, I would like to make these shrimps available to other chefs. But for the time being I use most of them to make my first signature dish, in combination with the wonderful dune asparagus provided by Marc Deswarte, a farmer who lives over the French border. His asparagus are grown at the foot of the Dune Fossile, a series of fossilised dunes that are more than five hundred years old. This gives them a softer, silkier taste than the classic white asparagus. The beef in my second signature dish comes from the Lonnewille breeding farm in Vivekapelle, run by the brother of Pieter Lonneville of Restaurant 'Tête Pressé', one of my former colleagues at Sergio Herman's. The meat comes from a Holsteiner breed, better known as our black-and-white milking cow, but is only taken from animals that are three to four years old and have already calved once. It is full of flavour, with just a hint of spice and beautifully streaked with fat. We let the meat mature further for two to three weeks on the carcass, following which we cut it, vacuum pack it and let it mature for a further four weeks. This results in super-tender flesh of an exceptional quality. I present it before cooking to the guests at table and explain which part of the animal it has been cut from. This helps to create a bond between the customer, the product and its place of origin."

> *Something like eighty percent of my products are of Belgian origin. This is part of the strength of my cuisine.*

Pure and simple

Filip Claeys draws his inspiration from simple things, such as a meal in an everyday Bruges restaurant, where he was once served dogfish with sauerkraut. "You seldom see dogfish on restaurant menus these days. But this was a beautiful dish: classical and brilliantly well done. Since then, I have included dogfish in my own menu, served in combination with smoked eel. Now that a number

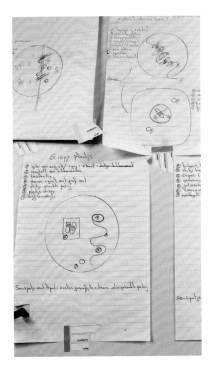

of fish sorts are threatened with extinction, it is becoming necessary – and it is also an interesting challenge – to put less well-known species on our menu cards. And I certainly prefer less well-known fish to farmed fish." Filip finds less to inspire him in cooking programmes on television, cooking articles in magazines and the cooking books which seem to fill half our bookstores nowadays. "I want to follow my own path, without being influenced by other chefs. I did buy Noma's book, but I only flicked through it once or twice, and then put it away in a cupboard. When I first started 'De Jonkman', I made a conscious decision not to eat in a star-restaurant during the first twelve months. I had already developed a method of thinking and working, based on what I had learned from the three head chefs for whom I had worked: Stéphane Buyens at 'The Fox', Geert Van Hecke at 'De Karmeliet' and Sergio Herman at 'Oud Sluis'. It is a synthesis of the ideas of these three that you can now see in my dishes. In the past, I sometimes used up to eight different ingredients on a plate; I now confine myself to a maximum of four. It is purer and simpler. For instance, I now have a dish on my menu with just scallops, cauliflower and turnip. The turnip is served caramelised, raw, marinated in slices, cooked in the microwave and as an escabèche. The cauliflower is also served more or less raw, as a puree and as a couscous. There are only three ingredients on the plate but I try to exploit their possibilities to the full, so that I can bring maximum flavour and structure to the dish."

De Jonkman
Maalse Steenweg 438, 8310 Sint-Kruis
050/36.07.67
www.dejonkman.be

In a nutshell

➜ **Who or what influenced your choice of profession?**
My parents, who also ran a restaurant.

➜ **What was your first culinary experience or memory?**
'Het Laurierblad' in Berlare, when I was five years old.

➜ **What can really make you mad in the kitchen?**
If someone has messed up but is not prepared to admit it. Or if someone doesn't answer when I ask something or say something!

➜ **What is your most important personal quality?**
Persistence. My motto is: never give in, always try harder.

➜ **What would you like to have more time for?**
My two children, Fleur and Jules.

➜ **What do you most enjoy doing in the kitchen?**
Last minute improvisation.

➜ **What do you least enjoy doing in the kitchen?**
Filling the pepper grinder!

➜ **What is your favourite vegetable?**
The dune asparagus of Marc Deswarte.

➜ **What is your favourite type or cut of meat?**
Entrecôte from my own self-reared cow: heavenly!

➜ **What type(s) of fish do you like to work with?**
Everything and anything from the North Sea.

➜ **What are your preferred herbs for fish and meat dishes?**
Tarragon.

➜ **What are you favourite aromas and smells in the kitchen?**
The smell of shrimp stock.

➜ **What is your favourite dish?**
Frogs legs in garlic butter.

➜ **Which small object could you not do without in the kitchen?**
My filleting knife.

➜ **Which chef has inspired you the most?**
Every chef who has vision and who gives 100% to his/her profession.

➜ **What type of cuisine do you not like?**
A cuisine that has no respect for its products.

➜ **What is your favourite aperitif?**
A Trappist beer from the abbey at West-Vleteren.

➜ **What do you most enjoy eating on your day off?**
Pizza carpaccio.

➜ **Which famous customer would you one day like to welcome, and why?**
Lady Gaga: a 'woman with balls', as the saying goes. It would, I think, be a challenge to cook for her.

➜ **Which famous person from the past would you like to have welcomed as a customer?**
Alexander McQueen.

North Sea shrimps with dune asparagus from Mark Deswarte, quail's egg and Leffe

For 4 people

4 slices of rye bread

For the shrimp oil:
50 g grey shrimps
corn oil
1 clove garlic
2 sprigs thyme
2 sprigs rosemary

For the hand-peeled shrimp stock:
40 cl water
1 onion
200 g grey shrimps
pepper and salt

50 g live grey shrimps
sea salt
shrimp oil (see above recipe)

For the shrimp gel:
50 cl shrimp stock (see the basic recipe above)
5 g agaragar

For the fried shrimps:
Maldon salt
50 g peeled grey shrimps
pepper
1 pinch of garlic
lime juice

For the shrimp powder:
boiled shrimp heads and shells
corn oil
1 pinch gold powder

For the Leffe gel:
39 cl Leffe 9° (beer)
11 cl sherry vinegar
5 g agaragar

4 quail's eggs
4 dune asparagus
pepper and salt
sherry vinegar
olive oil
fresh verbena leaves

› Pre-heat an oven to 185 °C. Slice the rye bread finely, cut out shapes to the desired form and bake in the oven until golden brown.
› For the shrimp oil, fry the shrimps in the corn oil with the garlic, thyme and rosemary. Immerse in oil and allow to simmer for 3 hours at 70 °C. Pass the mixture through a sieve and store the fluid in a cool place.
› Bring the water with the shrimps and the finely chopped onion to the boil and allow to 'brew' gently for 20 minutes. Season with pepper and salt. Pour the stock through a sieve and keep the shrimps separately. Boil the live shrimps for 1 minute in the stock. Peel them and flavour with sea salt and the shrimp oil. If you do not have live shrimps, you can use cooked but unpeeled shrimps (although there is no need to boil them). Also peel the shrimps used to make the stock.
› Bind the shrimp stock with agaragar. Allow to harden in the fridge and then mix until it forms a gel.
› Heat a frying pan and sprinkle with Maldon salt. Fry the shrimps for 20 seconds with the garlic and a little pepper and salt, and add a few drops of lime juice.
› Pre-heat an oven to 110 °C. Fry the boiled shrimp heads and shells with the gold powder in corn oil, until they are crisp. Dry in the oven at 110 °C for 2 hours and then for a further 24 hours at 60 °C. Grind half of the dried shrimp heads with half of the crisped rye bread to form a fine powder.
› Mix the Leffe beer with the sherry vinegar and bind with the agaragar. Allow to stiffen and mix until a gel is formed.
› Cook the quail's eggs for 90 seconds in boiling water. Cool them in ice water. Cook them again in boiling water, this time for 50 seconds. Cool them a second time in ice water. Peel off the shell and marinate the eggs in the shrimp oil for 15 minutes at 50 °C.
› Peel the asparagus and cook them for 3 minutes in boiling water. Cool them in ice water and cut them into nice chunks. Season half the chunks with salt, pepper, sherry vinegar and olive oil. Crisp fry the other half in a pan with some hot oil.
› Fill the lower part of the cut-through bottle with the shrimp crunch, asparagus, a quail's egg and some shrimps. Decorate with the gels, the rye bread and the fresh verbena leaves.

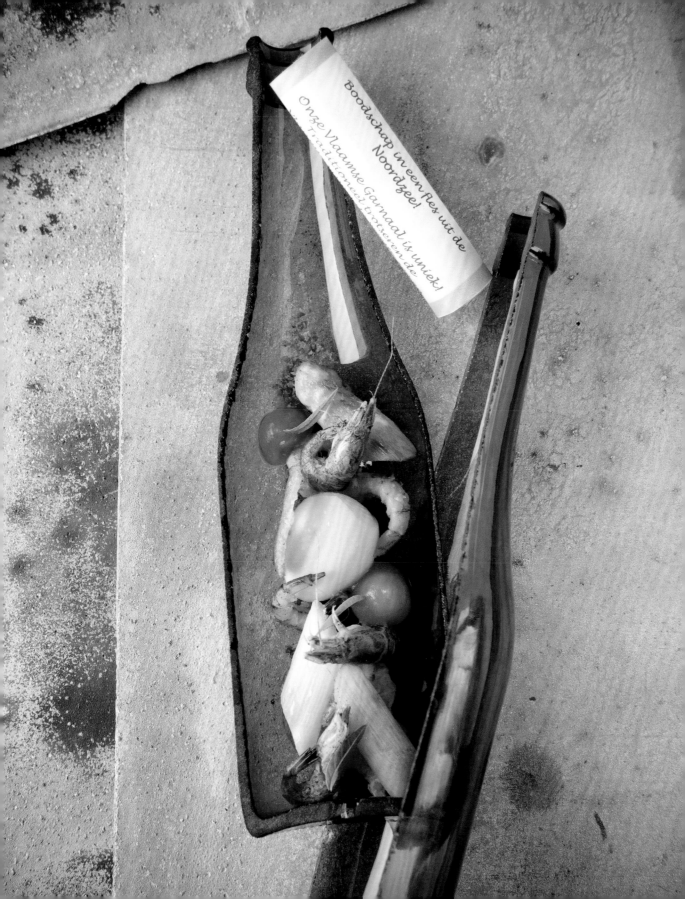

Boodschap in een fles uit de
Noordzee!
Onze Vlaamse Garnaal is uniek!
traditioneel

Grilled farm-bred beef from Vivekapelle with tomato, red onion and chips

For 4 people

1 kg entrecôte
coarse salt and pepper
farmhouse butter

For the red onion:
4 red onions
pepper and salt
5 cl olive oil
2 cl red wine vinegar

For the cherry tomatoes:
8 cherry tomatoes
20 cl water
50 cl white wine vinegar
30 g sugar

› Cut a thick slice from the entrecôte and season on both sides with coarse salt and pepper. Grill the meat on both sides for 4 minutes in a Green Egg or on a barbecue. Allow to rest for 5 minutes and then colour for 3 minutes with some farmhouse butter under a salamander.
› Remove the peel from the onions. Cook the peel for a few moments in boiling water, dab it dry and then dry further for 4 hours in an oven at 90 °C until crisp. Grind half of the peel into a fine powder. Keep the other half for plate decoration. Cut the onions into segments, season with pepper and salt and marinate them for at least a day in the olive oil and red wine vinegar.
› Blanch the cherry tomatoes for 10 seconds in boiling water. Remove the peel. Mix the water, white wine vinegar and sugar. Marinate the tomatoes for at least a day in this mixture.
› Blend the butter into the pureed potato and allow to stiffen for 2 hours in the fridge. Cut the puree into the shape of thick chips and dry them for 1 hour in an oven at 60 °C. Crisp-fry them in the beef dripping at 185 °C.
› Wash the chive stalks thoroughly and crisp-fry them in oil at 185 °C.

The preparation in 1, 2, 3

> Blend the butter into the pureed potato.
> Allow to stiffen for 2 hours in the fridge.
> Cut the puree into the shape of chips.
> Make sure that the chips are nice and thick.
> Dry them in an oven at 60 °C.
> Crisp-fry them in beef dripping at 185 °C.

Marinated pear with lemon and home-made lemonade

For the lemon cream:
250 g egg
18 cl lemon juice
188 g sugar
8 g vanilla powder
1 slice gelatine

100 g butter

For the lemon crumble:
500 g butter
500 g sugar
450 g flour
450 g powdered almond
17 g salt
grated peel of 2 lemons
grated peel of 2 oranges

300 g feuilletine

For the lemonade:
50 cl water
250 g sugar
10 cl lemon juice
1/2 bunch mint
1 stalk lemon grass

For the Italian meringue:
280 g sugar
5 cl water
140 g egg white

For the marinated pear:
1 pear
10 cl lemonade

For the quince puree:
4 quinces
50 g sugar
1/2 cinnamon stick
5 cl water

For the candied lemon peel:
grated peel of 1 lemon
150 cl water
150 g sugar

vanilla ice-cream or pear sorbet (ready-made)

› Stir the egg, lemon juice, sugar and vanilla powder together and warm to 80 °C. Add the gelatine. Remove the pan from the heat and allow to cool at room temperature. Stir in the butter.
› Beat the butter for the crumble until it is smooth. First add the sugar and flour, then the powdered almond, and then the salt. Stir in the grated lemon and orange peel. Roll the mixture into a sausage shape and place in the fridge, until it stiffens. Pre-heat the oven to 150 °C. Cut the sausage into slices and bake for 11 minutes in the warm oven.
› Mix all the ingredients for the lemonade, bring to the boil and allow to 'brew' for 30 minutes.
› For the meringue, bring the water and 200 grams of sugar to the boil at 121 °C. Beat the egg white with the rest of the sugar. Pour the boiling sugar mixture over the beaten egg and continue to beat occasionally, while allowing to cool in a kitchen robot.
› Peel the pear and cut out a number of balls with a parisienne scoop. Marinate these balls for 6 hours in the lemonade.
› Cut the quinces in two and remove the cores. Cut the flesh into pieces. Mix these pieces with the sugar, the half cinnamon stick and the water. Place on a low heat and allow the mixture to caramelise, until a compote is formed. Blend the compote until it becomes smooth.
› Using a slicer, cut wafer-thin slices of lemon peel. Mix the sugar and the water and bring to the boil. Cook the lemon peel slices three times in a mixture of 50 centilitres of water and 50 grams of sugar: the first time for 5 minutes, the second time also for 5 minutes and the third time until they are cooked through. After each cooking, pour away the water and make a fresh sugar-water mixture. Allow to drain.
› Arrange some blobs of meringue in a deep plate. Singe them with a blow torch. Add the pear balls, lemon cream and crumble between them. Serve with vanilla ice-cream or a pear sorbet, and a glass of lemonade.

Jacques Colemont

∫ Figaro ∖

Jacques Colemont has been working behind his stove at Restaurant 'Figaro' for more than four decades. He is still driven by the same curiosity and ambition, but he has now surrounded himself with a group of young chefs and embraces the new kitchen techniques with an open mind.

Starting young

Restaurants who have maintained the same high standards for forty years with the same chef in charge: you can count them on the fingers of one hand. Physical, financial or family problems force many to call it a day at a much earlier stage. Jacques Colemont has also had his share of woes. His first wife and only son both died at an early age of cancer. This hurt him deeply, but it did not break him. "After each new body blow, I was told to slow down, take things easier. But what was the point of that? Cooking is my life and working was the only way to keep negative thoughts at bay." Jacques Colemont comes from a farming family and is the oldest of five children. Aged just fifteen, he entered 'Salons Georges' in Leuven to learn the tricks of the restaurant trade. Next came further refinement of his skills under Roger Souvereyns, who was then at Restaurant 'Van Dijck'. "I grew up with the traditional smells of red cabbage and bacon, leek soup and sugared apples, bubbling away gently in a big pot on our old Leuven cooker," says Colemont. "I rediscovered these aromas in Souvereyns' kitchen, but in a much more refined form. He was a master at combining ingredients, had exceptional product knowledge and knew everything about herbs. He pioneered a number of products that were hardly known in the Belgian gastronomy of the day, such as wild quails, hop shoots and smoked salmon, which he first imported in 1965. In those days, the salmon was individually packed in oil in plastic bags. Souvereyns taught me all I know. After two years I was headhunted by a restaurant in Overpelt that offered me three times what Souvereyns was paying me. I was already married with a kid, so a higher salary was welcome. I stayed for three years but the owners had no real feeling for the food business."

> **My kitchen still contains the timeless aromas that we all grew up with, but refined and presented in a new and exciting manner. That is what makes Belgian cuisine so unique.**

Still searching for new ideas

"When I was twenty-three, I began my own restaurant on the Luikersteenweg in Hasselt. That was on 19 March 1969. I served simple dishes to begin with: mussels and chips, pork chops with Blackwell sauce, entrecôte 'Stroganoff', which I later turned into entrecôte 'Figaro' with a different garnish. It was all very classical. Then I came into contact with Willy Slawinski. He was the Belgian Ferran Adrià of the 1970s, a visionary chef who was far ahead of his time. But Slawinski was finding it difficult: his cuisine wasn't understood, but he stubbornly persisted. He was more or less cooking for himself. We became good friends and I helped him where I could. He introduced me to the techniques of nouvelle cuisine and I applied them readily. This allowed me to update my own dishes. By now, my son Luc was also working alongside me. I would have gradually given him much more of a free hand, but I was always planning to stay in the kitchen. But it was not to be. He became ill at an early age and had to stop. At about the same time, I found myself beginning my own fight against the ageing process. I decided to recruit some young blood into my kitchen team, but I never stopped searching for new ideas. I travelled to France, Switzerland and Italy in the hope of finding new eating experiences and I bought enough cooking books to fill a library. In the 1990s I discovered Spanish cuisine and twelve years ago I paid my first visit to 'El Bulli'. What Ferran Adrià served us was pure genius. It was like a rejuvenation cure! I decided to further explore his cooking methods and followed training sessions at 'Hacienda Benazuza', the El Bulli hotel in Sevilla, and also at the Rocca brothers in Restaurant 'Moo' in Barcelona. For the past few years I have been going to 'Noma' in Copenhagen, where I have almost become a regular. Curiosity has been the motor of my passion for innovation all my life. But I only apply new techniques little by little. I don't want to frighten off my customers! Slawinski might have been happy to cook for himself, but I want to cook for others. Besides, in order to be able to translate these new concepts into effective practice, you need a good classical basis. I sometimes make the wrong choices, but I am quick to put things right."

As natural as possible – and preferably regional

A constant feature of Jacques Colemont's cuisine is his use of regional products. This is reflected in his signature dishes: Maas (Meuse) bass, Limburg asparagus, goat's cheese, Loon syrup, watercress and cherries. "I would love to work exclusively with Belgian products, but this would mean finding enough suppliers who can provide ingredients of the necessary quality all year round. And that is the problem. There is no shortage of good fruit and

In a nutshell

→ **What was your first culinary experience or memory?**
Chicken curry, bought at a Chinese restaurant in 1964 with the money that I earned as a trainee with Roger Souvereyns.

→ **What can really make you mad in the kitchen?**
Products that are not perfectly fresh or staff who make errors through laziness.

→ **What is your most important personal quality?**
Perseverance and a passion for innovation.

→ **For you, what is the epitome of luxury?**
A gastronomic meal with fellow-believers and friends.

→ **What is your favourite vegetable?**
Asparagus and endive.

→ **What is your favourite type of cut of meat?**
Aubrac beef.

→ **What type(s) of fish do you like to work with?**
Sea arrow (short-finned squid) and North Sea sole.

→ **What are your preferred herbs for fish and meat dishes?**
A mix of thyme, rosemary and laurel is still the basis.

→ **What are you favourite aromas and smells in the kitchen?**
Star aniseed.

→ **What is your favourite dish?**
Langoustines with an oyster emulsion à la Roger Souvereyns.

→ **What was the last celebrated restaurant that you visited and what was your opinion?**
'Noma', which for me is like coming home. I am welcomed each time I go, which still gives me a kick.

→ **What do you most enjoy eating on your day off?**
My mother's meat stew with Savoy cabbage.

→ **Which famous person from the past would you like to have welcomed as a customer?**
Willy Slawinski.

vegetables: I am sitting in the middle of Belgium's premier fruit-growing region. I can also supplement North Sea fish with shell-fish from Brittany. You will also find whitefish – a relative of the trout – on my menu. I first ate this at Marc Gerard's and immediately became a big fan. But you can't find it locally. My fishmonger gets it for me from Switzerland. Most of my meat also comes from abroad. I have a supplier in Valkenburg, just over the Dutch border, who can supply good, natural game and also breeds Aberdeen Angus cattle. Another breeder in the same area provides me with Black Angus and Iberico beef. But it's very difficult to find good pigeons: these still need to come from Anjou or Bresse.

I try to work with all these ingredients in a manner that is as natural as possible. I want my customers' taste buds to be saturated with the full flavour of every product on the plate. As far as the wave of new ingredients associated with 'molecular' cooking are concerned, I have stored a dozen or so in my memory banks, but my 'hard disk' is now full! This is why I work with relatively few components per dish: it is the only way to deliver maximum taste."

A star? No thanks!

'Figaro' has been lavishly praised in restaurant guides for the past forty years. GaultMillau has consistently given Jacques a score of sixteen (out of twenty) but he has never been awarded a Michelin star. Does this bother him? "Throughout the years I have kept on telling the Michelin inspectors that I don't want a star. They only give you extra pressure and I am happy with the customers that I have now. My wife thinks that I am crazy, but even she can't change my mind on this point. I have customers who have been loyal to me for 40 years. I know them by name, know their family histories, know their joys and sorrows. In 'Figaro' they can find the familiar dishes that they like, as well as modern versions of classic recipes. I have a list of twenty customers who ask me each year to inform them when the first hop shoots arrive. The lists for asparagus, summer fruit and game are even longer. My kitchen still contains the timeless aromas that we all grew up with, but refined and presented in a new and exciting manner. That is what makes Belgian cuisine so unique. We draw our inspiration from the good plain cooking of yesteryear, partly based on regional products, but we add to this the refinement and quality of French haute cuisine. The combination is irresistible."

Figaro
Mombeekdreef 38, 3500 Hasselt
011/27 25 56
www.figaro.be

Maas bass with espuma, crumble of ham and asparagus ice

For 4 people

For the ham espuma:
1 dl consommé
50 g ham, finely chopped

2 dl cream, lightly whipped
pepper and salt

For the green asparagus ice:
12 green asparagus, washed and cut into chucks
salt
40 g glucose
1 cl lemon juice

For the ham crumble:
50 g ham
2 slices puff pastry

For the Maas bass:
4 x 150 g Maas bass
25 g tempura flour
25 g panko
olive oil

› Warm the consommé, add the ham and allow to cook gently on a low heat for 30 minutes. Dice finely in a thermomix and pass through a fine sieve. Season with pepper and salt. Place the mixture in an aerosol spray and pressurise with a single gas capsule. Keep in the fridge until needed for use.
› Boil the asparagus briefly in salted water, then rinse them in cold water. Keep 40 centilitres of the cooking fluid and pour away the rest. Add the glucose and heat at a high temperature for 2 minutes, and then allow to cool. Add the lemon juice and fill the pacojet pot three-quarters full with the glucose mixture and the asparagus. Place in the freezer and freeze until the core temperature drops to -20 °C. Mix to a fine consistency in the pacojet.
› Pre-heat the oven to 180 °C. Dry the ham for the crumble in the warm oven for 20 minutes. Bake the puff pastry at 180 °C until it is nice and brown, and then mix it with the ham, until a fine, crumbly consistency results.
› Cut up the Maas bass into portions. Mix the tempura flour and the panko. Coat the skin side on the bass with this flour mix. Heat the olive oil in a pan and fry the bass until it is nice and brown. Remove from the pan and allow to cook further in an oven for 5 minutes at 180 °C.
› Garnish according to your preference.

Smoked goat's cheese, Loon syrup, watercress and sweetleaf

For 4 people

200 g goat's cheese
3 egg yolks
1.5 dl milk
2 gelatine slices, soaked
1.5 dl cream, beaten until stiff
pepper and salt
5 sprigs watercress
2 sprigs stevia rebaudiana (sweetleaf)
Loon syrup

For the decoration:
50 g isomalt
50 g glucose
100 g fondant

1 larch twig (finely chopped stevia is an alternative)

› Smoke the goat's cheese for 30 minutes on beech wood chips and allow to cool.
› Warm the egg yolks and milk to 80 °C. Add the soaked and wrung gelatine slices. Allow to cool. Add the goat's cheese and fold in the cream. Season with salt and pepper. Place the pot containing the mixture in an ice-bath and continue stirring, until the binding process is almost complete. Roll into tubes and allow to harden in the freezer.
› Blanch the watercress and the sweetleaf for 30 seconds in boiling water, then immediately rinse under cold, running water. Dry for 35 minutes in a drying cabinet or in an oven at 80 °C. Reduce the dried leaves to powder in a blender. Keep the powder in a dry place.
› Remove the cheese from the freezer 15 minutes before serving and arrange on a plate.
› Dress with Loon syrup according to your preference.

The decoration in 1, 2, 3

> Collect together all the ingredients (see above)
> Allow the isomalt to melt in a pan.
> Add the glucose.
> Add the fondant.
> Heat to 160 °C.
> Pour the resulting caramel onto a silicone baking mat and allow to harden for 20 minutes.
> Pulverise the caramel in a thermomix (or blender).
> Spread the caramel powder evenly over the baking mat with a fine sieve.
> Decorate with young larch twiglets.
> Heat in an oven at 100 °C until the caramel has melted. Allow to cool and then cut or break into the desired shape.

Roasted foie gras with an almond salve and cherry juice

For 4 people

2 tablespoons elderberries
1 dl blackcurrant syrup (cassis)
150 g wheat
1 shallot
2 dl chicken consommé
1/2 slice gelatine, soaked in cold water
1 dl cream
50 g ground almonds
4 slices foie gras, each of 80 g
ca. 20 grains wheat germ

› Pick ripe elderberries during the summer. Wash them and add them to the blackcurrant syrup. Keep in a cool place.
› Sow the wheat on a wet cloth and allow it to germinate (it will take 14 days before you have usable plants).
› Make a wheat risotto by sweating the shallot and then allowing it to cook through in the consommé with the wheat, while stirring. Bind the risotto mixture with the melted gelatine. Pour into moulds of desired shape and allow to cool.
› Make a light bechamel sauce with the cream and stir in the ground almonds.
› Grill the foie gras for 2 minutes on both sides.
› Decorate and present according to your preference.

Maxime Collard

♪ La Table de Maxime ♪

Maxime Collard is the youngest of the Wallonian chefs to open his own restaurant, which he did in 2009. Just eighteen months later, he was chosen by GaultMillau as the 'most promising young chef of the year' in Wallonia and was also awarded his first Michelin star. What makes him so special?

Serene cuisine with roots in the Ardennes

The setting is the quiet, rural village of Our, the place where Maxime was born. The building is the property of the local village contractor, Thomas&Piron. Maxime has redecorated the interior in a contemporary, 'mondaine' style, which exudes the rustic charm of the village. After his initial training at the hotel school in Libramont, he started work at Restaurant 'Au Forges du Point d'Oie' in Habay-la-Neuve. He then did five years with Geert van Hecke at 'De Karmeliet' in Bruges. The difference between the two? Maxime: "More homely and traditional in 'Au Forges', more product-oriented and technical at 'De Karmeliet'. This illustrates the essential difference between Flemish and Wallonian gastronomy. In Wallonia, traditional cuisine is still the order of the day, since that is what people want. Cuisine in Flanders is more adventurous, more avant-garde; and this too has its own broad public. My own cuisine balances between the two. I see it as a 'serene' cuisine, with its roots in the Ardennes. First and foremost, it is a product cuisine with recognisable ingredients, some of which are of local origin. But it is also a classical cuisine, albeit in a 'light' version, in which new techniques are sparingly used. Yes, I take account of my customers and what they like, but even if that were not the case, I would still cook in the same way. Because that is my style."

Regional ingredients

Like many people from the Ardennes, Maxime Collard is a stay-at-home. He loves his native region, and this is reflected in his choice

of products. "'As far as possible, I like to work with regional products, because they help to better define the identity of a chef and his cooking. For this reason, for example, I have reintroduced a trout dish into my menu. Until ten or twenty years ago, you always used to see trout on the card in most gastronomic restaurants. Nowadays, you only find it in tourist-type restaurants. Finding fresh trout here is not a problem. There are several trout breeders in the area around Bouillon and from March onwards, if the weather allows, I even go and fish for wild trout in the local rivers. But I prepare it in a modern way. First I fillet the fish, but then I 'glue' the fillets back together, using transglutaminate, an enzyme that binds protein. It is one of my signature dishes.

My second signature dish involves pigeon. Unfortunately, pigeons are not bred around here, so I have to buy them in France. To compensate for this, I serve the pigeon breasts with a traditional Liege salad. This salad with beans, potatoes, bacon and onion is a typical regional dish, for which every housewife in Liege has her own particular recipe. In my version I use slices of Florenville, a firm local potato with a golden yellow interior and a fine, delicate flavour. For my third signature dish, I use Ardennes lamb, goat's cheese from Ferme des Sureaux in the neighbouring village of Maissin, and wild bear's garlic which I pick in the local woods. I use both the leaves and the flowers."

> *I like to work with regional products, because they help to better define the identity of a chef and his cooking.*

> *In Wallonia, traditional cuisine is still the order of the day, since that is what people want. Cuisine in Flanders is more adventurous, more avant-garde.*

Light and pure

For Maxime Collard, quality is always the most important criterion when selecting his products. Even his regional products. "I get my beef from Poncelet in Paliseul, a butcher who carefully selects his animals from the local breeders in the area. A gardener in the village grows herbs and edible flowers especially for me. I also use snails from Namur, Ardennes ham and pâté and game from the local forests. Sometimes, I am even my own supplier! I like to go for long walks in the countryside and I will often come back with wild herbs, ceps and other types of woodland mushroom. And what I can't buy locally, I buy elsewhere. About fifty percent of my ingredients are local or Belgian, the rest come from France."

Maxime Collard's cuisine is characterised by lightness and purity. "I am always looking for delicate harmonies of flavour. I don't use butter or cream, but prefer olive oil. I work with natural herb juices for emulsions and sauces, which I like to make as concentrated as possible. You can also find a number of oriental influences in my cooking, particularly in the herbs and spices, but I always integrate them into my dishes with subtlety. Good products don't need much tra-la-la."

La Table de Maxime
Our 23, 6852 Our (Paliseul)
061/23 95 10
www.tabledemaxime.be

➜ **What was your first culinary experience or memory?**
The meals prepared by my parents and grandparents. And the cuisine of Provence that I learnt to appreciate during our family holidays to the South of France.

➜ **What is your most important personal quality?**
The ability to keep silent but remain attentive.

➜ **What would you like to have more time for?**
Tennis, fishing, travel and friends.

➜ **What other job would you like to do?**
Banker!

➜ **For you, what is the epitome of luxury?**
The perfection of an object or product.

➜ **What are you best at in the kitchen?**
In general, cooking; in particular, bringing lightness to dishes.

➜ **What do you most enjoy doing in the kitchen?**
Preparing fish dishes.

➜ **What is your favourite vegetable?**
Peas.

➜ **What is your favourite type or cut of meat?**
The entrecôte from my butcher that I prepare at home for my family.

➜ **What type(s) of fish do you like to work with?**
Cod.

➜ **What are you favourite aromas and smells in the kitchen?**
The fragrances of the aromatic plants that I grow in my vegetable plot.

➜ **Which chef has inspired you the most?**
Geert Van Hecke and Michel Bras.

➜ **Who is your perfect table companion?**
Congenial people with respect for the staff.

➜ **What is your favourite aperitif?**
A glass of white wine.

➜ **What do you most enjoy eating on your day off?**
Entrecôte with chips and a salad.

Fillet of trout from our rivers, fried foie gras and smoked eel, with a tartar of peas with mint, caramelised tomatoes and onion juice

For 4 people

2 trout
pepper and salt
transglutaminate
120 g shelled peas
20 g conserved tomatoes, chopped
into chunks
6 fresh leaves of mint, finely chopped
olive oil
1 onion, finely chopped
10 cl port
20 cl white stock
4 x 50 g foie gras
50 g smoked eel

› Fillet the trout and remove the bones. Season the meat side (inside) of the fillets with pepper and salt. Sprinkle both meat sides with transglutaminate and stick them neatly back together. Allow to rest for half a day in the fridge.
› Make the pea tartar: fry the peas, add the conserved tomatoes, mint and some olive oil. Season with pepper and salt.
› Fry the onion and add the port and white stock. Allow the liquid to reduce for 2 hours and then mix thoroughly. Season as appropriate.
› Cut the trout fillets into two equal portions. Roast them for 2 minutes on the skin side.
› Fry the foie gras on both sides.
› Cut the smoked eel into chunks.
› Spoon the lukewarm pea tartar into a kitchen ring. Add the foie gras, trout, eel and onion juice.

The preparation in 1, 2, 3

Fillet the trout and remove the bones with tweezers.

Sprinkle both meat sides with transglutaminate and stick them neatly back together.

Allow the conserved onion, port and white stock to reduce for 2 hours and then mix thoroughly.

Fry the foie gras on both sides.

Cut the trout fillets into equal portions.
Roast them for 2 minutes on the skin side.

Spoon the onion juice around the
pea tartar and add the trout.

Spoon the lukewarm pea tartar into a
kitchen ring.

Finish by adding blocks of smoked eel, topped
with a slice of the foie gras. Decorate according
to preference.

Breast of Anjou pigeon, with conserved pigeon legs, a Liege salad, Florenville potatoes and a vadouvan juice

For 4 people

4 pigeons
200 g goose fat

For the stock:
1 carrot
1 stick blanching celery
1 stick leek
1 sprig thyme
1 laurel leaf
1 clove garlic
1 tablespoon tomato concentrate
1 tablespoon vadouvan

150 g French beans
8 potatoes
1 slice smoked ham, 0.5 cm thick

2 onions, finely chopped

2 tablespoons balsamico

› Bone the pigeons and cut away the meat: legs, breast, carcass, liver. Season the legs and conserve them slowly in the goose fat for 3 hours at 65 °C.
› For the stock, colour the carcass, the vegetables and the herbs. Add the water, tomato concentrate and vadouvan. Allow to reduce almost completely over a period of 3 hours.
› Cut the beans into equal-sized chunks and blanch them for 2 minutes.
› Boil the potatoes in their peel. Cut them into slices.
› Fry the ham and the onion, and deglaze with the balsamico.
› Fry the pigeon breasts for 1 minute on each side and allow to rest for 5 minutes.
› In the meantime, fry the pigeon liver.

Milk lamb cutlets with conserved leg of lamb, bear's garlic, fresh Ferme des Sureaux goat's cheese, couscous, candied fruit, and a ras-el-hanout juice

For 4 people

For the stock:
lamb bones: shank, leg, ribs
olive oil
1 carrot
1 stick blanching celery
1 onion
1 clove garlic
1 tablespoon tomato concentrate

200 g leg of lamb
pepper and salt
4 g ras-el-hanout
160 g couscous
olive oil
8 leaves bear's garlic
1 fresh roundel goat's cheese
8 lamb cutlets

4 candied apricots
4 candied prunes
20 g pine kernels

> For the stock, fry the bones in olive oil until they are fully browned. Add the chopped vegetables and the tomato concentrate, and allow them to colour. Take the ingredients out of the pan. Deglaze the stock, replace the ingredients, add water until everything is just covered and then allow to reduce for a further 5 hours.
> Season the leg of lamb with salt, pepper and ras-el-hanout. Roast on all sides. Place in a vacuum bag with the vegetables from the lamb stock and allow to cook slowly for 36 hours at 65 °C.
> Boil the couscous in water with some olive oil, salt and ras-el-hanout for 5 minutes.
> Blanch the leaves of bear's garlic for 5 seconds and immerse them immediately in ice-cold water. Allow them to drain and wrap them around the goat's cheese.
> Fry the lamb cutlets on all sides and then cook them further for 2-3 minutes in an oven at 180 °C.
> For the sauce, use the reduced lamb stock, seasoned with 2 grams of ras-el-hanout.

Gert De Mangeleer

∫ *Hertog Jan* ∿

Although he describes his cuisine as 'classic', his customers are mad about Gert De Mangeleer's food for its innovative combinations and diversity of products. And with the cultivation of micro-vegetables on his own farm, he has taken yet another step towards confirming his exclusive 'Hertog Jan' style.

A boyhood dream

Gert De Mangeleer already knew that he wanted to be a cook when he was just twelve years old. But his parents first insisted that he should complete his normal secondary education – which he did. Thereafter, he immediately enrolled in the 'Ter Groene Poorte' hotel school. Two years later he worked his way into the kitchen of Danny Horseele in 't Molentje' (Zeebrugge). "He immediately gave me carte blanche. I was given the cold kitchen and the pastry, and was even allowed to draw up the menu. He must have sensed that I had it in me, otherwise he would never have given a new boy that amount of trust. Horseele was the first and only chef for whom I worked. Because I was left to my own devices, I never had the chance to learn much from him. At first, I found this a bit of a problem. Other budding chefs go to Sergio, Peter Goossens or Geert Van Hecke with the specific intention of learning from the masters. At the time, I felt that I was missing out on something. Looking back, it was probably a blessing in disguise. I have always picked things up easily, and after my initial disappointment I soon began to find my own way. I worked in 't Molentje' for four years and had plenty of opportunities to test out my own ideas. In this way, I was gradually able to develop my own style. When I came to work with

sommelier Joachim Boudens in the 'Hertog Jan' in 2003, this style was still not fully defined. Two years later, we took over the running of the restaurant, and from that moment I was really able to work at perfecting my culinary identity."

Daring combinations

Gert De Mangeleer combines ingredients with an exceptional feeling for taste. In his desire to reduce flavours to their essence, he knows exactly what to put in and exactly what to leave out. "I combine flavours using my instinct. Experience plays an important role. I sketch almost everything out beforehand. If my gut feeling tells me that a combination will work, I will give it a try. In eighty to ninety percent of cases, it's an immediate bull's-eye. For the remaining ten to twenty percent, I try again, adding new accents. If the combination is a successful one, I still keep fine tuning, until I have found exactly the right dosage for each of the different flavours. The dish is then ready 'for production'. Amongst other things, I now make a preparation based on distilled wattle seeds (the seed from an Australian variety of the acacia tree) and a passion fruit cream with vanilla oil, served with smoked lobster and onion marinated in a soya sauce. I also have a combination of smoked aubergine with tomato and cinnamon. Or a dessert with a basis of ponzu, chicory, crisp-fried bacon and a lemon ice-cream with lemon pepper. These combinations are not always straightforward for my customers, but that's the way they seem to me. I am busy with them every day, so I don't really notice how daring some of the combinations actually are. But once you taste them, you know that they work. It then requires lots of further effort and testing to bring them to perfection. The combination of cacao with cherries and mustard is one of my signature dishes and the taste is phenomenal. It has been on our menu for more than three years. Originally with pigeon, then with lamb, and now with lobster from the Oosterschelde. The hint of almonds in the tonka bean acts as a perfect bridge between the chocolate and the mustard."

Vegetables from his own bio-farm

"My cuisine looks very innovative, but in reality it is very simple and very natural. The combinations are innovative, because they are not 'everyday'. This is why many people think that we serve molecular food, but we do nothing of the kind. I have one of the least technical kitchens, in comparison with many other restaurants. Our cuisine is actually characterised by the wide diversity of our products, in which vegetables play an important role. Our

> **My cuisine looks very innovative, but in reality it is very simple and very natural. The combinations are innovative, because they are not 'everyday'.**

In a nutshell

- Who or what influenced your choice of profession?
  My mother. She is an excellent cook.

- What was your first culinary experience or memory?
  Horsemeat sausages.

- What can really make you mad in the kitchen?
  Anger in the kitchen is a sign of weakness and poor organisation.

- What is your most important personal quality?
  The ability to organise.

- What would you like to have more time for?
  My family.

- What other job would you like to do?
  Architect.

- For you, what is the epitome of luxury?
  A free and unplanned Sunday with my wife and children.

- What are you best at in the kitchen?
  Organising.

- What do you most enjoy doing in the kitchen?
  Everything.

- What do you least enjoy doing in the kitchen?
  Nothing.

- What is your favourite vegetable?
  Tomato.

- What is your favourite type or cut of meat?
  Neck of lamb.

- What type(s) of fish do you like to work with?
  Sardines.

- What are your preferred herbs for fish and meat dishes?
  Fleur de sel.

- What are you favourite aromas and smells in the kitchen?
  Lemon.

- What is your favourite dish?
  Entrecôte on the grill.

- Which small object could you not do without in the kitchen?
  A potato peeler.

- Which chef has inspired you the most?
  Jonnie Boer.

- What type of cuisine do you not like?
  Macrobiotic.

- What was the last celebrated restaurant that you visited and what was your opinion?
  'Troisgras' in Roanne.

- What is your worst ever professional experience?
  The accident involving Joakim and Julie, two of our finest team members.

- Who is your perfect table companion?
  My wife.

- What is your favourite aperitif?
  Duvel (a strong Belgian beer).

- What do you most enjoy eating on your day off?
  Entrecôte.

- What are your favourite book and your favourite cooking book?
  Michel Bras.

- Which famous customer would you one day like to welcome, and why?
  Georges Leekens: he is our biggest fan and we are his.

- Which famous person from the past would you like to have welcomed as a customer?
  Willy Slawinski.

largest investment to date was the purchase in 2010 of a farm in the polders, with three hectares of ground. We have reserved two hectares for the cultivation of our own micro-vegetables. This was a big step financially, but the exclusivity that it gives us in culinary terms is beyond price. This will create new resources for further investment. I am thinking in the long term. If there is an over-production of a particular vegetable, we can store them, bottle them and sell them under our own label. We work biologically, almost bio-dynamically, because I feel that these are the methods that give the best results. I am not an eccentric or a do-gooder, and I am not trying to save the planet. I just want good, honest products, with plenty of flavour. This explains why we are not following the current hype for the purchase of regional products. Of course, I will always check first to see if we can buy quality products close to home, and I think it is very important to monitor our ecological footprint. But if I can't find what I want nearby, I will go abroad. I have never found a supplier of better lamb than the farmer with whom we work in the Limousin. The rest of our meat and poultry also comes largely from France. But if I want pigs' trotters, calf tongue, oxtail or a good entrecôte, I go to a small producer in Damme who slaughters and processes his animals on-farm. The best quality fish and seafood – sole, turbot, sea bass, cuttlefish and shrimps – can still be found at the quayside market in Nieuwpoort. Our eel and lobster come from the Oosterschelde (Scheldt estuary) and our mackerel and sardines from Brittany. We have a fine selection of cheeses in the restaurant, but I do not want to limit myself to local types. The identity of your kitchen is not only defined by the products you use, but also by what you do with them. Your own style is the decisive factor. If Belgian cuisine wants to establish a clear identity, then chefs need to look more in their own cooking pots and less in the pots of their foreign colleagues. Too many things in Belgium are copied from others. This is one of the reasons why I have been to so few other quality restaurants in Belgium in recent years: I want to protect myself from other influences (and so I go to a nice bistro instead!). During the Flemish Primitives in Ostend, we were constantly hearing that Flanders is at the forefront of culinary innovation. Does this mean that after the Spanish wave and the Scandinavian wave we can now expect a Flemish wave? I doubt it. Ferran Adrià must have had the feeling that he had invented something new. René Redzepi too. I do not feel that I have invented anything. I just do my own thing with my own farm and my own combinations, some of which may be special. If my customers tell me that they don't know where my inspiration comes from, that is the nicest compliment they can pay me. What I do is highly individual. If every Flemish and Belgian chef could strive for this type of individuality, then we might be able to speak of a culinary wave. But this will not be possible while all we have is a hundred copies of Ferran Adrià."

Hertog Jan
Torhoutsesteenweg 479,
8200 Sint-Michiels (Brugge)
050/67 34 46
www.hertog-jan.com

Marinated langoustines with raspberries, red beetroot and vanilla oil

200 g langoustine meat, finely
chopped
20 g shallot, finely chopped
8 tablespoons vanilla oil
coarse salt
4 raspberries
4 slices marinated beetroot
8 g wattle seed

10 g raspberry powder
chive flowers

› Mix together the chopped langoustines, shallot and vanilla
oil. Season with coarse salt. Cut the raspberries into pieces as
shown in the photograph (step by step).

Presentation in 1, 2, 3

› Take an empty plate.
› Place a slice of marinated red beetroot on the plate.
› Add the langoustine tartar.
› Sprinkle with some wattle seeds.
› Garnish with pieces of raspberry.
› Sprinkle the raspberry powder over the ingredients.
› Finish with vanilla oil and coarse salt.
› Decorate with the chive flowers.

Oosterschelde lobster with cherries and cacao

For the cherry cream:
2 dl cherry juice
5 cl red wine vinegar
100 g sugar
3 g agaragar

For the tonka bean foam:
1 dl half-cream milk
1 tonka bean
1 g sucro

2 Oosterschelde lobsters, each of 500 g
100 g farmhouse butter

For the decoration:
10 g ground cacao beans
5 g coarse salt
12 black cherries
12 sweet-sour red onions

12 sprigs of young mustard greens

› Mix all the ingredients for the cherry cream and bring to the boil. Beat the mixture until it forms a smooth cream. Pour out and allow to stiffen. Keep the cream in a piping bag.
› Bring the milk and the tonka bean to the boil. Pour the milk through a sieve. Set the pan on a warm stove and allow to simmer for 10 minutes. Add the sucro and work into a light foam with a hand mixer.
› Separate the lobster tails from the heads. Keep the heads and claws for another preparation. Cut the tails in two and place them in a vacuum bag with the butter. Cook for 12 minutes at 65 °C.
› Sprinkle a deep plate with the cacao powder. Arrange the lobster tails on the plate and season with coarse salt. Squirt three rosettes of the cherry cream between them. Dress with the cherries and sweet-sour onions. Pour the light tonka bean foam over the composition and decorate with the mustard greens.

Cream of polder potato and bear's garlic with morel mushrooms, juice of tarragon vinegar and young sorrel

For the cream of polder potato and bear's garlic:
250 g polder potatoes
12.5 cl milk
12.5 dl cream
20 bear's garlic leaves

For the morel mushrooms:
12 morel mushrooms
50 g farmhouse butter
coarse salt

For the tarragon vinegar juice:
1 dl tarragon vinegar
100 g farmhouse butter

For the decoration:
20 g young sorrel leaves
20 bear's garlic flowers
20 bear's garlic buds
12 slices gherkin

› Bring the polder potatoes, milk, cream and bear's garlic leaves to the boil and cook until the potatoes are soft. Remove the bear's garlic leaves, mash the remaining mixture into a smooth puree and place in a piping bag.
› Fry the morel mushrooms briefly in farmhouse butter and season with coarse salt.
› Heat the tarragon vinegar and butter. Beat up into a foam.
› Squirt three rosettes of cream into a deep plate. Arrange the morel mushrooms between them. Drizzle the tarragon foam over the composition. Decorate with the bear's garlic flowers and buds, the slices of gherkin and the sorrel.

Kwinten De Paepe

℘ Trente ℘

With just a simple stove and a kitchen robot, Kwinten De Paepe makes complex dishes as though a whole battery of kitchen equipment and technical aids are at his disposal. This makes him the master of minimalism, but also the champion of taste.

Most promising youngster

For three years Kwinten De Paepe was the cook at the popular 'Oesterbar' in the Muntstraat in Leuven. After the owner had to close the bar following an accident, Kwinten and his mates found themselves unexpectedly out of a job. The young chef had long dreamed of opening his own business before he was thirty. The sudden closure gave him the push he needed to go and look for suitable premises. He found them on the other side of the road from the Oesterbar and promptly (and appropriately) named his new eating house 'Trente' – the French word for thirty. He also had the good fortune to have a ready-made kitchen team: his old colleagues from the Oesterbar! Right from the very first day, Kwinten made a big impression with his highly individual style. In 2010 GaultMillau chose him as the 'Most Promising Youngster' in Flanders.

Virtual cooking

The dishes which come out of his tiny kitchen are presented as though they have been cooked 'molecularly'. However, all he uses is an ordinary stove and a kitchen robot. His combi-steamer is only used to warm his plates and bake his cakes. "We thought seriously about getting some other equipment, like a thermomix, roner or pacojet, but we decided it wasn't necessary. It was a choice which deliberately limits us, but this is precisely what inspires us to find ways to offer contemporary dishes with contemporary presentation by different methods. The creation of new dishes is a continual process. We work together in a kitchen just a few metres square and are constantly exchanging ideas. Every idea is written down in a notebook and explored further when we have the time. My chef and I are very good at virtual cooking. Before I put together a new menu, I have already cooked the dishes in my head. During our closing day on Mondays, I write out the recipes in full for the first time. On Tuesday we cook and serve them. We don't do any tests or preparations: we don't have time for any of that. If something is not good, we keep on changing it until it is right. Our basic starting point is always a single product that we build into the recipe. We then look for other ingredients that can provide a balance in terms of taste, temperature and structure. Bitter and sour, fresh and salt: these must form the basis for contrasts. The first dish on the menu must contain sufficient minerals; the last dish must be sweet in combination with fresh tasting acids."

Art as a source of inspiration

"Some of our dishes return at regular intervals, but in a different guise. For example, a combination of quail with onions and raisins has been on our menu every since we opened, but each year we develop a different version of the recipe. At the moment, we are serving it with salted praliné, added baby onions (to change the

texture), and glazed legs of quail (whereas they were previously just fried). Similarly, we have had an endive dish on the menu for the past four years, but with a new variation each year. The most recent changes are the addition of a chicory cream and cacao biscuits. These changes are always small, not revolutionary. Our style and our presentation essentially remain the same. The real evolution is in the taste, which is better thought-out, more refined and better balanced. The dessert that we offer – white achrome – is a cheese dish that is already into its second year. It is based on 'The Chromatic Diet' by the French performance artist Sophie Calle, who ate a meal of the same colour every day. For us, this was a great starting point for a completely white dessert. In fact, we often find our inspiration in art. For example, we have also made a dish that mirrors a painting of water-lilies by Renoir."

Over the borders

As far as possible, Kwinten likes to shop for his ingredients in Belgium, but he goes international when he has to. "Ours is not a 'terroir' cuisine, although we would like to buy more local regional produce, since this gives your cooking a clearer identity. I don't work enough with local suppliers, because most of them are exponents of monoculture and therefore offer too little variety. If we want Belgian cuisine to have a specific identity, we must learn to give greater value to our own products by using them to make outstanding gastronomic dishes, which people are then prepared to try out at home. As chefs, we are in a position to introduce new products and, through our recipes, encourage their use by the wider public. Fortunately, I can see a growing interest in our own 'territorial' cuisine and chefs are rediscovering the classic recipes, some of which have been a part of our culinary heritage for centuries. In particular, new and interesting forms are being created of old standards, such as paling 'in the green', shrimp croquettes and endives in ham and cheese sauce.

I often eat out at the restaurants of other colleagues, whether they be experimental, contemporary or classical. I also closely monitor developments abroad. First there was the Spanish wave, launched by Ferran Adrià, and now there is the Scandinavian wave, with 'Noma' as its figurehead. Sadly, with each new evolution there are always Belgian chefs who copy the new ideas blindly, without stopping to think whether they are compatible with our culinary traditions. For instance, it is almost impossible to make a good imitation of a Japanese dish. All you can do is give the Japanese ideas a Belgian twist in a Belgian context. This brings me back to the question of the identity of Belgian cuisine. We are too modest and self-effacing. We behave as though all the best chefs live abroad, whereas we have dozens of really excellent chefs right here on our own front doorstep. You don't find this in France. Flanders is roughly the same size as Provence, but has far more Michelin stars (seventy-two). The young generation of Belgian chefs is exercising a growing influence, but it does not yet fully appreciate (or exploit) its full potential. Someone like Peter Goossens is often regarded as arrogant, whereas in other countries he would be heralded as a hero. This is typically Belgian – and it is this kind of negative, self-deprecating attitude that we need to change."

> **The young generation of Belgian chefs is exercising a growing influence, but it does not yet fully appreciate (or exploit) its full potential.**

Trente
Muntstraat 36, 3000 Leuven
016/20 30 30
www.trente.be

→ **Who or what influenced your choice of profession?**
Definitely my father. He taught me that you have to make choices in life.

→ **What can really make you mad in the kitchen?**
The chef is ultimately responsible for everything that happens in the kitchen, so you should be angry at yourself if things go wrong. The things that most frequently disrupt a service are not worth getting upset about; otherwise, none of us will ever live to be old. Keep calm and try to find the right solution for the problem as quickly as possible. It is this challenge that makes our job such fun.

→ **What is your most important personal quality?**
Organisation and logistics.

→ **What would you like to have more time for?**
For my darling daughter, of course.

→ **What other job would you like to do?**
Designer or project developer.

→ **For you, what is the epitome of luxury?**
Getting up in the morning and realising that every day is a blessing. Many people are far worse off than we are.

→ **What do you most enjoy doing in the kitchen?**
The morning and evening preparations. The kitchen machine gradually getting into gear.

→ **What is your favourite vegetable?**
All vegetables, as long as they are in season and have been grown correctly and with respect.

→ **What is your favourite type or cut of meat?**
The (so-called) less worthy cuts, such as shank, neck and the cheeks. It is fun to do something fantastic with these undervalued pieces.

→ **What type(s) of fish do you like to work with?**
Any type, as long as they are not farm-grown, small and tasteless.

→ **What are your preferred herbs for fish and meat dishes?**
No doubt about it: rosemary, full-flavoured but always fresh.

→ **Which small object could you not do without in the kitchen?**
Tweezers to extract bones from fish.

→ **Which chef has inspired you the most?**
No one chef in particular, but several; starting with my own team, who are always searching for the new ideas, while continuing to respect the old ones. I also admire the persistence bordering on stubbornness that I see in so many chefs.

→ **What was the last celebrated restaurant that you visited and what was your opinion?**
Jacques Decoret in Vichy (France). A perfect meal: delightfully playful and the restaurant all to ourselves.

→ **What is your favourite aperitif?**
Manzanilla (young fino sherry), a glass of lager or a 'geuze' (a Belgian beer based on a mix of lambics).

→ **What are your favourite book and your favourite cooking book?**
No need to think long about this one: *Eten en Koken* by Harold McGee.

→ **Which famous customer would you one day like to welcome, and why?**
Louis Tobback, burgomaster of Leuven: there is never a dull moment with that man.

→ **Which famous person from the past would you like to have welcomed as a customer?**
If it were possible, a long table with Auguste Escoffier, Marie-Antoine Carême, Jean-Anthelme Brillat-Savarin, Ferdinand Point, Bernard Loiseau and Willy Slawinski.

Quail with onions, raisins and a salted praliné

For 4 people

4 quails
500 g goose fat
2 sprigs thyme
2 laurel leaves
2 Spanish peppers (poivres longs)
4 juniper berries
1 carrot, finely chopped
1 onion, finely chopped
1 stalk blanching celery, finely
chopped
2 tablespoons tomato puree

10 stalks parsley

1 clove garlic, crushed
40 g white raisins
5 cl sweet sherry
4 sweet white onions
10 g butter
15 cl amontillado sherry (dry sherry or
Madeira)
2.5 dl strong quail stock
50 g praliné nuts

For the crumble:
115 g butter
50 g sugar
50 g praliné nuts
175 g flour
2 g salt

pepper and salt

4 quail's eggs
8 shoots tahoon cress

› Clean the quails and the legs, until the form of the shank becomes clear. Conserve the legs by cooking them slowly for 4 hours at 67 °C in the goose fat, together with the thyme, laurel, Spanish pepper and a few juniper berries.
› Fry the quail carcasses in a pan. Add the carrot, onion and celery, together with the laurel, thyme, parsley, garlic, Spanish pepper, a few juniper berries and a little tomato puree. Add water and bring to the point of boiling for just a moment, then allow to simmer for 5 hours on a low heat. Drain and reduce the stock to a quarter.
› Soak the raisins for at least an hour in the dry sherry.
› Clean the sweet onion and cut it into slices. Stew the slices in a little butter in a covered pan. Dilute with the dry sherry and the quail stock. Add the soaked raisins and allow to cook lightly for 20 minutes on a low heat, with the lid removed.
› Pre-heat an oven to 170 °C. Make a crumble by dry mixing all the ingredients. Bake for 10 minutes in the warm oven. Allow to cool. Grind the crumble into a coarse powder with the kitchen robot.
› Further reduce the quail stock with the dry sherry and the praliné nuts until it has the consistency of a smooth sauce. Pass this sauce through a sieve and season with pepper and salt.
› Fry the quail fillets until they are nice and pink.
› Lightly fry the conserved quail legs.
› Crack the quail's eggs and fry them like a 'normal' fried egg. Cut them into roundels with a kitchen ring.
› Spoon the onion compote neatly onto a plate, place a quail fillet on top, with a quail leg resting against it and the praliné sauce around it. Put a quail's egg on top of the fillet, and sprinkle some crumble around it. Pour some extra sauce around the whole composition and dress with the tahoon cress.

Endives with chicory cream, cacao and foie gras

For 4 people

2 tablespoons crystal sugar
2 tablespoons chicory powder
4 g agaragar
20 cl milk
2 tablespoons ordinary sugar
1 tablespoon ground wattle seeds

8 endives (grown in full ground)
butter
1 l chicken stock
100 g terrine of foie gras
1 tablespoon of cacao powder (for the coating)
achillea flowers (for decoration)

For the crumble:
115 g butter
150 g sugar
150 g flower
20 g cacao
1 g salt
4 achillea stems

› Add the crystal sugar to 20 centilitres of water and allow to 'brew' for 20 minutes with the chicory. Pass through a sieve, mix in half the agaragar and bring briefly to the boil. Allow to cool and then whisk into a smooth cream.
› Put the ordinary sugar and the wattle seed powder in the milk and allow to 'brew' gently for 2 hours. Pass through a sieve and bring briefly to the boil. Add the remaining agaragar, bring to the boil again and then allow to cool, before whipping into a smooth cream.
› Stew the endives in a little butter. Remove four of the endives and keep them to one side.
› Put the other four endives into the chicken stock and simmer until they are cooked through. Drain the fluid and puree the vegetables into a smooth cream.
› Cut the terrine of foie gras into small cubes and roll them gently in the cacao powder, until covered on all sides.
› Pre-heat an oven to 170 °C. Dry mix all the ingredients for the crumble and bake them for 10 minutes in the warm oven. Allow to cool. Grind the crumble into a coarse powder with the kitchen robot.
› Fry the four remaining endives in a pan until they are golden brown. Finish the dish with the crumble, serve with the creams and the foie gras cubes and decorate with the achillea flowers.

White achrome (coconut, lemon and white curry with jasmine rice)

For the rice flan:
4 jasmine tea-bags (or loose tea)
1 stalk lemon grass
40 g sugar
200 g jasmine rice
25 cl coconut milk
2 g agaragar

For the white curry:
25 cl coconut milk
20 cl palm sugar syrup
1 bundle coriander
2 kaffir leaves
1 kaffir lime
1 stalk lemon grass
1/2 galanga root

1 green chili pepper
1/2 vanilla stick
4 g agaragar

For the lime meringue:
10 cl lime juice
10 g ovoneve (powdered egg white)
30 g sugar

For the malto powder:
20 g maltodextrine powder
20 g icing sugar
1 tablespoon coconut fat

For the coconut mousse:
20 cl coconut milk

3 dl whipped cream
120 g sugar
1/2 vanilla stick
juice of 1/2 lime
3 slices gelatine
2 tablespoons powdered coconut flakes

For the coconut sorbet:
60 cl coconut milk
20 cl glucose syrup
20 cl milk

jasmine flowers
grains of puffed rice (ready-to-buy)

› Make some jasmine tea and add the lemon grass and the sugar. Boil the rice for 15 minutes in this jasmine stock. Drain the rice and cook again, this time with the coconut milk. Add the agaragar. Tip the mixture onto a baking tray and allow to cool. Cut out a number of roundels with a kitchen ring. Work the remaining pieces into a fine cream in a mixer.
› Mix together all the ingredients for the curry, apart from the agaragar, and warm them lightly in a pan. Remove the pan from the heat and allow the lukewarm ingredients to cool and mingle for an hour and a half. Pass the mixture through a sieve and bring the resulting fluid to the boil with the agaragar. Allow to cool and then work into a smooth cream in a mixer.
› Beat together all the ingredients for the lime meringue in a kitchen robot, until they form a snowy-white foam. Spread this foam onto a sheet of baking paper and bake for 4 hours in a warm oven at 90 °C, until this white mass becomes firm.
› Cold mix all the ingredients for the malto powder.
› Stir the coconut milk into the whipped cream. Add the sugar, vanilla stick, lime juice and the drained, melted gelatine. Allow to stiffen for 3 hours. Make a number of mousse balls with a scoop and coat them with the powdered coconut flakes.
› Mix together all the ingredients for the sorbet and bring them briefly to the boil. Stir well and allow to cool. Put this mixture into an ice-cream machine and make the sorbet.
› Decorate the plated-up ingredients with a jasmine flower and some puffed rice.

Presentation in 1, 2, 3

Draw a line of rice cream across the plate.

Add two of the round rice flans.

Add a ball of coconut mousse.

Drizzle some drops of the rice curry over the plate and over the different ingredients.

5

6

Decorate with jasmine flowers and some puffed rice.

Spoon on some malto powder.

7

8

Use two spoons to form a coconut sorbet quenelle.

Finish with a piece of lime meringue.

Bart De Pooter

♪ *Pastorale* ♪

For Bart De Pooter running a restaurant is a form of self-expression. But this was something of which he was not immediately aware, when he opened his restaurant 'Pastorale' in Reet at the tender age of just twenty. "It was only gradually that I came to realise that working in a kitchen is much more than a question of simply preparing food. It was not until later that I understood that 'Pastorale' was also a means to give expression to what I think and feel."

Work in progress

At the start of his career, Bart De Pooter was more concerned with putting all the many skills and techniques he had learned into faithful and effective practice. He had already worked for a number of years under the guidance of three-star chef Pierre Romeyer. Even after the opening of 'Pastorale', he still spent his free days for a year finishing off his culinary education under the expert eye of Roger Souvereyns. "But as soon as I was able to stand on my own two feet, I started to ask myself some telling questions. This is when my real search began. I wanted to make an impression, to create an identity, but it soon became clear that this was easier said than done. In fact, I realised that this was likely to be a never-ending process, since many of the things that I do are in a state of continuous development. This helps to explain my favourite expression: 'Pastorale' is and will remain 'a work in progress'." Bart De Pooter regards the realisation of his culinary vision as an evolutionary project. And in 1991, together with his wife, he found the ideal setting in which to lay the basis for this project: the historic surroundings and serene atmosphere of an elegantly renovated vicarage. Authenticity and purity, combined with technical skill and artistic flair, are the key elements which allow Bart De Pooter to give depth and personal identity to his culinary creations. At the same time, they are also the means by which he seeks to involve his customers in an intense and highly intimate manner in his restaurant project.

As a chef, I keep on looking for personal accents which can help me to give a new twist to basic products.

A never-ending search for the personal touch

"It is possible that 'Pastorale' will eventually evolve into a smaller restaurant with fewer places, so that we can focus more sharply on our ultimate goal. It is something I often think about, but it is not yet a practical option. Even so, the idea itself shows that for me the running of a restaurant has its own dynamic, a dynamic in which we, as a team, should always be striving to achieve perfection. In everything: tableware, glassware, service, entourage, atmosphere... This is not a one-man show. I am constantly on the look-out for people who share the same ideas and who are as keen as I am to give those ideas shape and form. Our project is very much team-driven, but I sometimes need to be able to take a step back, so that I can see what still needs to be improved. Most of my spare time is also taken up with 'Pastorale'. I read, I search and I explore possible solutions for the problems with which I am likely to be confronted. For example, products with unique taste and a strong identity are destined to become scarcer. This is a real worry for the future, and one for which I need to find an answer. As a chef, I keep on looking for personal accents which can help me to give a new twist to basic products. I work primarily with vegetables and increasingly with herbs that I grow myself. I have a seed bank with more than two thousand different varieties, of which I have currently planted about two hundred. I have no real idea what to expect from most of them. It is a matter of feeling my way: testing, testing, testing and tasting, tasting, tasting. Only then will I understand what they might be able to bring to my cooking. But I am always pleased when an experiment of this kind shows that a new flavour accent can give added length and depth to another product. This is often a time-consuming process of trial-and-error, but it helps to create its own kind of dynamic in the kitchen. Not that I am the only chef working in this manner. Many of my colleagues share the same concerns and are also on the hunt for new and more intense flavour combinations. By working together and sharing our findings, we can also enrich each other's expertise."

Stimulating the senses and conjuring up emotions

The cuisine at 'Pastorale' is characterised by depth of taste and a more than usual concern for the 'feel' of food in the mouth. By using feminine, almost coquettish, accents, Bart De Pooter gives a playful nervousness to his light and fluid recipes. His dishes stay with you and give his cooking strong personal cachet. "The desire to stimulate all the senses and to conjure up different emotions is the inspirational basis of my cooking. Of course, the main emphasis is placed on natural, well-balanced flavours, with a hint of nuance. Nowadays, there are all sorts of techniques available which allow you to create healthy and easily digestible food of high quality. Applying these

In a nutshell

➜ **Who or what influenced your choice of profession?**
Fascination for fresh things from the garden, pots and pans, love of good food, job security and social contact with customers, the chance to be of service...

➜ **What was your first culinary experience or memory?**
The peas and carrots prepared by my mum for my first communion party.

➜ **What can really make you mad in the kitchen?**
When good products are rendered tasteless through incompetence.

➜ **What is your most important personal quality?**
Honesty, passion, drive, determination.

➜ **What would you like to have more time for?**
Children.

➜ **What other job would you like to do?**
Architect or spatial planner.

➜ **For you, what is the epitome of luxury?**
Feeling good, the surge of adrenalin, the freedom to think and do what I want.

➜ **What do you most enjoy doing in the kitchen?**
Tasting.

➜ **What is your favourite vegetable?**
Super-fresh, season-ready young peas, asparagus and salsify.

➜ **What is your favourite type or cut of meat?**
A thick, tender, juicy, fat-laced, well matured, not overcooked côte à l'os from Aubrac.

➜ **What type(s) of fish do you like to work with?**
Blue fish: mackerel, sardines, anchovies.

➜ **What are your preferred herbs for fish and meat dishes?**
Vervain, star aniseed.

➜ **What is your favourite dish?**
This varies from place to place and season to season: pigeon with peas, sauerkraut, bouillabaisse.

➜ **Which small object could you not do without in the kitchen?**
A paring knife.

➜ **Which chef has inspired you the most?**
I get most of my inspiration from my surroundings; in other words, from mother nature. But I admire certain chefs who continually strive for perfection, such as Pierre Gagnaire.

➜ **What was the last celebrated restaurant that you visited and what was your opinion?**
'De Leest' in Vaasen (The Netherlands). Whenever I visit chef Jacob Boerma, a friend, I always have the feeling that I am coming home: enjoyment, conversation, surprises, tasting, teasing and very good food. 'De Leest' has it all.

➜ **What is your worst ever eating experience?**
A meal which ended with a visit to the doctor. I think its called salmonella.

➜ **Who is your perfect table companion?**
Jolien and Karen, my two children.

➜ **What is your favourite aperitif?**
A fine, dry Riesling or sherry.

➜ **What do you most enjoy eating on your day off?**
A mixed salad with a juicy piece of red meat and thick, fat chips.

➜ **What are your favourite book and your favourite cooking book?**
Favourite book: a collection of Chinese fairy tales. Favourite cookery book: The El Bulli Collection. Also works by Joachim Wissler ('Vendôme'), Kobe Desmaraults ('In De Wulf') and Rene Redzepi ('Noma').

➜ **For whom would you one day like to cook, and why?**
For everyone who I like and respect; to give back a little something for all the things I have been so fortunate to receive.

➜ **Which famous customer would you one day like to welcome, and why?**
Madonna: rhythm, passion, perfection, colouring outside the lines.

➜ **Which famous person from the past would you like to have welcomed as a customer?**
August Escoffier – stories from the past which are still meaningful today.

techniques correctly represents an additional challenge. In essence, however, eating and preparing food is about the discovery of new tastes and textures. The greatest pleasure is to be found in the development phase, in the process of conceptual thinking. This is followed by the phases of production and reproduction, which also have their charm, but are generally less interesting (if I am perfectly honest!). For this reason, I am still focused on the search for new forms of expression that can make my cooking stronger. Not simply by copying other people's ideas, but by transforming them and making them my own. For my plate presentation, for example, I am continually drawing on ideas from art in general and architecture in particular, which allows me to create a field of tension through the interplay of different lines. I try to use the surface of the plate in a spatially pleasing manner, which brings added strength to the dish. In much the same way that an artist hopes to give shape and form to something expressive, so I hope to give shape and form to a sensory experience. I want my cooking to surprise, to amaze, to question, to evoke memories, to provoke discussions. In addition to stimulating the five basic senses of my guests, we also want to engage their emotions. With a smile, a wink, a tongue-in-cheek accent or an element taken out of its usual context, we hope to activate their hidden sixth sense. This is why I love the work of Jan Fabre. I have two of his most powerfully expressive pieces in the restaurant, one at the entrance and one in the garden. No other artist is better able to release the emotions with his sensitive and evocative creations than Fabre. If we can do the same with our food, then we will have achieved our goal."

Pastorale
Laarstraat 22, 2840 Rumst-Reet
03/844.65.26
www.depastorale.be

Fried eel, turnip puree with young garlic and a quinoa salad with Jabugo ham

For 4 people

600 g river eel
20 g transglutaminate
olive oil
80 cl soya sauce

For the puree:
100 g young garlic
100 g turnip
20 cl honey vinegar

For the quinoa salad:
2 turnips
honey vinegar
20 cl grape seed oil
pepper and salt
1 shallot
4 tablespoons pine kernels, soaked
80 g Jabugo ham, finely sliced
80 cl stock
80 g quinoa, cooked

For the finishing:
10 cl lime juice
1 teaspoon of grated lime peel
2 tablespoons of quinoa, puffed
2 tablespoons of pine cone seeds, roasted
60 g smoked eel
20 g spring onions, finely chopped

> Remove the lateral fins and heads from the eel. Cut through the belly of the fish. Fillet the tail and the belly. Sprinkle with transglutaminate. Place the fillets back together and roll tightly in plastic foil. Seal them in a vacuum and cook for 40 minutes at 52 °C. Cut the eel into portions and fry in olive oil. Caramelise them with the soya sauce.
> Cut the young garlic bulb in two. Blanch just once. Place the garlic in a pot with the turnips and bring to the boil. When cooked through, mix the garlic and the turnip in a mixer, seasoning with a little honey vinegar.
> Finely slice the two turnips for the salad. Season with honey vinegar, grape seed oil, salt and pepper. Stew the shallot. Add the pine kernels and the brunoise of Jabugo ham. Add the stock and the previously cooked quinoa toe. Allow the mixture to simmer until done.
> Plate up the ingredients and dress with the lime juice, grated lime peel, puffed quinoa, roasted pine cone seeds, smoked eel and spring onions.

The preparation in 1, 2, 3

› Remove the lateral fins.
› Remove the head and cut through the belly.
› Fillet the tail.
› Fillet the belly.
› Sprinkle with transglutaminate.
› Place the fillets back together and roll tightly in plastic foil.
› Seal the fillets in a vacuum and cook for 40 minutes at 52 °C.
› Cut the fillets into portions and fry in olive oil.
› Caramelise the eel with soya sauce.

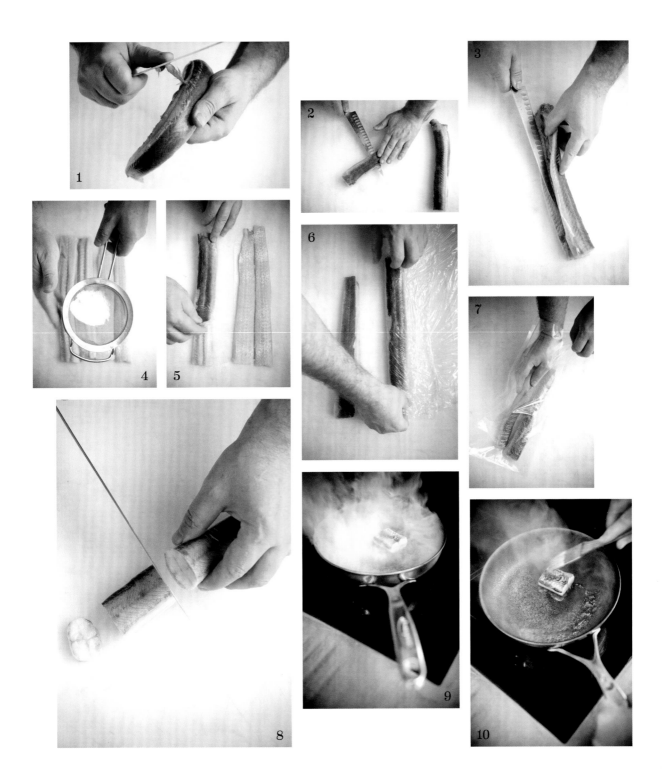

Fried sea bass with celeriac, blanching celery and lovage shortbread

For 4 people

600 g sea bass

For the celery strips:
200 g blanching celery
20 cl grape seed oil
pepper and salt
lemon juice

For the pickled celery cream:
500 g blanching celery
250 g white wine vinegar
250 g crystal sugar
2 g kitchen salt
1 l water
1/2 green pepper
vinegar water
400 g celeriac
milk
1 knob of butter
80 cl cream

For the lovage biscuits:
250 g butter
4 eggs
150 g trisol
20 g malto
500 g flour
10 g baking powder
10 g salt
40 g almond powder
pepper
60 g lovage powder (dried lovage
leaves, powdered in a mixer)

› Fry the sea bass slowly and on the skin side only.
› Peel the blanching celery and make thin strips with the peeler. Season with the grape seed oil, pepper, salt and lemon juice.
› Peel the blanching celery and cut it into fine blocks. Make a pickling fluid with the white wine vinegar, crystal sugar, kitchen salt and water. Bring this mixture to the boil and then pour it over the celery. Allow the cooled mixture to stand for at least 24 hours. Remove the seeds from the green pepper and blanch it in the vinegar water. Peel the blanched pepper and cut into a fine brunoise. Stir the pickled celery into the pepper brunoise. Peel the celeriac, cut it into fine cubes and soften in the milk. Press the softened celeriac through a sieve and then process in the thermomix. Flavour with the butter and finally add the cream.
› Mix together all the ingredients for the lovage shortbread. Roll out the dough to a depth of 8 millimetres and cut into cubes. Bake for 7 minutes in an oven at 130 °C.

Cherries and blackberries with caramel ice-cream, chocolate and hazelnuts

For 4 people

For the cherry syrup:
350 g red wine
200 g dark cherry puree (Boiron)
300 g cherries (Boiron)
150 g water
400 g sugar
5 g star aniseed powder
zest of 1 orange

200 g cherries

For the cherry jelly:
300 g cherry syrup
2 g agaragar
2 slices of gelatine

For the cherry foam:
500 g cherry syrup
2 g sucro

For the lemon cream:
270 g lemon juice

270 g sugar
270 g eggs
4 g agaragar
350 g butter

For the cherry pâté à fruit:
500 g cherry juice (Boiron)
100 g glucose
575 g sugar
18 g yellow pectin
6 g citric acid
dextrose

For the cherry jam:
800 g cherry syrup
20 g lemon juice
300 g sugar
1 l water
15 g kappa
15 g agaragar
50 g cherry vinaigrette (Vom Fass)

For the caramel ice-cream:
1 litre milk

20 g chicory
200 g sugar (for the caramel)
60 g sugar
60 g pro-cream (Sosa)

For the praliné feuilletine:
250 g milk chocolate
500 g praliné paste
600 g feuilletine

For the chocolate praliné cream:
250 g milk
250 g cream
120 g egg yolk
120 g sugar
2 slices of gelatine
170 g nyangho
90 g praliné

For the decoration:
12 blackberries
roasted hazelnuts
shiso purple cress

> Make the cherry syrup by mixing all the ingredients together and letting them boil for 10 minutes.
> Remove the stones from the cherries, seal them in a vacuum bag and put them in the roner for 30 minutes at 70 °C.
> Make the cherry jelly from the cherry syrup, agaragar and gelatine. Pour onto a gastronorm plate. Allow to harden and then cut out as desired.
> Make the cherry cream by mixing the cherry syrup and the sucro together, and then working up into a foam with a hand mixer.
> Make the lemon cream by mixing together the lemon juice, sugar, eggs and agaragar. Allow to boil for 1 minute. Pour the mixture into the thermomix at a low speed. Add the knobs of butter. Allow to cool for 12 hours in the fridge.
> For the fruit pâté, cook the cherry juice, glucose, sugar and yellow pectin in the thermomix at level 8 until the mixture reaches 106 °C. Then add the citric acid. Pour out, allow to harden and then cut into pieces, before coating in the dextrose.
> Stir together all the ingredients for the cherry jam in a pan and allow to come to the boil for 2 minutes. Mix further in the thermomix and pour the jam into an aerosol spray.
> Make the caramel ice-cream by infusing the milk and the chicory. Pass the resulting mixture through a sieve. Caramelise the sugar in a pan and then pour in the infusion. Add the sugar and the pro-cream. Stir well and finish in the pacojet.
> Make a praliné feuilletine by mixing all the ingredients together.
> Make a chocolate praliné cream by mixing all the ingredients together.
> Arrange all the ingredients elegantly on a plate and dress with blackberries, hazelnuts and the shiso.

Sang-Hoon Degeimbre

ʃ *L'Air du Temps* ∿

Sang-Hoon Degeimbre was once a sommelier with no cooking experience at all. Now he is one of the most progressive chefs in the country. He uses almost scientific techniques to create dishes with unexpected flavours and textures. In this way, he has found his own unique and very personal style.

The greatest challenge of his life

Sang-Hoon Degeimbre was born in South Korea. He came to Belgium as a four-year-old orphan. He still likes to recall the memories of his childhood with his adoptive parents and he still remembers vividly the first time he cooked for his nine brothers and sisters. A career in cooking might have seemed an obvious choice, but he initially wanted to be a chemist. However, his parents thought differently and sent him to butcher's school. By the age of sixteen, he was qualified to open his own butcher's shop – but this was not what he had in mind for himself. He started as an apprentice in Pickeim Castle, a hotel-restaurant in Namur. A year later, he was joined there by his brother, Sang-Ho. He continued to learn the skills of the sommelier's art and went to work (amongst other places) at 'La Truffe Noire' in Brussels and 'L'Eau Vive' in Arbre. In 1997, he opened (with his wife, Carine) his own restaurant, 'L'Air du Temps': he had never stood behind a stove to cook for paying guests in his life! For this reason, he still refers to the experience as his greatest ever challenge. "I had absolutely no kitchen experience," says Sang "But I had plenty of inspiration and imagination. I set about creating my first dishes in the same way I approach good wine: dismantle and analyse the flavours and aromas, and then search for the best possible new combinations. One of my first recipes was for weever fish, which contained all the same elements as a white Bourgogne wine, including the same roasted aromas, vanilla and butter. The physical and chemical processes which occur during the preparation of food have always fascinated me. But my understanding of these processes was limited by my lack of technical knowledge. Molecular

cooking was my salvation. I followed training with Hervé This, the French founder of molecular cuisine, and there I found an answer to all my questions. He explained to me the chemical reactions which take place when food is heated, how proteins work and how acids and alkalis can affect the end result. My dishes are based first and foremost on technique. I use molecular principles to control and shape the physical-chemical processes, thereby creating a texture that is as close as possible to the original product. A technical style of cooking does not means that the ingredients suddenly become unrecognisable, and that they no longer taste like they are supposed to taste. It is amazing how many misconceptions people still have about molecular cuisine. For example, René Redzepi of 'Noma' has been portrayed as a naturalist who simply transfers pure dishes straight from nature onto a plate. Whereas in reality his food is hyper-technical and crammed full with molecular techniques! The vegetable plot that I set up in 2002 in Couthuin with gardener Benoît Blairvacq was my first step in the world of molecular cooking. I needed the best products to exploit the full potential of the molecular skills I now possessed. This plot taught me a great deal about the physics and chemistry of plants and vegetables. For example, if you peel the leaves of an onion, you can see that it contains a kind of gelatine. And if you understand how this gelatine was formed, you can try to create it in your dish. One of my new techniques is the use of ultrasound. We use a mixer which has an ultrasonic detector instead of standard blades. This detector can extract the aromatic molecules from ingredients without the need to use chemical agents. This is particularly useful for fragile products that are easily damaged. It allows us to harvest the sap in its purest form. In this way, we make a rose sorbet with sap taken from rose petals, without using a single gram of artificial additives."

> **My dishes are based first and foremost on technique.**

A thousand and one original dishes

Sang-Hoon's culinary repertoire contains more than one thousand original dishes, some of which are truly ground-breaking, such as kiwêtre (kiwi-oyster) of chimera (octopus-egg).

"The combination of kiwi with oyster came into being when I was slicing kiwis and suddenly smelt an aroma that reminded me of the sea. I then consulted Bernard Lahousse, a scientist specialised in food-pairing, and he discovered that kiwi has fourteen aromatic molecules in common with oyster. And so I was able to create my marriage of kiwi and oyster, with coconut puree and cuttlefish ink. With chimera, I wanted to invent a new kind of egg, with the texture and appearance of a soft-boiled chicken's egg, but with a surprise in the middle. The result is a black-and-white dish, with lightly fried octopus in water with a thickener, which is then 'cast' in an egg-shaped

mould. The 'yolk' is from a mixture of fluid risotto and octopus ink. When all the different elements are put together, it looks just like an ordinary chicken's egg. But the structures are very different. With chimera, I wanted to create an imaginary world with which I could tell a story. Narrative is very important for me. Each of my dishes must have its own tale to tell. If a chef is able to explain why he has created a specific dish in specific way, you can understand the taste better and the interrelationship between the different components. Our story begins with the aperitif and ends with the dessert. This allows us to immerse our guests in our visionary world."

In 2009 Sang-Hoon returned for the first time to the land of his birth. "The powerful flavours of the cuisine in Korea really opened my eyes. If Japan created the umami flavour, Korea has something every bit as good with kimchi: an assortment of fermented vegetables and vegetable pasta, which acts as a basis for most Korean cooking. The fermentation in lactic acid which the vegetables undergo results in strong flavours and aromas, but also for high concentrations of amino acids, vitamins and minerals. In other words, the fermentation process makes the basic product more nutritionally valuable. I first experimented with this ingredient during the Flemish Primitives in 2010 and it has now become a fixture in my kitchen. We apply the lactic acid fermentation process to any spare vegetables we have in our garden plot. This makes it possible to keep them for longer, so that we no longer need to throw away part of our harvest, if it is a large one. This allows us to serve vegetables that are very healthy and packed full with flavour, almost all year round."

Back to the roots

"My visit to Korea also gave me deeper insights into my own personality and identity. Throughout the centuries, Belgium has frequently been occupied by foreign powers. So too has Korea. Both countries are a crossroads, where different influences come together, so that it is difficult to establish a real identity. I also see this in the culinary world in Belgium, where many chefs follow the latest trends from here, there and everywhere, but without developing a real personality of their own. We need to get back to basics, back to our roots. Our uniqueness lies in our use of our own products and an innovative approach to traditional Belgian cuisine. In every region there are interesting ingredients and cooking methods to be found, which only the local people know, but which will allow a creative chef to develop something new and exciting. What we lack in Belgium is a standard bearer like Ferran Adrià in Spain or René Redzepi in Scandinavia, someone who can launch a new wave of culinary inventiveness. It must be someone with a broad vision, someone who is unattached and who does not need to behave in a protectionist manner. A personality who can carry us all forwards, dragging us by the scruff of the neck, if need be. We badly need this knight in shining armour – and we need him now."

L'Air du Temps
Rue de la Croix Monet 2
5310 Liernu
081/81.30.48
www.airdutemps.be

In a nutshell

➜ **Who or what influenced your choice of profession?**
My parents steered me in this direction, because they knew I loved food. But I never realised just what an adventure it would be.

➜ **What was your first culinary experience or memory?**
I began my culinary training in a hotel-restaurant where they used local products and local game, hunted nearby. We did everything from A to Z: very basic, but very well done.

➜ **What can really make you mad in the kitchen?**
Laziness and lack of will-power.

➜ **What is your most important personal quality?**
Judging everyone on their merits.

➜ **What would you like to have more time for?**
For my children.

➜ **What other job would you like to do?**
When I was a child, I wanted to be a chemist. As I grew older, so I became more interested in art and architecture.

➜ **For you, what is the epitome of luxury?**
Endless space.

➜ **What are you best at in the kitchen?**
I know almost no boundaries, but still regularly question what I am doing.

➜ **What is your favourite vegetable?**
Artichoke and beets.

➜ **What is your favourite type or cut of meat?**
Filet-mignon of Belotta pork.

➜ **What type(s) of fish do you like to work with?**
Shellfish.

➜ **What are your preferred herbs for fish and meat dishes?**
Lemon verbena for fish and ginger for meat.

➜ **What are you favourite aromas and smells in the kitchen?**
Bread fresh out of the oven and roasted aromas in general.

➜ **What is your favourite dish?**
Meat balls in tomato sauce.

➜ **Which small object could you not do without in the kitchen?**
My small curved spatula.

➜ **What was the last celebrated restaurant that you visited and what was your opinion?**
'Noma', with my whole team. We shared fantastic emotions.

➜ **What is your favourite aperitif?**
Manzanilla sherry from Gutierrez Colosia.

➜ **What do you most enjoy eating on your day off?**
Very light, raw fish.

➜ **What are your favourite book and your favourite cooking book?**
Most recently: *Le Cuisinier* by Martin Sutter.

➜ **Which famous person from the past would you like to have welcomed as a customer?**
Magritte, because surrealism is transforming the boundaries of the understandable.

Jogaetang

300 g Venus shells
300 g cockles
1.2 l water
16 g salt
10 g garlic
80 g fine spring onions
40 g red paprika
2.4 l water
16 g fine salt
1/2 teaspoon gochu powder
(Korean pepper, chili powder is an
alternative)
elderflower (optional)

› Wash the Venus shells and allow them to stand for 3 hours in salted water in a cool place.
› Peel, clean and finely chop the garlic. Cut the spring onions into fine slices.
› Boil the shells in salted water and add the garlic, spring onions, paprika and gochu powder. Cook until the shells open. Pour the cooking fluid through a sieve.
› Serve the shells with the vegetables in a deep plate, with a little of the cooking juices. Decorate with elderflowers.

Variations on a colour theme. Purple duck: breast of duck, red cabbage and red onion

For the breast of duck:
1 breast of Mulard duck
salt

For the red beetroot:
mayonnaise
100 g egg white
33 cl grape seed oil
5 cl red beetroot juice
5 cl sushi rice vinegar
5 g salt

For the red cabbage jelly:
20 cl red cabbage juice
3 cl rice vinegar

1 cl white vinegar
2.4 g agaragar

For the red cabbage brunoise:
50 g red cabbage, blanched
3 cl rice vinegar
2 g salt

For the red onion at low temperature:
10 red onions
25 g salt
50 g sugar
20 cl white vinegar
50 cl water

For the tapioca with souffléd red cabbage:
100 g tapioca
150 g red cabbage juice
arachide oil
salt

For the East Indian cherry jam:
5 g agaragar
50 cl juice of East Indian cherries

For the onion puree:
500 g cooked red onion

200 g cooking juices
170 g grape seed oil

For the red cabbage sauce:
250 g red onions, chopped
50 cl red wine
1.2 l poultry stock
50 cl red cabbage juice
7 cl sushi rice vinegar
120 g butter

some stems of atsina cress

› Season the skin side of the duck breast with salt. Fry briefly to colour both the skin side and the meat side of the fillet. Allow to cool to 3 °C and then vacuum cook for 90 minutes at 56 °C. Allow to cool. Re-fry the meat side briefly and keep warm in the Alto Shaam (warming cabinet).
› Prepare the red beetroot mayonnaise by mixing all the ingredients together until they form a smooth substance.
› Make the red cabbage jelly by mixing all the ingredients together in a pot. Allow the resulting mixture to rest for a few hours in the fridge. Remove from the fridge and bring to the boil. Pour into a tray and allow to cool. When the mixture has stiffened, cut it into four equal squares.
› Finely chop the blanched red cabbage. Mix this brunoise well with the rice vinegar and salt.
› Peel the red onion. Mix with the salt, sugar and vinegar. Vacuum cook for 90 minutes at 83 °C.
› For the tapioca with souffléd red cabbage, boil the tapioca for 12 minutes. Allow to drain, clean in cold water and stir in the red cabbage juice (which should be one and a half times the volume of the tapioca). Spread on a silicone baking mat and allow to dry. Soufflé this mixture in oil at 180 °C. Season lightly with salt.
› For the East Indian cherry jam, mix together the juice and the agaragar and allow to rest for a few hours in the fridge. Remove and bring to the boil, then pour into a tray. Allow this mixture to set in the fridge, then mix it, pass it through a sieve and spoon it into a squeeze bottle.
› Make the onion puree by mixing all the ingredients together.
› For the red cabbage sauce, mix the onion puree with the wine and allow to reduce almost completely. Add for three-quarters the chicken stock and the red cabbage juice. At the last moment, add the sushi rice vinegar and thicken with butter.
› Place a rectangle of the red cabbage jelly on the plate. Cover with the red cabbage brunoise and coat with the red cabbage sauce. Put a few slices of onion on top. Squeeze on some East Indian cherry jelly and decorate with a few stems of the atsina cress and a piece of the souffléd red cabbage tapioca. Cut the duck breast into rectangular slices and arrange neatly. Drizzle some drops of the red beetroot mayonnaise and the East Indian cherry jam over the meat. Serve.

Lacquered sweetbreads, carrot pickles and romanesco

For the red beetroot:
1 red beetroot
5 l water
60 g salt

For the romanesco:
1 cauliflower stalk
7 cl water
2 g salt

100 g broad beans

For the sauce:
100 g shallots, finely chopped
20 cl red wine
10 cl port
1 teaspoon tomato concentrate
5 cl rice vinegar
40 cl brown veal stock
3 juniper berries
2 tablespoons Worcestershire sauce
(English sauce)
butter
salt and pepper

300 g heart sweetbreads, cut into neat
medallions
hard flour
grape seed oil

For the lacquer:
300 g dark mirin (rice cooking wine)
100 g ganjang (Korean soya sauce;
Japanese soya sauce is an alternative)
50 g black rice vinegar

1 spring onion stalk
12 tablespoons of atsina cress leaves

› Boil the red beetroot until it is cooked. Allow to cool and then hand peel. Cut into slices 1.5 millimetres thick. Use a kitchen ring to cut out circles with a diameter of 2.5 centimetres. Keep in the fridge.
› Cut the cauliflower stalk into slices 1.5 millimetres thick. Use a kitchen ring to cut out circles with a diameter of 2.5 centimetres. Blanch the circles briefly in water with a pinch of salt.
› Shell the broad beans and blanch them for 1 minute in boiling water. Drain well and cut into slices.
› Make the sauce by heating together the shallots, red wine, port and tomato concentrate. Allow to reduce and then add the rice vinegar and the veal stock. Crush the juniper berries and add the Worcestershire sauce. Allow to reduce by half. Thicken slightly with butter. Season as necessary.
› Dip the sweetbreads in the hard flour and fry in grape seed oil until golden brown. Warm the lacquer and place the sweetbreads into the mixture. Continue warming until the sweetbreads are fully lacquered.
› Place the sweetbreads in a kitchen ring. Add the beetroot and cauliflower slices. Top with the broad beans, finely cut spring onions and the atsina leaves. Drizzle the sauce over and around the composition.

The preparation in **1, 2, 3**

Cut the cauliflower stalk into slices and make circles with a kitchen ring.

Cut the red beetroot into slices and cut out circles with a kitchen ring.

Cut the spring onion into slices.

Shell the broad beans.

Fry the sweetbreads.

Lacquer the sweetbreads.

Arrange the sweetbreads and the slices of beetroot and cauliflower in a kitchen ring.

Decorate with the broad beans, spring onions and leaves of atsina cress.

Bart Desmidt

ʃ Bartholomeus ʅ

Bart Desmidt is blessed with a good dose of realism and common sense. He cooks with gut feeling, does not like unnecessary frills and concentrates on getting the most out of the flavour of his products. Making maximum use of all the richness offered by the North Sea, he has acquired a reputation as one of the best seafood cooks in Belgium.

A child of the sea

Bart Desmidt grew up in the toy shop run by his parents on the promenade at Heist. His grandfather and uncle were both fishermen, so the family was used to having fresh fish and shellfish as a regular part of their weekly diet. Moreover, his parents used to like talking about food. In short, it was the ideal background for launching the young Bart into a career in the restaurant business. Even so, it was relatively late before he discovered his calling. He first attended normal secondary school and it was only at the age of eighteen that he decided to become a cook. "I worked for three different restaurants on training contracts. I thought that there was a lot of show on the outside and very little substance on the inside. I saw chefs who suddenly 'went missing' when suppliers called to settle their bills and learnt all other kinds of 'tricks of trade'. It was only at the third restaurant – 'L'Echiquier' in Knokke – that I finally saw how it might be possible to make a living from cooking. I worked there for two years and it was also there that I first met my wife, Sandra – on Christmas Eve. Five months later we were married and in June we opened our own restaurant in my parents' old toy shop. We were careful right from the very beginning, making sure that we didn't over-invest. For the first three and a half years there was just the two of us. It stretched us to the limit, but we were determined to succeed. We worked day and night and never looked at the clock or took a holiday. That was not the way my parents had brought me up, but we did it anyway – and it worked. We are now seventeen years further down the line and have a staff of ten working for us. We also have a Michelin star. My quality of life is much better than it once was and I have become calmer. Perhaps for that reason, my cuisine has also evolved and improved."

All taste and no nonsense

Bart Desmidt is very clear about his style of cooking: good tasting products, prepared simply, honestly and without frills. "No nonsense: just like I am. I can't be bothered with too much fiddly work on my plate. Of course, the dishes need to look attractive, but there is no need to go overboard. I stick to just three or four ingredients per plate: this gives a maximum of flavour. For example, I might serve sea wolf with lamb's ear and salicornia, accompanied by just a light juice with a few slices of tomato and some new potatoes. Or I might do some eight-week matured beef with cauliflower, pickles and ensope tomatoes. Or perhaps asparagus with cockles, parsley and some smoked butter. I cook with my instinct, based on the flavours I learnt at home. This means that classic Flemish dishes form the basis of my cuisine. If I am cooking fish, I will usually go for celery and onions as flavourers. These are the tastes that I remember from eating mussels as a lad. But I also try to make these 'classics' a little lighter and more interesting. Even so, taste remains the no.1 priority, much more so than inventiveness. For instance, tartar of wagyu with oyster has been on my menu for six years and is a big success. What makes the combination so interesting is the way that the silt taste of the

I have become calmer. Perhaps for that reason, my cuisine has also evolved and improved.

oyster replaces the salt in the meat. I usually serve it with a mustard ice-cream, but an ice-cream based on horseradish would work just as well. To this I add some blocks of tomato or cucumber, dressed with caramel mixed with a little citric acid. The acid reduces the sweetness of the caramel and gives a better balance of flavours. If you put too much sweetness in your food, you are on the wrong track – at least in my book. My recipe for North Sea sole contains pickles. I love pickles and often prepare it myself. But the best pickles come from Widow Tierenteyn on the Graanmarkt in Ghent. Pickled vegetables can bring a new and unexpected freshness to many dishes. And try putting pickles on your chips from the local chip shop: I can guarantee you that the chips won't lay heavily on your stomach afterwards. In my desserts I include waffles, strawberries and 'babelutten'. These are three local Flemish products. As far as 'babelutten' are concerned, they are very local indeed: there is a shop just around the corner from our restaurant! Their typical 'seaside sweet' taste combines perfectly with waffles. If I can, I like to buy Belgian wherever possible. My fish, shellfish and even my scallops mostly come from Zeebrugge. For my meat, I have found local butchers who are prepared to mature blue-white beef for me for eight weeks. Hares, pheasants and partridges all come from local hunters who I know and trust. The feathered game is all plucked cold, as it should be. (I draw the line, however, at deer and boar: they are not for me.) And eighty percent of our vegetables are Belgian-grown."

More attention for home-grown products

Bart Desmidt does not often eat out: he prefers to define his own culinary agenda. "There is no need to keep on looking over the garden fence. Of course, we can use influences from other people and other cultures, but

In a nutshell

→ **Who or what influenced your choice of profession?**
My parents. Food and drink were important in our house. We also went out eating a lot and often had family and friends around for a meal.

→ **What was your first culinary experience or memory?**
Dining as a young lad at 'La Poularde'** in Nice.

→ **What can really make you mad in the kitchen?**
Dishonesty, failing to own up to your mistakes, keeping your feelings to yourself when you are upset.

→ **What is your most important personal quality?**
Perseverance, keeping constantly busy, always in a good mood (even early in the morning!).

→ **What would you like to have more time for?**
For my wife, Sandra, and our son, Arnaud.

→ **For you, what is the epitome of luxury?**
Being able to enjoy all the big and small moments in life.

→ **What are you best at in the kitchen?**
Seasoning and organising.

→ **What do you most enjoy doing in the kitchen?**
Service: the busier, the better.

→ **What is your favourite vegetable?**
Asparagus and tomatoes.

→ **What is your favourite type or cut of meat?**
'Blue-white' beef, matured for eight weeks.

→ **What type(s) of fish do you like to work with?**
Any fish from the North Sea, as long as they are super-fresh.

→ **What are your preferred herbs for fish and meat dishes?**
Parsley.

→ **What are you favourite aromas and smells in the kitchen?**
Baking bread and pastries, simmering stocks and sauces.

→ **What is your favourite dish?**
Asparagus with tomatoes and hand-peeled Zeebrugge shrimps.

→ **Which small object could you not do without in the kitchen?**
A good knife.

→ **Which chef has inspired you the most?**
Michel Troisgros.

→ **What type of cuisine do you not like?**
Any type which does not use fresh ingredients.

→ **What was the last celebrated restaurant that you visited and what was your opinion?**
'Per Se' in New York: super.

→ **What is your worst ever eating experience?**
Being served fish that was already stinking.

→ **Who is your perfect table companion?**
My wife, son and friends with their children, all together at a single, long table.

→ **What is your favourite aperitif?**
A nice, cold glass of beer.

→ **What do you most enjoy eating on your day off?**
Pasta with shellfish.

→ **What is your favourite book and your favourite cooking book?**
Livre de Cuisine by Alain Ducasse. However, in recent years I have not had the time (or the inclination) to look at many cookery books.

→ **Which famous customer would you one day like to welcome, and why?**
Anyone and everyone, as long as they love food and behave like ordinary human beings.

→ **Which famous person from the past would you like to have welcomed as a customer?**
Louis de Funès.

we should do it with our own products. I now work a lot with whiting, a much underrated fish. Raw whiting is delicious and much more flavoursome than raw tuna. Our lobsters are also excellent, providing you eat them in season. Before June we get them from the Oosterschelde (the estuary of the River Scheldt), and until October they come from the North Sea. Our scallops also come from the North Sea: I get them live in the shell and you cannot taste the difference with their more famous Breton counterparts. We need to be more chauvinistic about our own products, and I am starting to notice that more and more of my fellow chefs are becoming aware of this fact. I hope that this will help to promote a more quality-based approach to food production. Our farmers are currently being forced to produce everything at the lowest possible price. The result is tasteless food. It would be a huge step in the right direction if the restaurant sector as a whole could encourage producers to aim for greater flavour and better quality. I, for one, would be perfectly happy to pay more to hunters, fishermen, farmers and breeders – providing I can get the quality I want. And if they know that they are going to be paid more for their end product, they will be more willing to expend the time and effort needed to improve that product. Because it is only with products of quality that we will be able to make a difference – and keep Belgian cooking on the world map!"

I cook with my instinct, based on the flavours I learnt at home.

Bartholomeus
Zeedijk 267, 8301 Heist-aan-zee
050/51.75.76
www.restaurantbartholomeus.be

Tartar of wagyu beef with oyster, tomato and mustard

For the tartar:
300 g bavette of wagyu
1 cl olive oil
1 shallot, finely diced
black pepper
3 drops of Tabasco

For the tomato:
1 tomato (coeur de boeuf)
1 g cayenne pepper
10 g sugar
1 cl vinegar
olive oil
Tabasco

For the mustard ice-cream:
15 cl milk
13 g glucose
20 g sour cream
1 g gelatine
50 g mustard

For the caramel:
10 g icing sugar
7 g glucose
10 g soya sauce
2 g citric acid

20 g capers
8 oysters

› Dice the meat with a sharp knife into a fine brunoise. Mix with a little olive oil, the shallot, black pepper and Tabasco.
› Immerse the tomato for 15 seconds in boiling water. Remove the skin. Dice the flesh into a brunoise and mix with the cayenne pepper, sugar, vinegar, a little oil and the Tabasco.
› Heat the milk and dissolve the glucose in it. Add the other ingredients. Mix in an ice-cream machine until the consistency is smooth and firm.
› Mix all the ingredients for the caramel and bring them to the boil at 160 °C. Allow the mixture to harden and then chop it to a fine powder in a blender. Shake the powder onto a silicone baking mat and place in an oven pre-heated to 160 °C for 3 minutes, so that it melts to form a thin, crispy layer of caramel. Allow this to cool and then cut to the desired shape.
› Wash the capers and deep-fry them at 180 °C.
› Open the oysters and remove the adductor muscle. Cut each oyster into three pieces.

North Sea sole, polder puree, pickles and tarragon

4 North Sea sole
butter

50 g green beans
50 g string beans
50 g broad beans
butter

1 fresh stem of savoury, finely
chopped
salt and pepper
50 g peas
1 cl cream
1 cl milk

4 large polder potatoes
150 g butter

20 g sour cream

100 g pickles
50 g fresh tarragon
10 cl mousseline sauce

› Fry the sole in butter and fillet them.
› Clean the beans thoroughly. Cut the string beans into pieces and shell the broad beans. Blanch them both and immerse them in ice-cold water, so that they retain their green colour. Mix the beans with a little melted butter, the savoury and the salt and pepper.
› Cook the peas for 6 minutes. Mix them in the blender with the cream, milk, salt and pepper. Spoon the resulting puree into a piping bag.
› Pre-heat the oven to 200 °C. Let the potatoes cook in their peel for 1 hour. Cut them in two, remove the pulp and puree it in a stirring sieve (passe-vite). Add the butter and sour cream and mix again in a blender, until the consistency is smooth.
› Blend the pickles and the tarragon and then stir lightly into the mousseline sauce.
› Arrange all the resulting ingredients elegantly on the plate.

The preparation in 1, 2, 3

› Shell the broad beans.
› Immerse the blanched green beans, string beans and broad beans in ice-cold water.
› Cook the potatoes for 1 hour in the oven.
› Cut them in two and remove the pulp.
› Puree the pulp in a stirring sieve (passe-vite).
› Mix the puree with the butter and sour cream in a blender.
› Blend the pickles and stir them into the mousseline sauce.
› Mix the beans with the melted butter and savoury.
› Fry the sole in butter.
› Fillet the fried sole.

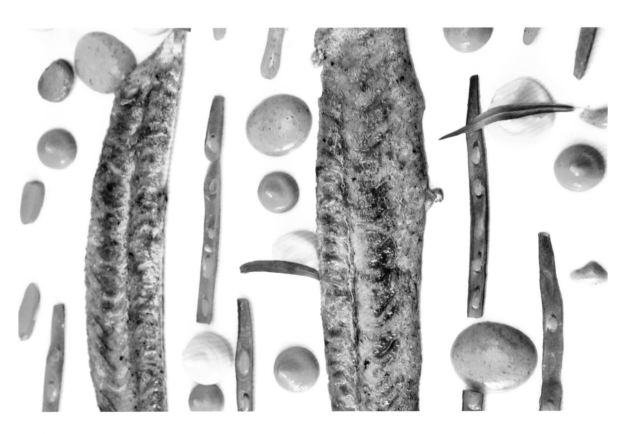

60 watt, strawberries, babelutten and waffle

300 g strawberries
50 g strawberry jam

For the waffle:
10 cl milk
10 cl water
50 g butter
10 g sugar
15 g vanilla sugar
2 g salt
5 g yeast
1 egg
100 g flour

sugar
1 vanilla stick
50 g sour cream

For the babelutten ice-cream:
25 cl milk
75 g babelutten
3 egg yolks
5 cl cream
25 g glucose

For the caramel:
100 g icing sugar
50 g glucose

› Cut the strawberries into a brunoise and mix with the jam.
› Mix all the ingredients for the waffle together, apart from the egg white. Beat the egg white separately and then fold it into the other ingredients. Let the mixture rest for 1 hour. Bake the waffle in a hot waffle iron, trim the edges and cut into neat squares. Dry the remaining pieces in an oven for 2 hours at 120 °C. Blend the dried pieces with the sugar.
› Cut the vanilla stick along its full length and scrape out the marrow with a sharp knife. Add the marrow to the sour cream and beat thoroughly.
› Mix all the ingredients for the babelutten ice-cream together and heat to a temperature of 84 °C. Allow to set for 24 hours in the fridge. Mix in an ice-cream machine until smooth and firm.
› Mix the sugars and heat them to 154 °C. Pour the caramel into a mould, pour it out and then pour it back in again. Allow to harden, then remove carefully from the mould.
› Fill the moulded caramel with strawberries. Add a scoop of ice-cream in the shape of a bulb. Place a piece of waffle alongside and sprinkle it with the powdered waffle. Finish with a few drops of sour cream.

60 Watt

Kobe Desramaults

In De Wulf

By being creative with local produce and reviving the fortunes of a number of other supposedly 'lost' ingredients, Kobe Desramaults has developed a strong culinary identity, all his own. His ambition is to further deepen and refine the taste of his top quality products, until he finally reduces them to their essence.

Local Food Express

Pork from Borre, nest-bred pigeons from Steenvoorde, lambs from Lo-Reninge, dune asparagus from Ghyvelde, finest beef from a rare breed of red West Flanders cattle in Westouter, fruit, vegetables and wild herbs from Dranouter and wines from vineyards on the sun-kissed slopes of nearby Heuvelland. The hill country which straddles the border between south-west Flanders and northern France is blessed with dozens of small-scale farmers and breeders of top quality products. Even so, it was only four years after he took over the running of 'In De Wulf' from his mother that Kobe Desramaults finally discovered the culinary richness of the region in which he lives and works. I was only twenty-three when I first started here. I had already worked with Sergio Herman in 'Oud Sluis' and Carles Abellan (a pupil of Ferran Adrià) in 'Commerç 24' in Barcelona. I was still strongly influenced by these former mentors and tried to recreate their manner of working in my own cooking. In these early years, I was primarily concerned to 'make an impression'. Technical mastery came before everything. Nowadays, there is much more feeling to my dishes; they have a much stronger personal identity. This change in style first started after I paid a number of visits to Michel Bras and Alain Passard. I was particularly impressed by the way that they were able to work local products into their recipes and this inspired me to see if I could do something similar in Flanders. However, it soon became clear that it was not going to be as easy as I had hoped. Although I live in a predominantly agricultural region, the most interesting producers are very hard to find. Our local farmers are all very modest and self-effacing, almost to the point of invisibility. They do little or nothing to advertise their produce. I first got started four years ago, by persuading one of my neighbours to grow fruit and vegetables for me. Two years later, I found someone who was prepared to drive around the countryside, hunting for the best products. It was at this point that I received a phone call from Rik Delhaye, a dynamic bio-farmer from Westouter. He thought that I was wasting too much time and energy, and so he suggested setting up a cooperative venture with bio-farmers and other small scale producers in the region. The idea was that we would collect the produce with our own logistical service and then sell it to other interested restaurants. This made perfect economic sense: on the one hand, it guaranteed small farmers a market for their produce; on the other hand, it guaranteed top chefs a reliable supply of high quality, day-fresh ingredients. And so the Local Food Express was born. To begin with, we worked with just six farmers, supplying the same number of restaurants in locations as far away as Bruges. We now operate with a group of some twenty farmers, offering a variety of foodstuffs to restaurants as far away as Ghent. The good thing about the Local Food Express is that all our production is small-scale and quality-driven, so that you can only get the products that are available at any given time; in other words, authentic products that are in season.

Back to the essentials

"If you work with farmers, this automatically creates a link with both the region and with local products. It also automatically gives your cooking greater personality. What's more, these local growers and breeders also provide me with a kind of spiritual inspiration. To a large extent, they are responsible for what happens in the kitchen at 'In De Wulf'. They bring me herbs, shoots, buds and vegetables that I have never seen before, let alone worked with! And there are a number of farmers in the cooperative who love to experiment. For example, they will let their cabbage grow for longer than usual, so that they begin to develop shoots. They will then test different ways to see if these shoots have any possible culinary value. They also taught me how bits of meat that most cooks regard as 'waste' can be used to make 'krakeling'. Krakeling – known as crackling or scratchings in English - is an old tradition in this part of the world, and is made by frying pieces of bacon rind in sugar until it becomes crispy and caramelised. In the past, it was often used as sweets for children, but I like to make a dessert with it. In addition to picking up traditions of this kind, I also love to listen to their stories about the 'old days' and about how the processes of cultivation have changed throughout the years. This allows me to develop my own individual style and identity."

In these early years, I was primarily concerned to 'make an impression. Nowadays, there is much more feeling to my dishes; they have a much stronger personal identity.

In a nutshell

→ **What can really make you mad in the kitchen?**
I can be really irritated by sloppiness or laxity. Everyone has their own responsibilities and we must all learn to take them seriously. This is the only way to get ahead in life.

→ **What would you like to have more time for?**
Family and friends. I know this sounds like a cliché, but it is becoming more and more important to me than in the past.

→ **What other job would you like to do?**
Ever since I was a kid, I have been fascinated by graphics. When I was young, I was always drawing – so I would probably have done something in that direction, if I had not become a chef.

→ **For you, what is the epitome of luxury?**
Quality time with my mates.

→ **What do you most enjoy doing in the kitchen?**
I love playing about with exciting new products, until I arrive at new recipes, often by sheer chance.

→ **What do you least enjoy doing in the kitchen?**
Moaning and groaning.

→ **What is your favourite vegetable?**
That depends on the season.

→ **What are you favourite aromas and smells in the kitchen?**
Roasted onions.

→ **What was the last celebrated restaurant that you visited and what was your opinion?**
'Septime', a restaurant recently opened by Bertrand Grébaut, an old boy of 'L'Arpège'. It was the max: no nonsense, top quality.

→ **Who is your perfect table companion?**
Blond, with lovely eyes.

→ **What is your favourite aperitif?**
Redor lager from the Dupont Brewery.

→ **What are your favourite book and your favourite cooking book?**
The Forager Handbook by Miles Irving, a guide to edible plants in Great Britain.

→ **Which famous person from the past would you like to have welcomed as a customer?**
Jean Berquin, a legendary Flemish chef. He was a master in everything related to pork.

> **" I also love to listen to stories about the 'old days' and about how the processes of cultivation have changed throughout the years. This allows me to develop my own individual style and identity. "**

In his most recent recipes, Kobe is searching for greater purity. This means that the preparations can sometimes take longer than normal, but the final result brings him much closer to the true essence of the product. This is the case, for example, with the pigeons from Steenvoorde, which he hangs with their innards in place for a period of two to three days, before cleaning them, stuffing them and packing them with roasted hay. The total 'ripening' process can last from four days to a week, following which the birds are cold smoked on hay, after which they are vacuum-packed and left to ripen for a further week. "The meat is first lightly warmed and then roasted in an oven. A little winter butter (from cows reared exclusively on hay) and a sprinkling of salt – and that's it. The product must be able to speak for itself. If I am able to reduce a single ingredient in each of my recipes

back to its essence, I will feel that I have succeeded. But the final dish still needs to form a harmonious whole. There is a huge difference between deepening a flavour and pushing it right over the edge. There has to be overall balance between the different taste elements. A dish is only a good dish if it contains an identifiable logic."

In De Wulf
Wulvestraat 1, 8950 Heuvelland (Dranouter)
057/44 55 67
www.indewulf.be

North Sea cuttlefish with chard and asse

For the North Sea cuttlefish:
10 North Sea cuttlefish
Xeres vinegar
salt
lemon oil
onion oil

For the stock:
sunflower oil
1 dl white wine
1 dl shellfish juice
2 onions
1 carrot
1 leek
1 bundle celery
1 bulb garlic
2 tablespoons fennel seeds
2 tablespoons aniseed
1 finely chopped shallot
2 dl wine (Entre-Deux-Monts)
20 g reduced cream
30 g sepia (cuttlefish ink)

For the roasted chard:
1 bundle of chard
roasted onion oil
salt
smoked oil
Xeres vinegar

8 young spring onions with roots
oil

For the asse:
100 g sourdough breadcrumbs
1 tablespoon of sepia (cuttlefish ink)
1 tablespoon of onion asse

› Clean the cuttlefish thoroughly. Keep the heads. Remove the membranes from all the pouches. Lay four cuttlefish bodies on top of each other in a vacuum bag and put them in the freezer. Remove the frozen cuttlefish from the freezer and cut them into very fine slices, using a slicer. Arrange approximately 40 grams on each plate. Cover with plastic film and heat for 1 minute in a steam oven. The slices must be warm, but raw. Marinate lightly with Xeres vinegar, salt, lemon and onion oil. It is important to retain the natural flavour.

› Next, make the stock. Wash the cuttlefish heads thoroughly. Cut out the eyes. Fry the heads in sunflower oil in a hot pan. Add a little white wine and allow the mixture to reduce until it caramelises. Add the shell fish juice. Place the heads in a pot with a mirepoix of roughly chopped onions, carrot, leek and celery. Add the unpeeled bulb of garlic, sliced in two. Roast the fennel and aniseed, and add this also. Dilute with water until the heads are just covered and allow this to simmer at a low temperature for 4 hours. Boil the resulting fluid until just 1.5 litres remains. Add the finely diced shallot and the wine (Entre-Deux-Monts) and allow this to reduce by half. Add the reduced cream and the cuttlefish ink. Bring to the boil for just a few seconds and then remove the pot from the stove.

› Remove the outer skin from the chard shoots. Cut the shoots into pieces approximately 6 centimetres in length. Sprinkle the pieces with the roasted onion oil and place them in a warm grill pan, cooking them until they are almost black on both sides. Remove from the heat and marinate immediately with roasted onion oil, salt, smoked oil and Xeres vinegar.

› Wash the spring onions thoroughly and deep fry them at 180 °C until they are golden brown.

› Mix the sourdough breadcrumbs with the cuttlefish ink. Allow the resulting mixture to dry out completely in a drying oven at 60 °C. Mix the black breadcrumbs with the onion asse.

Young cucumbers with Pas de Rouge and house-smoked bacon

10 small cucumbers
elderberry vinegar
100 g Pas de Rouge cheese (2 years old)
milk
8 finely cut slices of bacon
herbs: chervil, roman chervil, wild chervil

› Peel 8 cucumbers, cut them in half and remove the seeds with a spoon. Heat a grill pan and cook the cucumbers until they are very dark on both sides. Remove them from the grill and marinate them with the elderberry vinegar.
› Blend the cheese (Pas de Rouge) and dilute it with milk until the structure becomes smooth and creamy. This will also result in a softer flavour.
› Cut the remaining 2 raw cucumbers in slices and marinate them immediately before serving with the elderberry vinegar.
› Cover the hot roasted cucumbers with the slices of bacon and let them melt.
› Dress with the herbs.

Nest-bred pigeons from Steenvoorde, cooked in hay

2 nest-bred pigeons
roasted hay
500 g butter

› Hang the pigeons for 2 days, without removing the innards. This ensures a more complex flavour. Remove the innards after 2 days and stuff the birds with roasted hay. Pack the stuffed birds completely in moist, roasted hay and let them rest in the fridge for a further 4 days.
› Pack the pigeons in a vacuum bag and seal the vacuum. Immerse the bag for a few seconds in boiling water. Remove and cool immediately in ice-cold water. Take the pigeons out of the vacuum bag, tie the legs together and smoke the pigeon for 2 hours with hay in a cold smoking oven.
› Mix the butter with a handful of roasted hay and let this draw slowly on the stove for 3 to 4 hours at 70 °C.
› Pre-heat the oven to 200 °C. Warm the pigeons to 55 °C by letting them stand in a warm place in the kitchen. Fry them in the hay butter until they are brown on all sides, then place them for a further 2 minutes on a bed of roasted hay in the heated oven.
› Fillet the pigeons.
› Decorate with a sprig of hay.

The preparation in 1, 2, 3

Roast the hay on a baking tray.

Stir regularly until all the hay is roasted.

Stuff the pigeons with the roasted hay.

Pack the pigeons completely with moist, roasted hay and let them rest for 4 days.

Smoke the pigeons for 2 hours with hay in a cold smoking oven.

Frank Fol
alias De Groentekok®

Frank Fol alias 'The Vegetable Chef' has worked harder than any other chef in our country to win a more prominent place for vegetables in the menus served up daily both at home and in restaurants. A place which – in his opinion – their status fully deserves. Because for him, Belgium is the No.1 vegetable country in Europe, if not the world. It's just that we all failed to realise it – until The Vegetable Chef appeared on the scene!

Frank Fol and his vegetable kitchen

Frank Fol was head chef in his own restaurant – the 'Sire Pynnock' – in Leuven. It was only in 2005 that he took up his self-appointed role as Belgium's vegetable ambassador to the world. At first sight, this might seem a somewhat strange career move, but it was one that was written in the proverbial stars. From the very first day of the opening of his very first restaurant, Frank Fol showed that he was serious in his new approach towards vegetables. His first menu card bore the heading: 'Frank Fol and his vegetable cuisine'. This new battle-cry – for such it was – caused a good deal of furore and confusion back at the beginning of the 1990s. "People thought that I wanted to start a vegetarian restaurant. But my only intention was to give vegetables a proper place in my menu, the place that they deserve. In my opinion, most kitchens pay too little attention to the possibilities offered by vegetables, whereas in reality they are an almost limitless and health-giving source of creativity, texture and flavour. What's more, the range of vegetable produce in our country is wide. In fact, they represent an important part of our nation's culinary identity and tradition. People also tend to associate particular vegetables with a particular dish or technique. This has a limiting and impoverishing effect on our national cuisine. I now know no fewer than forty different techniques, which allow me to prepare vegetables in a varied, healthy and (above all) tasty manner."

From kitchen prince to vegetable ambassador

Frank Fol enjoyed a classical culinary education. "I followed cooking at the COOVI School and followed this up with a training period at Restaurant 'Villa Lorraine' under chef Freddy Vandecasserie. He offered me a job before I had even finished my studies and I grabbed at the offer with both hands. I learnt a huge amount in his kitchen: not only about cooking techniques, but also about the importance of organisation, discipline and efficiency. It was a flourishing restaurant with a large kitchen team, so that I was given the opportunity to try my hand at every different position, even as a pastry cook. Those seven years really shaped me as a chef. But before I could start up on my own, I felt the need to follow a further year of finishing at Restaurant 'L'Ecailler du Palais Royal', where I had the good fortune to work under Attilio Basso. I regard both Freddy and Attilio as my professional godfathers." It was at a culinary festival with Freddy Vandecasserie in Thailand that Frank Fol learnt for the first time to appreciate the full potential of cooking with vegetables and spices. As soon as he was back in Belgium, he began to experiment with ways to give vegetables a more prominent place in the professional kitchen. "Until then, vegetables where seen as, something secondary that you needed to go with fish, meat, game or poultry. Ever since, my aim has been to ensure that vegetables are given the same 'star' treatment as these other ingredients. Why? Because they can be so deliciously tasty and also because they are an important part of a healthy and balanced diet.

My passion for vegetables gave me a new drive. They still do. When I started the 'Sire Pynnock' with my wife back in 1989, we had two guiding principles from which we were not prepared to budge: firstly, that vegetables would play a leading role in my cooking and, secondly, that we did not intend to stay in this restaurant for the rest of our lives! After 15 years, I felt that the time had come to find a different way to pursue my professional career, a different way to give expression to my culinary talents. This made the decision to sell the business that much easier. Moreover, my television work in the mid-1990s also meant that my methods and ideas were fairly well known and had met with favourable response. Many different companies began to ask me for advice and information. One thing soon led to another, and I gradually began to find myself slipping more and more into the role of a consultant. It was an almost organic process. Finally, in 2005 I decided that I would only continue to operate as an advisory chef – and so The Vegetable Cook was born. In the end, it was a question of time management: I could no longer combine my consultancy work with the full-time running of a restaurant. The decision was quickly made. I have always loved the idea of new challenges and the work that I now do is project-based, clearly defined, but with a great deal of variety. I am probably no less busy than in the past, but now I at least have more control over what I do and when I do it. Some of my projects need following up over a number of years, such as new recipes, the training of personnel or the quality management processes at the Exki fast service chain. In fact, the first brainstorming sessions for Exki were held while I was till in the 'Sire Pynnock'. I was instrumental in helping to set up this successful chain, which now has more than 60 outlets in different European cities. The distribution sector in our own country is also becoming more interested in vegetable-based dishes. This is an area where I am still actively creating new 'ready-to-eat' recipes and salads.

My passion for vegetables gave me a new drive.

To use even more fruit and vegetables in a creative manner Frank Fol developed his 'Think Veg-Think Fruit' philosophy, which is based on a number of simple steps and aids. With this philosophy as his cornerstone, Fol organizes lectures and demonstrations all year round in Belgium and The Netherlands. He also takes part in a number of eye-catching promotional events, such as 'The Fruit and Vegetable Week', in which local growers are deservedly put in the spotlight in a bonanza of nationwide workshops, cooking demos, expositions and talks. One of the highlights is the choosing of the 'Best Vegetable Restaurant in the Benelux', which was also the inspiration for the publishing of the first Green Gault & Millau. In this new guide, all the nominated vegetable restaurants were included, together with a summary of the best fruit and vegetable markets in the Benelux and the best specialist suppliers. And so the 'Think Veg-Think Fruit' philosophy of Belgium's very own Vegetable Chef has made an international breakthrough - at last.

Frank Fol
www.degroentekok.com
www.deweekvangroentenenfruit.info
www.degroenegaultmillau.info
www.denkgroenten.info

In a nutshell

→ **Who or what influenced your choice of profession?**
My parents are both bon-vivants who enjoy life to the full and my mother and grandmother were constantly – and creatively – busy in the kitchen. In addition, we used to go once a year to the Bourgogne region of France, where we always ate in the best restaurants. This is where I learnt to appreciate gastronomy.

→ **What was your first culinary experience or memory?**
My first culinary milestone was experienced at Kayserberg in the Alsace region of France: quenelle de brochet with a Nantua sauce and a farmyard chicken with Riesling. The flavours were heavenly and I can still taste them, even today. Much later, I went back to the same restaurant but the original owner and cook were no longer there. And the dishes on the menu bore no comparison with what I remembered.

→ **What can really make you mad in the kitchen?**
When someone is not honest.

→ **What is your most important personal quality?**
A positive attitude: I whistle my way through life.

→ **How would you most like to be described by others?**
As someone who enjoys life and who believes passionately in his open and honest message about vegetables.

→ **How do you deal with set backs?**
By evaluating, drawing the right conclusions and trying to move on (although it isn't always easy!).

→ **What would you like to have more time for?**
Family, friends and travel.

→ **What other job would you like to do?**
Photographer and/or winemaker. Two subjects over which I have long pondered as possible career avenues: hence my passion for wine and the numerous books on cooking that I have been fortunate enough to make!

→ **For you, what is the epitome of luxury?**
Spending time with my family and having enough money to make it fun.

→ **What do you like to give as a present to your friends?**
Good wine and friendship!

→ **What are you best at in the kitchen?**
Being creative!

→ **What do you most enjoy doing in the kitchen?**
Cooking?

→ **What do you least enjoy doing in the kitchen?**
Washing up!

→ **What is your favourite vegetable?**
Witloof (chicory in Belgium, endive in France).

→ **What is your favourite type or cut of meat?**
Top skirt (onglet) of veal.

→ **What type(s) of fish do you like to work with?**
Dover sole, halibut, pollack, turbot and brill.

→ **What are your preferred herbs for fish and meat dishes?**
For meat: mace. For fish: fresh mixed herbs.

→ **What are you favourite aromas and smells in the kitchen?**
Tomato, peas, fresh herbs and spices, stock, lobster...

→ **What is your favourite dish?**
Endive purée, vegetable hot-pot or a Thai vegetable salad.

→ **Which small object could you not do without in the kitchen?**
The classic small kitchen knife.

→ **Which chef has inspired you the most?**
In the past, Michel Bras and Pierre Gagnaire. I still have great respect for them both.

→ **What type of cuisine do you not like?**
Cooking with heavy cream sauces!

→ **What was the last celebrated restaurant that you visited and what was your opinion?**
Comme Chez Soi. Delicious! Lionel Rigolet is in top form and gives quality products the added value they deserve.

→ **What is your worst ever eating experience?**
At a famous star-rated restaurant in Paris.

→ **Who is your perfect table companion?**
Anyone with the right frame of mind to enjoy themselves, but with respect for the restaurant, its food and its staff.

→ **What is your favourite aperitif?**
Bollinger champagne.

→ **What do you most enjoy eating on your day off?**
Soup, pasta or a salad.

→ **What are your favourite book and your favourite cooking book?**
Food: Het Grote Ingrediëntenboek (The Big Ingredients Book).

→ **For whom would you one day like to cook, and why?**
Michelle Obama, because she is mad about fresh vegetables and herbs. Just to show her what you can really do with them.

→ **Which famous customer would you one day like to welcome, and why?**
Arne Quinze. He is a bon-vivant who enjoys good food and good wine. He is also a fine friend.

→ **Which famous person from the past would you like to have welcomed as a customer?**
Salvador Dali, to philosophise about ingredients and cooking.

→ **In which city would you like to live and work?**
None!

Glazed pigeons with a potato puree with parsley, ginger, mustard and soya, grilled rhubarb and a salad with pointed cabbage, black radish, pimpernel and elderflower

For 4 people

For the pigeons:
2 pigeons
pepper and salt
butter
2 teaspoons honey
2 dl veal stock
soya sauce
1 shallot, finely chopped

For the puree:
200 g potatoes, soft-boiling
salt
1 clove garlic
1 handful curly parsley
fresh ginger, grated
soya-yuzu sauce
1 teaspoon mustard

For the rhubarb:
1 thick stick of ripe rhubarb
arachide oil
pepper

For the salad:
some elderflower stems
0.5 dl white wine vinegar
1 pointed cabbage leaf
60 g black radish
some pimpernel stems
black pepper from the mill
sea salt

elderflowers, for the garnishing

› Clean the pigeons and season them with pepper and salt. Colour them on both sides in a pan with some butter. Brush them liberally with the honey, then cook further in a hot oven for 4 to 5 minutes. During the cooking, baste them regularly with the meat juices. When tender, remove from the oven and allow to rest. Remove the legs from the carcass. Keep the feet and claws separately. Bone the lower part of the leg and remove the skin. Carve the breast meat from the carcass and keep it warm for later. Remove the fat from the roasting tin. De-glaze with the veal stock and a little soya sauce. Add the shallot and allow to reduce.

› Peel the potatoes. Wash them and cut them into pieces. Bring to the boil in water with a clove of garlic. Also parboil the parsley in some water. Rinse in cold running water and puree in the blender with some of the cooking fluid. Mix the potato puree and the parsley together, adding the grated ginger, soya-yuzu sauce and the mustard. Make sure the consistency is smooth and creamy.

› Peel the rhubarb and cut into thick pieces. Brush these pieces with arachide oil and season with pepper. Grill the pieces briefly until cooked through.

› Soak the elderflowers for at least 30 minutes in the white wine vinegar. Cut the pointed cabbage and the black radish into fine, short strips. Allow these to stiffen for 10 minutes in ice-cold-water. Drain the water, dry the strips and stir in the pimpernel, pepper from the mill, sea salt and a little elderflower vinegar.

› Draw two lines of puree centrally on the plates. Warm the pigeons briefly in the oven. Slice the breast fillets and divide equally over the plates. Likewise divide the grilled rhubarb and add a piece of the boned pigeon leg. Top with a little of the pointed cabbage salad. Stand a pair of pigeon feet on each plate. Mix the sauce and pour over the pigeon. Finish with pepper from the mill and some of the elderflowers.

Asparagus, mangetouts and peas with garden cress, young shoots, rape flowers and hazelnuts

For 4 people

2 shallots
salt

6 thick Mechelen asparagus
60 g peas
2 mangetouts (sugar peas)

For the asparagus vinaigrette:
cooking fluid from the asparagus
1 cooked asparagus (or some leavings)
pepper and salt
white wine vinegar
rape seed oil

For the pea foam:
40 g cooked peas in some of their
cooking fluid
rape seed oil
pepper and salt
white wine vinegar

some stems of garden cress
a selection of other young shoots
rape flowers
some hazelnuts, finely chopped

› Smoke the shallots. To do this, sprinkle 5 grams of sawdust in the bottom of a low but wide cooking pot. Cover the sawdust with a deep plate and arrange the shallots on the plate. Close the pot with the lid. Place on the stove and turn up the heat. Continue until the sawdust begins to smoke. Remove from the heat and allow the pot to cool, with the lid on. Cut the shallots into fine rings and cook for 1 minute in some salted water. Rinse them in cold water and allow them to dry.

› Clean four asparagus and cook them al dente in some salted water. Allow them to cool in a little of the cooking fluid. Clean the remaining asparagus and cut them lengthwise into thin tagliatelle-like strips with a shredder. Immerse them for 30 seconds in boiling asparagus cooking fluid. Remove and cool under cold, running water. Allow them to drain on some kitchen paper. Cook the mangetouts and the peas for 1 minute in some salted water. Cut the mangetouts into fine slices lengthways.

› Make the asparagus vinaigrette with some of the asparagus cooking fluid, a cooked asparagus (or some cooked leavings), pepper and salt, a splash of white wine vinegar and a splash of rape seed oil.

› Make the pea foam by mixing the peas with a splash of their cooking fluid, pepper and salt and a splash of white wine vinegar.

› Place on each plate an asparagus, cut lengthways (dry them first). Arrange the other ingredients one by one: the asparagus tagliatelle, some garden cress, some mangetouts, a few other vegetable shoots, the smoked shallot rings, the peas, the rape flowers and some hazelnuts. Sprinkle the composition with the asparagus vinaigrette. Mix the pea foam and add to the plates as appropriate. Serve cold or lukewarm.

Marinated ravioli of kohlrabi with passion fruit and a sweet pesto of chocolate and banana

For 4 people

1 large kohlrabi
2 dl passion fruit juice
water
2 tablespoons caster sugar
some green stems from the kohlrabi
(or some fresh mint)
some flowers (blue bean flowers,
cucumber flowers, blue violets)

For the pesto:
80 g pure Belgian chocolate
1/2 ripe banana
rape seed oil
a few drops of lemon juice
20 g almonds, chopped

› Peel the kohlrabi and cut 12 very thin, round slices (for the ravioli) with a mandolin. Stir together the passion fruit juice and the sugar in a good splash of water. Gradually increase the heat, stirring continually. Place the kohlrabi slices one by one in this warm mixture and let them simmer gently for a maximum of 1 minute. Remove from the stove and spoon the ravioli onto a dish or tray. Cover them with part of the passion fruit juice as a marinade and place in the fridge. Reduce the remaining passion fruit juice until it forms a smooth coulis. Be careful to ensure that the colour does not change.

› Melt the chocolate for the pesto on a low heat. Mix the warm chocolate in a blender, together with the banana, a splash of oil and the lemon juice. Add the chopped almonds and mix again.

› Put three spoonfuls of pesto onto a long plate and cover this with the kohlrabi ravioli. Pour a little of the passion fruit juice and the coulis over the ravioli and decorate with kohlrabi leaves or a sprig of mint and with dried and ground passion fruit seeds, if desired.

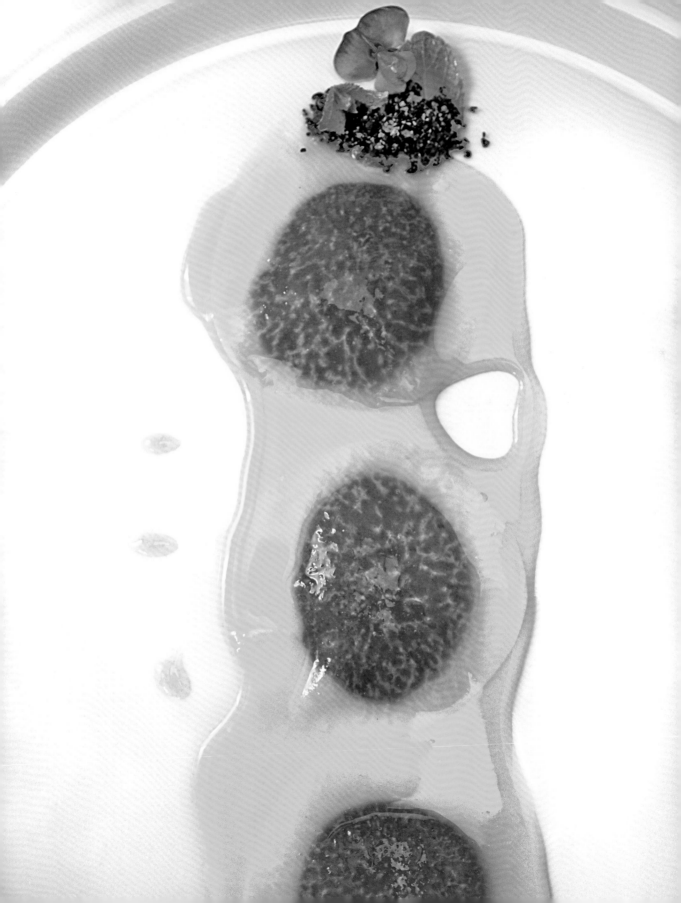

The preparation in 1, 2, 3

1

Peel the kohlrabi.

2

Add the rape seed oil to the banana.

3

Slice the kohlrabi to make 'ravioli'.

4

Put the kohlrabi ravioli into the passion fruit sauce.

5

Melt the chocolate.

Add the banana to the chocolate.

Mix the warm chocolate and banana into a pesto.

Add the almonds.

Place the kohlrabi ravioli on top of the chocolate pesto.

Pour a little passion fruit coulis over the ravioli.

Finish with the kohlrabi leaves a sprig of mint and dried and ground passion fruit seeds.

Viki Geunes

∫ 't Zilte ∫

A striking visual signature makes the self-taught Viki Geunes something of an exception amongst Belgian chefs. Driven by a desire for perfection, this outstanding food designer has built up a strong personal repertoire. But he is also driven by taste: food must be pleasing to the eye – very pleasing in his case – but the palate must likewise be titillated. And this is something that he achieves with brio in Restaurant ''t Zilte'.

A personal touch

"Whether I work with seemingly simple products such as turnips or carrots or more noble ingredients such as langoustines or turbot, I always respect the basic taste of the product to a maximum degree and try and make the difference with the presentation," says Viki Geunes. Flavours and textures are his basis. He seeks to give added value, a personal touch, with the visual aspects of his dishes. Through a decorative accent or an unusual plate presentation, he hopes to offer his customers something extra. Herein lays the strength of his signature. "I do not only choose products that are already well-known, but also ingredients that are new on the market. A combination of the two gives more power. Classic products have already proven their value: they are recognisable and inspire confidence in the customers. But new ingredients can also tickle their interest and make them curious. They fascinate and offer new possibilities for unusual combinations." As might be expected, however, this top chef also gives pride of place to his products. Techniques – visual or otherwise – are secondary, just a means to get the very best out of the ingredients. Even though he has a very strong technical repertoire, he understands that this must not take precedence in his kitchen. On the contrary, these skills must be used in the service of the product to enhance its final taste. "I see that chefs sometimes use new techniques because they are 'innovative', whereas in many cases the use of a classic method will still give them a better result. For example, I like to make an aioli or a tapenade in the traditional manner, because that gives a better overall character and flavour. We have reached a point in time where many chefs are able to properly assess both classic and new techniques, so that they can choose and use them consciously in function of the end result that they are trying to achieve. The days when everything 'new' was automatically 'good' are now gone, but this period has nonetheless given us a stronger type of cuisine."

Talking and stimulating – the visual way

Viki Geunes always seeks to arrive at a product result with a high concentration of flavour, but he feels that it is equally important that it should look good on the plate. "When a plate of food is placed on a table in a restaurant, the customer's first contact with that food is visual. That is the starting point for my cuisine. In many areas of life, good initial eye-contact is a prelude to a deeper relationship and a better understanding," he adds with a grin. He wants his dishes to talk to his guests, to excite them and stimulate them. A dish that repels or poses too many questions will seldom be able to convince. "If that first visual contact is inviting, the subsequent 'meeting' between food and customer will be that much easier. You can certainly be creative with patterns of flavour, but the visual aspects of cooking offer almost limitless possibilities for innovation. Of course, what you serve must not only be 'pretty': it must also remain recognisable

for the customer. You can add a few details that may raise questions or arouse curiosity, but the overall composition must always look appetising to eat. This is the whole point: the aesthetic elements must encourage the appetite. In the very best cases, they might even provoke a little excitement." Viki Geunes searches for triggers and question-marks that can stimulate, but then quickly provide the necessary answers, once the food is tasted. Flavour always remains the main determining factor. "An umami effect in sweetbreads or a slightly burnt caramel flavour in lacquered eel is the end result I am looking for. But a creative garnish can enhance this end result, without the sweetbreads or the eel becoming unrecognisable. I have been trying for many years to give my dishes added power in a personal manner. This is a process that is continually evolving. I follow many different paths, but the ultimate goal remains the same: to create a result and style that is ever more refined."

We have reached a point in time where many chefs are able to properly assess both classic and new techniques, so that they can choose and use them consciously in function of the end result that they are trying to achieve.

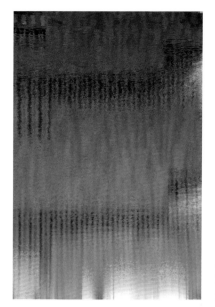

An exceptional location

For Viki Geunes, the accentuating of the visual element is not confined to the food on his plates or the interior of his dining area. He believes that eating out must be a total experience. This belief was clearly reflected in his first restaurant in Mol. But he felt that the space available to him there was insufficient to grow with his vision. He needed a new location to be able to give proper shape and form to his bubbling creativity. As a result, Viki and Viviane Geunes loaded up their pots and pans and moved to Antwerp. Not to a fashionable or elegant location in the city, but to the ninth floor of the Museum on the River (MAS). In this new element in the urban landscape, which is designed to link the old harbour area more closely to the neighbouring city centre, people can discover all they need to know about the rich past and present of Antwerp. Various exhibition areas allow a broad thematic picture to be painted, and the building itself serves a vertical boulevard which offers a unique view of the city. And it is in this architecturally striking and ground-breaking location that Viki and Viviane have built their new culinary nest. "At a height of some sixty metres above the ground, we are literally working on a different level. It has taken everyone a little time to get used to it. I think that there are few other chefs in the country who take a lift to work every morning with such a spectacular view to inspire them! The new location has meant new challenges for everyone in the team. And to reflect the exceptional nature of the location, we have also created an exceptional interior which we feel is in keeping with the remarkable exterior of the building. This, too, was a challenge. But the final result is exactly what I wanted and matches my vision of what eating out should be: a total experience. To achieve this result, we worked with people such as architect Vittorio Simoni and artist Koen van den Broeck. Together, we have been able to provide the restaurant with just the right atmosphere."

On cloud nine!

With such a location, it is understandable that the new 't Zilte' now attracts a different public than in Mol. The MAS acts as a magnet for a much broader clientele. "I always worked with great passion in Mol, but this new location is of a completely different order. In Mol, I used to play in a small local theatre; I now feel as though I am starring in a musical on Broadway! This makes it possible to reach so many more people. It is a dream platform which allows us to adopt our personal approach to every aspect of a restaurant visit. The location has its own unique dynamic, and this also stimulates us to make even greater efforts. And all with the aim that our guests should leave here feeling like they're on cloud nine!"

't Zilte
Hanzestedenplaats 5, 2000 Antwerpen
014/32 24 33
www.tzilte.be

In a nutshell

→ **Who or what influenced your choice of profession?**
My mother's cooking, certainly on Sunday with a nice glass of wine to go with it!

→ **What was your first culinary experience or memory?**
Too long ago to remember with any degree of certainty!

→ **What can really make you mad in the kitchen?**
Chaos or lack of control.

→ **What is your most important personal quality?**
Always moving forward, never taking 'no' for an answer.

→ **How would you most like to be described by others?**
Hard but fair in my job, a job that I truly live for.

→ **How do you deal with set backs?**
Ever onwards, ever upwards!

→ **What would you like to have more time for?**
My family, daughter and wife.

→ **What other job would you like to do?**
Is there another job?

→ **For you, what is the epitome of luxury?**
Happiness in all its simplicity.

→ **What do you like to give as a present to your friends?**
Friendship!

→ **What do you most enjoy doing in the kitchen?**
Cooking, cooking and cooking!

→ **What do you least enjoy doing in the kitchen?**
Seeing how things sometimes go wrong.

→ **What is your favourite vegetable?**
Artichoke.

→ **What is your favourite type or cut of meat?**
Côte de boeuf (side of beef).

→ **What type(s) of fish do you like to work with?**
Turbot, langoustines and scallops.

→ **What are your preferred herbs for fish and meat dishes?**
Tarragon for meat, verbena for fish.

→ **What are you favourite aromas and smells in the kitchen?**
Vegetable stock with plenty of aromatics.

→ **What is your favourite dish?**
Steak tartar.

→ **Which small object could you not do without in the kitchen?**
Kitchen palette knife.

→ **Who is your perfect table companion?**
People with whom you can enjoy a good meal in a relaxed manner.

→ **What is your favourite aperitif?**
A good glass of champagne.

→ **What do you most enjoy eating on your day off?**
That depends on the season and the amount of time I have: a tasty piece of bread with fine olive oil, a good stew or a top dish with quality products.

→ **What are your favourite book and your favourite cooking book?**
Spelen met Vuur by Robert Kranenborg, because he gives a clear description of the dishes and because of his very non-classic photography.

→ **In which city would you like to live and work?**
Where I am now.

Lobster, carrot, sambal and kumquat

2 European lobsters, each weighing
800 g
court-bouillon

For the tomato compote:
2 shallots
1 clove garlic
1 tablespoon chermoula
6 clusters of cherry tomatoes
3 carrots

For the marinade:
Equal quantities of sugar, water and
sushi vinegar
1/2 clove garlic
1 tablespoon orange zest
a pinch of salt
1 large carrot
12 young carrots

For the sambal:
2 shallots
1 clove garlic
1 red pepper
1 stalk lemon grass
20 g ginger
4 tablespoons sushi vinegar
1 tablespoon tomato puree
2 dl vegetable stock
1 tablespoon Poudre Grande Caravane
(Olivier Roellinger)

250 g kumquats
sugar (half the weight of the
kumquats)
5 tablespoons sushi vinegar
a pinch of salt

1 nori skin
pepper and salt
sushi rice
150 g squid, cleaned
100 g sea salt

For the garniture:
flowers
fresh herbs

› Cook the lobster for 1 minute in the court-bouillon, freshen
  in cold water and cut the meat into medallions. Fry the
  medallions briefly on the plancha.
› Make a thick tomato compote by mixing together the shallot,
  garlic, chermoula and the tomato brunoise. Add the finely
  chopped carrot brunoise when the compote is nicely cooked
  through.
› Make a marinade from equal quantities of sugar, water and
  sushi vinegar, together with a little garlic, orange zest and salt.
  Marinate the carrot strips in this mixture.
› Cook the young carrots al dente and serve part of them as finely
  cut slices, marinated in the sushi vinegar marinade.
› Make a sambal from stewed shallots, garlic and red peppers.
  Add the lemon grass, ginger and sushi vinegar, and allow to
  reduce. Next add the tomato puree and then the poultry stock
  with the Poudre Grand Caravane. Allow to simmer dry, stirring
  all the time.
› Cook the kumquats five times in cold water. Bring to the boil
  each time and then refresh. Cook for the last time with half
  their weight in sugar and a little sushi vinegar. Add salt and
  allow to simmer for 5 minutes. Drain and make into a puree.
› For the sushi, roll the lobster claws in a nori skin and wrap this
  in a layer of boiled sushi rice, seasoned with salt and pepper.
  Cut into small sticks.
› Pickle the cleaned squid for 10 hours in sea salt. Rinse well, cut
  into thin slices and allow them to dry until crispy.
› Serve all the ingredients neatly arranged on the plate. Dress
  with the kumquat cream and decorate with different flowers
  and fresh herbs.

Chocolate, kalamansi and Earl Grey

For the chocolate ganache:
150 g kalamansi juice
310 g milk
100 g cream
75 g sugar
90 g egg yolks
30 g maïzena (thickener)
220 g chocolate

For the chocolate ice-cream:
700 g water
250 g chocolate 72 %
100 g sugar
50 g trimoline
100 g pro-cream (Sosa)
50 g cacao powder

For the Earl Grey granité:
1 l water
20 g Earl Grey tea
100 g sugar
50 g lemon juice
8 g gelatine

For the kalamansi mousse:
200 g water
150 g kalamansi juice
300 g egg white
1.5 g xantana

For the kalamansi gel:
4 dl kalamansi juice
5 dl water

50 g sugar
12 g agaragar

For the kalamansi cream:
200 g kalamansi juice
200 g water
300 g eggs
350 g sugar
12 g gelatine
400 g butter

For the golden crisp:
200 g fondant
100 g glucose
100 g isomalt
5 g gold powder

› Make the chocolate ganache by bringing the kalamansi juice to the boil with the milk and the cream. Beat the sugar, egg yolks and maïzena to a frothy consistency and pour this into the boiling kalamansi mixture. Bring to the boil again, whisking all the time. Stir in the chocolate, remove from the heat and allow to cool. Mix later in the thermomix.
› For the chocolate ice-cream, melt the chocolate in lukewarm water and then add the rest of the ingredients. Place the mixture in a pacojet bowl and allow it to freeze.
› For the Earl Grey granité, mix the water with the Earl Grey tea, sugar and lemon juice and allow to boil briefly. Add the gelatine, dissolve and allow to cool. Put the mixture in the freezer and scrape regularly, so that attractive ice crystals are formed.
› For the kalamansi mousse, mix the water with 150 grams of kalamansi juice, the egg white and 1.5 grams of xantana. Fill a siphon with this mixture and warm to 60 °C.
› For the kalamansi gel, bring the kalamansi juice, water and sugar to the boil. Add the agaragar and allow to harden. Mix to a smooth consistency in the thermomix.
› For the kalamansi cream, mix together the kalamansi juice, water, eggs, sugar and gelatine. Heat the mixture to 85 °C, allow to cool to 37 °C and then stir in 400 grams of butter.
› For the golden crisp, heat 200 grams of fondant, 100 grams of glucose and 100 grams of isomalt to 155 °C. Allow to harden and then mix to a fine consistency. Stir in the gold powder. Pour out the mixture and allow it to melt under a salamander.
› Draw a ganache stripe across the plate with a spatula. Spray nice roundels of kalamansi cream and gel. Add the chocolate ice-cream, Earl Grey granité, kalamansi mousse and the golden crisp.

Mackerel, radish, freshly-smoked cheese and langoustines

150 g fresh white cheese
400 g rettich (summer radish)
0.5 dl red beetroot juice
0.5 dl elderflower juice
3 cl Mizshio (purified seawater from van Minami Sangyo)
2 dl grape seed oil

150 g different types of radish
5 tablespoons olive oil
1 tablespoon lime juice
pepper and salt

12 langoustines (size 6/9)
1/2 tablespoon cumbava oil
2 tablespoons grape seed oil
1/2 tablespoon lime juice
pepper and salt
1/2 tablespoon light ponzu

1 mackerel
a pinch of sea salt
a pinch of sugar
1 teaspoon lime zest

4 dl water
50 g sugar
1 lemon, sliced
3 bunches of fresh elderflower

5 cl red beetroot juice
5 cl elderflower juice
5 cl grape seed oil
3 tablespoons sushi vinegar
1 tablespoon lime juice
pepper and salt

4 tablespoons herring eggs
some fine red-veined dock leaves

› Allow the white cheese to hang for a night in a hemp cloth. Cold smoke the cheese the next day for 15 minutes with dried pine needles.
› Cut thin, round slices of rettich. Seal in a vacuum bag with the red beetroot juice, the elderflower juice and the purified seawater and allow to marinate for 24 hours. Place the marinated slices in 'tile' fashion on some plastic foil and spray over the white cheese. Roll up the plastic foil tightly. Boil the remaining rettich until cooked through and then make into puree. Finish with a little grape seed oil.
› Cut thin slices of the different types of radish and marinate them briefly in a mixture of olive oil, lime juice, pepper and salt.
› Marinate the langoustines in a mixture of cumbava oil, grape seed oil, lime juice, salt, pepper and light ponzu.
› Fillet the mackerel and remove the bones. Salt briefly in the sea salt, with an added pinch of sugar and some lime zest. Rinse thoroughly after 5 minutes. Poach the skin side briefly with boiling water and divide into portions.
› Make a vinaigrette by boiling the sugar in the water, adding the slices of lemon and then pouring over the fresh elderflowers. Allow to brew for 24 hours. Mix together the red beetroot juice, the elderflower juice, the grape seed oil and the sushi vinegar, and flavour with a little lime juice, pepper and salt.
› Put some rettich cream on the plate and spread it with a spatula. Add the langoustine, white cheese roll and the mackerel. Dress with the herring eggs, mixed radish slices and red-veined dock leaves. Drizzle the vinaigrette and juice over and around the composition.

Presentation in 1, 2, 3

› Put some rettich cream on the plate.
› Spread it half out with a spatula.
› Add a langoustine and a white cheese roll.
› Place a piece of mackerel alongside.
› Dress with herring eggs.
› Decorate with slices of mixed radishes.
› Garnish with red-veined dock leaves.
› Drizzle vinaigrette and juice over the plate.

Peter Goossens

Hof van Cleve

It was a first in the world of journalism. A chef was chosen by a quality magazine as its 'Man of the Year'. Until then, chefs had only occasionally made the news if they won a competition or were awarded a star. But to be recognised as someone who had dominated the news in a positive manner for a whole year and helped to give it shape and form? No, no other chef had ever managed to achieve that. And you might easily ask yourself whether or not any other chef is ever likely to do it again. Who is ready to follow in the illustrious footsteps of Peter Goossens?

I just love things that are tasty! And I am not the only one.
We live in a country full of good food and good cooking.
It is part of our tradition.

From 'unknown Belgian' to the top of the world

The chef of Restaurant 'Hof van Cleve' is not just a natural talent in the kitchen. He has also turned his hand – with great success – to television. There, too, he has blazed a trail for the new generation of younger chefs. Peter Goossens has been in the very top echelons of European cuisine for a number of years. He is now being heralded by colleagues worldwide as one of the best chefs of his era. The number of Belgians with an international reputation is limited, but for a relatively small country we do not do too badly. All the more reason to let Peter Goossens head the list of most influential Belgian chefs: as a prominent ambassador and the leading exponent of Belgian culinary expertise.

In media terms, as a VIB (very important Belgian) Peter Goossens has superstar status. Thanks to his fascinating and widely-praised television appearances since 2008, he has become a household name. His face is seldom off the screen or out of the magazines. It is sometimes easy to forget that he is first and foremost an outstanding chef. But he is also much more than that. He regrets that he was never able to follow management training, although you would hardly know it: his leadership qualities and his ability to delegate, to organise and to think ahead are second-to-none. This, too, is a natural talent – and one without which it would have been impossible to reach the very top of the international cooking world. His equally natural talent for seamlessly combining tastes of exceptional purity was first recognised in the trade press in 1993, the year in which as a relative 'unknown' he won the 'Best Cook in Belgium' at the Golden Delta awards. A year earlier, the twenty-eight-year - old chef had opened his own restaurant – 'Hof van Cleve' – in Kruishoutem. Prior to that, he had received his initial training at the 'Ter Duinen' hotel school in Koksijde, followed by a number of years working in the famous Parisian restaurant 'Le Pré Catalan'. He started there as an ordinary trainee, but the owner and head chef, Gaston Lenôtre, soon gave him a permanent contract. He also gave him responsibility for the traiteur and catering service. The 'little Belgian' made a big impression, and when he returns to 'Le Pré Catalan' he is still welcomed as one of the family. His experiences there clearly made a big impression

on Goossens as well: if you talk to him about his Parisian period, he will regale you with tale after tale about great food and humorous incidents (the man is a born story-teller). 1994 brought another milestone in his professional career: the award of his first Michelin star. In that same year, GaultMillau gave 'Hof van Cleve' a score of fifteen out of twenty. A second star quickly followed in 1998, by which time GaultMillau has raised its opinion to eighteen out of twenty. His sensitive touch with products of exceptional quality and his unparalleled technical ability to create richly-detailed dishes of great refinement and freshness led in 2005 to the ultimate recognition: the awarding of a third Michelin star and an unheard of nineteen-and-a-half out of twenty in the GaultMillau guide. As far as his own country was concerned, Goossens had reached the very top of the tree. But he now made his entrance into the very exclusive 'inner circle' of three-star chefs who represent the very best in world gastronomy. Since 2006, this status has been confirmed by the unbroken inclusion of 'Hof van Cleve' at a high position in The World's 50 Best Restaurants, an authoritative list compiled by a highly respected international jury (on which Goossens also sits as Belgium's only representative).

A remarkable signature

His ability to create bridges with great sensitivity between classical and modern cuisine gives his signature a deeper significance, perhaps even a historical significance, in culinary terms. His passionate desire for perfection and an extreme form of consistent high quality are two other characteristics that typify his cooking. Goossens' dishes are light, refreshing and pure. He is able like no one else to create a harmonious and uniform whole from a diverse number of subtle ingredients. He has a preference for shellfish, but he is equally capable of dazzling his guests with deep-tasting and homogenous meat recipes. This is based on his uncanny sense of taste and his exceptional knowledge of his products. In addition, he can also count on the support of his wife Lieve, who marshals her strong and professional serving team with great competence and style. Together, they provide proof that a three-star restaurant can still be pleasant, homely and relaxed. The couple look forward to the prospect of welcoming their guests with food and service of the very highest quality for many years to come. But behind Goossens' personal and charismatic style (already imitated by so many), keen observers are already identifying the first sharp contours of what is destined to become a culinary legacy of great significance.

Respect for both product and producer

Apart from his reputation as a great stylist, Peter Goossens is also famed for his legendary sense of taste and his outstanding knowledge of his products. He always talks about his products with great respect. But in contrast to many chefs, he likes to take that respect a step further. "The producers also deserve our respect," he emphasises. "Without their care, knowledge and dedication, and in some cases even real passion, we would not have such delicious carrots, fine hop shoots, crispy radishes or fat, juicy asparagus. We need these super-products. We buy them, cut them, prepare them and serve them. They are the basis of our profession. Without them we are nothing. Fortunately, in our country we have a large number of producers who deliver products of quality. As chef, we have the task to finish off in style the excellent work that they have begun in their fields and greenhouses. This is an obligation we have not only to the products themselves, but also – even more so – to the men and women who make them what they are. And the same applies to the breeders of cattle, sheep, pigs and poultry. And to the fishermen, who are sometimes out on the high seas in storm-force winds. Top chefs all want top-quality turbot, but finding it and fishing it is another matter. This is true for several other 'typical' restaurant products, such as langoustines and scallops. We are dependent upon our trawlermen and divers, just as we are dependent on the knowledge and skill of our cattle and poultry farmers for the excellence of our meat. It takes four or five years of careful feeding before beef cattle are capable of yielding rich-tasting, fat-laced, finely-marbled meat. We need to treat that meat with the respect it deserves, not least out of respect for all the time and hard work that has gone

> *People no longer have the time to stand for hours in a kitchen, preparing a meal. But I hope that one day people will again learn to find the time to cook properly. Because few countries have the same rich culinary culture as Belgium.*

into its production. We chefs are at the very end of the food chain. People expect us to provide a fitting finale to everything that has gone before. Happily, in Belgium there are a large number of chefs who are professional enough to realise this. To a large extent, this determines the nature of our restaurant cuisine. And there are few other countries which can match us in this respect."

A young head of lettuce

"My cuisine has evolved strongly in this direction in recent years, because in our sector standing still is the same as going backwards. Ever since the opening of 'Hof van Cleve' I have consistently asked myself the same question: how can we make the use of our products even more refined, but without losing their essential character and respect. For example, serving products raw was once taboo. But some products have even more flavour and purity if they are served uncooked. Finesse is the key. Take, for example, sun-ripened fresh tomatoes. It is a shame to do anything with them except cut them in half and add just a little salt, pepper and a sprinkling of olive oil. My very best lettuce still comes from my father, who grows them in a large allotment. Young lettuce that is harvested in the spring is crispy and juicy. Products of this quality don't need much added to them. Even the veins are tasty." This last word is pronounced by Peter Goossens in an intense, no-holds-barred tone, as if to emphasise the

essence of the matter. "In 'Hof van Cleve' we serve salad raw, but also worked into a cream, which we can use for contrast. And also to bring extra nuances or variations of flavour to different textures. Our preference is for local products and these form the basis of our menu. The turbot, sole, plaice, shrimps, whiting and weever that come from our own North Sea taste better than the same varieties from the Atlantic Ocean. I don't know why – but it's true. There are probably specific factors which play a role – so that it is not unreasonable to speak of a 'terroir' effect. But of course, we also use products from other lands if they can offer added taste value. I am thinking in particular of a number of products from Japan, such as soya sauce or ponzu. We use them sparingly, to support our own 'home-grown' flavours. After all, we are running a Belgian restaurant – not a Japanese one."

Merveilleux!

"Our cuisine – in fact, cuisine in general – has become much more complex. We serve fewer dishes in a menu, because that is what people want. But the taste of the individual dishes has become richer and more intense. We are also giving more and more thought to lighter flavours and more easily digestible meals. We first serve a selection of hors d'oeuvres; culinary fun-and-games with the aperitif to sharpen the appetite. Then we offer a couple of light starters; mostly shellfish or fish. We build up gradually, so that when the main course arrives the guests are still hungry for more. This main course is something with a little more punch, followed by cheese or a dessert. But just because something is sweet, it doesn't need to be heavy. This is something else that has changed over the years. Our desserts are now feather-light. To finish off, we have a dessert trolley from which our guests are free to choose whatever they want. Classics such as rum-baba, eclairs, financier... all pure nostalgia for me. Or a merveilleux cake with moist meringue, cream and chocolate shavings, something that I always find super-tasty [that word again!]. It reminds me of Sunday mornings when I used to visit my grandmother for coffee. It is noticeable that these kinds of desserts seem to recall happy memories for quite a lot of my guests." Peter Goossens also traditionally serves 'smoutebollen' – doughnut balls. This fairground treat is not only delicious, but also gives people a good feeling. Just like his oven-warm Madeleine biscuits. "A legendary, finger-licking classic that few guests are able to resist, even after a hearty lunch or dinner. I just love things that are tasty! And I am not the only one. We live in a country full of good food and good cooking. It is part of our tradition. And long may it continue to be so!"

Pig's cheeks

Once he starts talking about food, he can't mention the word 'taste' enough. Peter Goossens speaks about it as though he is trying to convince a public meeting and continues in his well known hundred-miles-an-hour style. "In the old days, pots stood simmering on an old Leuven stove. Nowadays, people have modern cookers and ovens, but they still cook as much as they ever did, because they still love good food. This is ingrained in our cultural heritage. But we don't emphasise this fact enough. We have tremendous products, which are unique in Europe, if not the world. Here in East Flanders, for example, we have the most magnificent pigs, which provide the very best pork and pork mince. I was already serving pig's cheeks on my menu fifteen years ago. This dish (and calf's cheeks as well) are now a common site on many menu cards. But you need to serve pork products with sufficient fat to make them tasty. Tenderloin of pork with a good layer of fat, roasted in the oven, gives a far better juice than beef. We need to move away from pork that is sold and cooked without fat. That is just a waste! A little fat gives taste, character and body. Certainly in a country where people love eating. This is an area that we still need to work at. When I walk into a butcher's in France, I can immediately find different cuts of beef, pork, lamb and veal. All perfectly presented and neatly tied, just as you would expect. You can even find less highly-valued pieces, such as tails, ears, trotters and so on. Nowadays, a butcher's window in Belgium is full of lasagne, soup and vol-au-vent. People no longer have the time to stand for hours in a kitchen, preparing a meal. Everything needs to be 'fast' and 'ready-to-serve'. But I hope that one day people will again learn to find the time to cook properly. Because few countries have the same rich culinary culture as Belgium. It would be a shame to lose it, and it is up to all of us to see that this does not happen!"

Hof van Cleve
Riemegemstraat 1, 9770 Kruishoutem
09/383 58 48
www.hofvancleve.com

Anjou pigeon with a potato mousseline, winter truffle and crispy bacon

For 4 people

For the potato mousseline:
800 g potatoes (Rattes)
salt
150 g unsalted butter
50 g full cream milk
pepper
2 tablespoons winter truffle, grated.

150 g unsalted streaky bacon
salt

For the pigeons:
4 pigeons from Anjou
coarse salt
black pepper
1 l goose fat
pepper and salt
80 g unsalted butter

For the sauce:
1 shallot
1/2 clove garlic
100 ml red wine
1 laurel leaf
150 g brown stock
1 tablespoon winter truffle
25 ml truffle juice
1 splash of banyuls
butter

350 g chanterelle mushrooms
50 g unsalted butter
pepper and salt

For the decoration:
60 g truffle
butter
fleur de sel

› Peel and boil the potatoes in salted water. Drain and press them through a sieve. Stir in the butter and milk, and beat up until smooth and creamy. Season with pepper and salt. Finish with the grated truffle.
› Cut fine slices of bacon. Cook these in a dry non-stick pan until their texture becomes crispy. Allow to cool. Season with salt.
› Cut off the pigeon legs and cover them for 15 minutes in coarse salt and black pepper. Remove, rinse and dry. Immerse the legs in the heated goose fat (max. 90 °C). Cook for 30 minutes in an oven at 100 °C. Allow the legs to cool briefly in the fat. Remove the legs from the fat. Take out the leg bone and roll the meat in plastic foil. Remove the innards from the pigeon carcasses and season, both inside and outside, with pepper and salt. Fry the pigeons on both sides in a little butter, basting them continually with the cooking fat. Put the pan into the oven and cook for a further 3 minutes at 165 °C. Remove the pigeons from the pan and allow them to rest for about 5 minutes in a warm place.
› Degrease the pan for the sauce. Stew together the shallot and the garlic in the same pan until they make a compote. Dilute with the red wine, add a laurel leaf and allow to reduce briefly. Then add the brown stock and reduce further. Pass the mixture through a sieve and return it to the heat. Cook briefly with the grated truffle and then add the truffle juice and a splash of banyuls. Pass through a sieve for a second time and thicken with the butter.
› Clean the chanterelles thoroughly by cutting off any dirty pieces with a knife. Rinse briefly in water and dab them dry with a cloth. Fry them in foaming butter and season with salt and pepper.
› Fry the legs briefly in butter. Season with pepper and salt. Cut of the crown. Place the fried mushrooms on the plate and cover them with a layer of truffle puree. Cut the pigeon fillets into fine slices and arrange them on the puree, like tiles on a roof.
› Cut 15 grams of truffle per person in fine slices. Warm lightly with a little melted butter and fleur de sel, then place on top of the pigeon fillets, together with the fried bacon. Finally, add the sauce.

Squid with paprika, pickles and avocado

1 cuttlefish
olive oil
pepper and salt

For the mayo-pickles:
80 g mayonnaise
50 g pickles
100 g cream (40 %)
pepper and salt

For the black tapioca pearls:
50 g tapioca
1 bag of squid ink
1 tablespoon soya sauce
1 tablespoon mirin
1 tablespoon of olive oil
zest of 1 lime

For the guacamole:
2 creamy avocados (Hass)
1 tablespoon coriander
1 teaspoon lime juice
1 teaspoon lime zest

For the lemon condiment:
145 g lemon juice
60 g cane sugar
10 g white soya
36 g olive oil
fleur de sel

For the conserved paprika:
1 paprika
olive oil
pepper and salt

For the marinated shiimeji:
120 g shimeji's (white beech mushrooms)
2 tablespoons sushi vinegar

For the paprika sorbet:
450 g paprika coulis
92 g conserved tomatoes
38 g lime juice
2 tarragon leaves
13 g tarragon vinegar
4 basil leaves
37 g olive oil (Arbequina)
75 g water
150 g white wine
20 g soya sauce
230 g peeled tomatoes
8 g red pepper
black pepper from the mill (20 twists)
11 g sherry (Capirete)
107 g palatinose
5 g stabiliser
8 drops Tabasco

For the squid dressing:
2 tablespoons olive oil
1 tablespoon ponzu
2 tablespoons basil oil
2 tablespoons pine kernels, finely
chopped and roasted
conserved paprika, finely chopped
basil, finely chopped

For the ink tuile (cookie):
300 g panko
35 g sushi vinegar
4 bags of squid ink

50 g soya sauce
550 ml water
26 g pine kernels
12 g lemon zest
70 g miso
9 g bonito flakes
30 g black olives
16 g trisol
60 g malto

For the sweet-and-sour shallot:
1 portion of sweet-sour (see basic recipe
below)
1 shallot

For the sweet-sour:
25 g crystal sugar
35 g tarragon vinegar
250 ml water
1 g coriander seed
1 g white pepper
0.5 g thyme
1.5 g tarragon

For the mustard seed:
55 g mustard seed
15 g sushi vinegar
15 g mirin

For the decoration:
pickles (Tierenteyn)
violets
atsina cress (liquorice)
mojama (dried and salted tuna), finely
grated
salmon eggs

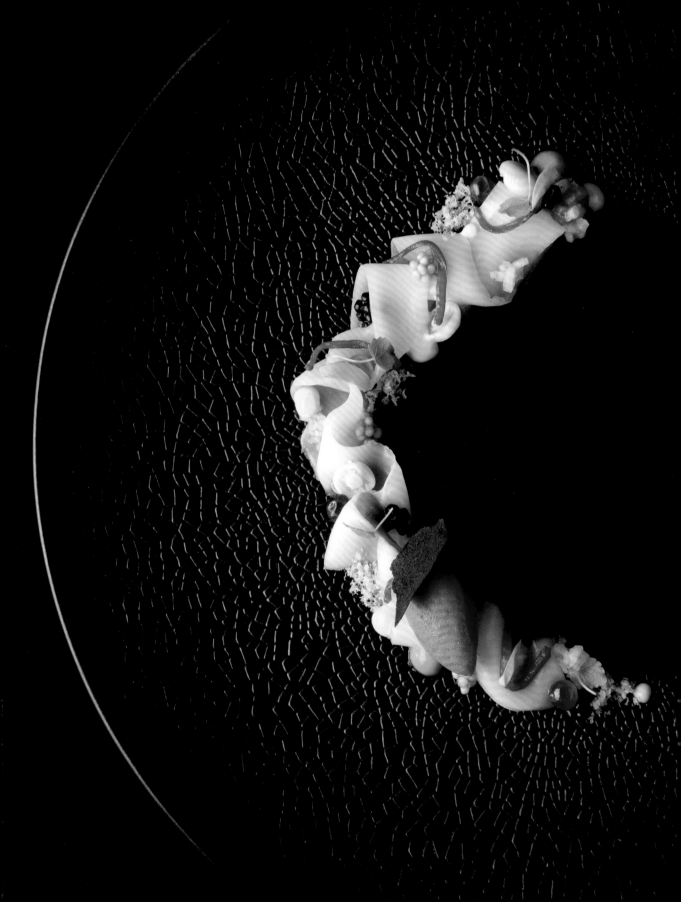

> For the squid, use a well-cleaned cuttlefish (see step by step). Put the cuttlefish in a vacuum bag with some olive oil and cook for 30 minutes. Allow to cool. Cut very fine, long strips and sprinkle them with olive oil, pepper and salt. Fry these strips in a dry, non-stick pan for just a few moments. Remove and store in the fridge.
> Mix together the mayonnaise and the pickles, then add the whipped cream. Season with pepper and salt.
> Boil the tapioca three times, each time in fresh water. Rinse well. Marinate with the squid ink, soya sauce, mirin, olive oil and lime zest.
> Fine mix all the ingredients for the guacamole in a mixer and pass through a sieve.
> Heat the lemon juice and the cane sugar until they form a syrupy mass. Add the white soya and the olive oil. Flavour with fleur de sel.
> Pre-heat the oven to 190 °C. Place the paprika in an oven dish with some olive oil. Allow the paprika to roast for 20 minutes, until it turns black. When cool, peel the paprika and pass the cooking juices through a sieve. Mix these juices with a few tablespoons of good quality olive oil. Cut fine slices of paprika and place them in this mixture in a pan. Season with pepper and salt and heat to boiling point. Remove and cool immediately.
> Cut the caps off the shimeji mushrooms. Heat up the vinegar and pour it over the mushrooms when hot. Allow to marinate for at least 10 minutes.
> Stir together all the ingredients for the paprika sorbet. Mix finely in the thermomix. Allow the mixture to rest briefly. Pass it through a sieve and use it to make the sorbet in the ice-cream machine.
> Mix together the olive oil, ponzu, basil oil, the pine kernels, the conserved paprika and the basil.
> Mix the panko with all the liquids and allow to soak for an hour, until everything is black. Put this mixture in the thermomix with all the other ingredients, except the malto. Mix to a super-fine consistency and pass through a fine sieve. Finally, stir in the malto. Spread the resulting dough thinly on a silicone baking pad and dry in the drying drum at 60 °C until crisp.
> For the sweet-and-sour shallot, first cut the shallot into the desired shape. Add the (cold) sweet-sour sauce and vacuum pack three times, in order to 'cook' the shallot.
> Boil all the ingredients for the sweet-sour sauce and pass them through a sieve.
> Boil the mustard seeds for 45 minutes in the poultry stock. Allow to cool and then marinate the seeds in mirin and sushi vinegar.
> Place the cold squid (cuttlefish) on the plate and dress with the following ingredients: small, finely chopped pickles, the mayo-pickles cream, black pearls of tapioca, guacamole, the lemon condiment, strips of paprika, violets, atsina cress (liquorice), mustard seeds, finely grated mojama, salmon eggs, the paprika sorbet, a piece of ink tuile and the marinated shimeji's. Serve the dressing separately.

The preparation in 1, 2, 3

› Cut off the tentacles and cut lengthwise along the back.
› Remove the hard, chalky matter.
› Remove the mantle.
› Remove the membranes (as far as possible).
› Wash the mantle, pat dry and cut.
› Put in a vacuum-sealed bag with olive oil.
› Cook for 30 minutes at 50 °C.
› Remove the mantle and cut into thin strips.
› Season with pepper and salt, and sprinkle with olive oil.
› Dry fry in a non-stick pan and dress on the plate.

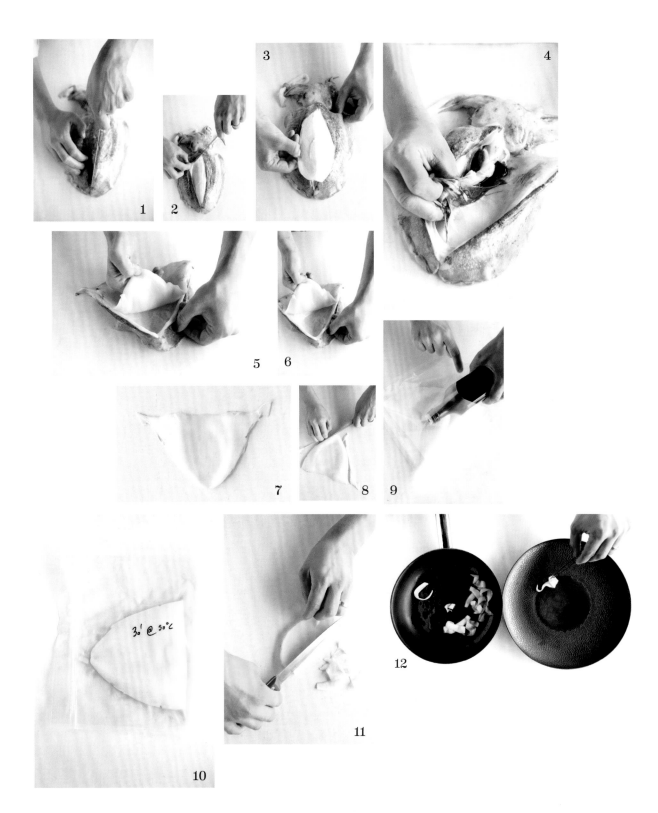

'Les Dombes' frog legs with parsley, parmesan and pesto

For the coated frog legs:
12 frog legs
white flour
egg white
panko
salt

For the watercress and parsley flan:
1 bundle of watercress
1/2 bundle of parsley
salt
180 ml poultry stock
pepper
1.3 g iota

For the parsley pesto:
100 g pine kernels
1 dl olive oil
70 g curly parsley
2 cloves garlic

For the parsley coulis:
200 g m'hamsa
300 ml poultry stock
parsley pesto (see basic recipe above)
2 tablespoons parmesan
pepper and salt

For the parmesan espuma:
1 l full cream milk

600 g cream (40 %)
240 g parmesan
30 g pro espuma caliente
30 g parmesá en pols

For the Bellota crumble:
7 slices of Bellota ham
olive oil
100 g panko
pepper and salt

For the decoration:
some parmesan flakes
some rucola leaves

› Cut the frog legs in two. Cut off the end of the foot and remove the small muscles. Pull the meat of the leg over the bone which has just been made free and cut off the other top piece of bone. Pull the meat back into its original position. Dip the meat (but not the bone) in the sieved flour, then in the beaten egg white and finally in the panko. Deep-fry at 180 °C until golden brown.
› For the flan, blanch the watercress and the parsley in salted water. Cool in ice-water. Puree the herbs in the poultry stock and a little of the cooling water. Season with salt and pepper and pass through a fine sieve. Boil 300 millilitres of this substance with 1.3 grams of iota. Pour into a deep plate and allow to cool.
› Put all the ingredients for the pesto into the bowl of a kitchen robot, mix to a fine puree and flavour with pepper and salt.
› Cook the m'hamsa (hand-rolled couscous) in the poultry stock until it is al dente. Mix together with the parsley pesto and flavour with pepper, salt and parmesan.
› Warm all the ingredients for the espuma and mix them to a smooth consistency in the thermomix. Pour into a siphon and pressurise with a gas tablet. Serve warm.
› For the Bellota crumble, cut the fat off the ham and allow the slices to dry for 2 hours on baking paper in an oven at 110 °C. Put some olive oil (or the fat from the ham) into a pan and gently fry the panko. Season with pepper and salt, and chop more finely. Mix the panko with the dried ham.
› Place a large kitchen ring on top of the watercress flan and fill it with warm couscous, the coated frog legs, some flakes of Bellota ham, the Bellota crumble, some dots of parmesan espuma, some flakes of parmesan cheese and a some rucola leaves.

Oosterschelde lobster with hemp seed, cucumber and avocado

For the court-bouillon:
1 onion
1 carrot
2 sticks blanching celery
1 teaspoon black pepper
150 ml white wine
2 sprigs thyme
2 laurel leaves
pepper and salt

For the lobster salad:
2 Oosterschelde lobsters (each weighing 500 to 600 grams)
2 tablespoons mayonnaise
some coriander leaves, finely chopped
1 tablespoon raw shallot, finely chopped

For the Granny Smith jelly:
250 ml apple juice (Granny Smith)
1 g xantana

For the hemp seed mixture:
2 tablespoons hemp seed, roasted
1 tablespoon sesame seeds, roasted
3 tablespoons fresh coconut
2 tablespoons Granny Smith jelly (see basic recipe above)
some drops of sesame oil (for taste and aroma)
2 tablespoons of hemp seed oil
pepper and salt

For the sweet-and-sour cucumber:
2 tablespoons crystal sugar
1 tablespoon water
3 tablespoons alcohol vinegar
1 tablespoon coriander balls, crushed
1 cucumber

For the avocado cream:
2 creamy avocados (Hass)
1 tablespoon coriander
1 teaspoon lime juice
1 teaspoon lime zest

For the basic coconut sauce (cold):
6 coconuts
6 dl poultry stock
20 coriander leaves
20 mint leaves

For the vinaigrette salée (salty):
50 g mustard
1 egg yolk
600 g grape seed oil
30 g salt
6 g pepper
80 ml water
1 dl chardonnay vinegar

For the finishing of the coconut sauce:
1 l coconut sauce (see basic recipe above)
2 g sesame oil
300 g coconut oil
96 g grape seed oil
71 g olive oil
200 g vinaigrette salée (see basic recipe above)
juice of 1 lemon
185 g apple juice (Granny Smith)
25 g white condiment

For the nut mix:
50 g cashew nuts
20 g hazelnuts
1 tablespoon pumpkin seed oil
1 tablespoon hazelnut oil
1 teaspoon lemon juice

20 g fresh coconut rasp
5 cl reduced shrimp stock

For the hijiki marinade:
1 tablespoon hijiki
50 g mirin
50 g soya sauce
1 teaspoon lime zest

For the mayo-curry:
50 g mayonnaise
2 g curry
3 g honey
1 g soya sauce
1 g kirsch

For the avocado ice-cream:
500 g avocado
140 g olive oil
1380 g poultry stock
190 g palatinose
92 g egg white
1 pinch of guar gum
5 coriander leaves
25 g lime juice
3 teaspoons vanilla oil
175 g apple juice (Granny Smith)
6 g ginger
90 g yuzu sap
4 g stabiliser
75 g white soya
48 g mirin
45 g sushi vinegar

For the decoration:
100 g raw round steak, finely sliced
olive oil
pepper and salt
violets

› Mix together all the ingredients for the court-bouillon, bring them to the boil and allow to simmer for 20 minutes. Flavour with pepper and salt.
› Cook the lobster claws and tails for 3 minutes in the court-bouillon. Remove the tails and cook the claws for a further 3 minutes. Cool in ice-water. Cut the lobster meat finely for the salad and mix with the mayonnaise, coriander and shallot.
› For the Granny Smith jelly, mix the apple juice with the xantana.
› Roast the hemp seeds and let them cool. Mix them with the sesame seeds and fresh coconut rasp, and flavour with the Granny Smith jelly, sesame oil and hemp seed oil. Season with pepper and salt
› Dissolve the sugar in the water and vinegar. Add the coriander balls and heat on the stove. Remove, allow to cool and pass the mixture through a sieve. Cut the cucumber into sticks and fine slices. Put them in the cold sweet-sour mixture in a receptacle and place in the vacuum machine. Apply the vacuum three times.
› Mix all the ingredients for the avocado cream to a fine consistency and pass through a sieve.
› Remove the coconut flesh from the nuts and cut into blocks. Put the blocks and the juice in a pan, together with the poultry stock, coriander and mint. Bring to the boil and then allow to stand overnight in the fridge.
› Put all the ingredients for the vinaigrette salée into a mixer and mix to a fine consistency.
› Take 1 litre of the cold basic coconut sauce. Add the sesame oil, coconut milk, grape seed oil, olive oil, vinaigrette salée, apple juice, lemon juice and the white condiment. Stir well and cool. Serve ice cold.
› Roast all the nuts and chop them finely. Flavour them with the pumpkin seed oil, hazelnut oil, lemon juice, coconut rasp and the shrimp stock.
› Soak the hijiki for 20 minutes in cold water. Press them through a sieve and marinate them in the mirin, soya sauce and lemon zest.
› Mix together all the ingredients for the mayo-curry.
› Put all the ingredients for the avocado ice-cream into the thermomix. Mix to a smooth consistency and pass through a sieve. Use the mixture to make ice-cream in the ice-cream machine.
› Roll up some of the lobster salad in slices of the steak. Sprinkle with olive oil and season with pepper and salt. Dress the cucumber sticks with the nut mixture and roll up the fine slices of cucumber into neat spirals. Arrange the rest of the plate as follows: put two mounds of hemp seeds centrally; alongside and between these mounds, place the lobster-beef rolls, two small mounds of the lobster salad, the cucumber rolls, the cucumber sticks, the avocado cream, the mayo-curry, the hijiki, some violets and – just before serving – two small spoonfuls of avocado ice-cream with a sprinkling of freshly grated coconut rasp. Finish with the Granny Smith jelly, to add a hint of sourness.

Pig's cheek with langoustine, peas, cauliflower and Belotta ham

For 4 people

For the pig's cheek:
700 g pig's cheek
80 g onion
1 sprig thyme
1 clove garlic
15 g mustard
150 g Westmalle 'dubbel' (brown abbey beer)
350 g brown stock

For the pig's ear wedges:
300 g cooking juices from the cheeks
200 g brown stock
3.5 g agaragar
2 slices gelatine
300 g pig's cheek, in a brunoise

For the 'puffed' pig's skin:
a large piece of pig skin, preferably from the belly

For the langoustines:
4 langoustines, 'size 7 to 9'
olive oil
pepper and salt

For the pea cream:
250 g deep-frozen peas
salt
100 ml poultry stock
5 leaves mint
25 ml cream (40 %)
pepper

For the cauliflower cream:
1 cauliflower
80 g butter
pepper and salt
200 g vegetable stock
120 g cream (40 %)
nutmeg

For the crispy potatoes:
400 g potatoes (Bintjes)
30 g unsalted butter
salt
1 teaspoon curry

For the decoration:
affilla cress (shoots of sweet peas)
blocks of goose liver terrine (5 blocks per person)
blocks Iberico ham (8 blocks per person)

› Clean the cheeks and cut them into equal portions. Colour them in a pot and add the onion. Allow to simmer until cooked through, then add the aromatics. Dilute with the beer and stock. Cook further in the oven for 1 hour at 180 °C. Allow the meat to rest for at least 2 hours in the juice, so that it can absorb the liquid. Pass the juice through a sieve and degrease it. Return it to the heat and reduce by a half. Add some olive oil (extra virgin) and stir well.
› For the pig's ear wedges, boil some of the cooking juices with the brown stock and the agaragar. Remove from the heat and dissolve the previously soaked gelatine in the liquid. Pour over the pig's ear brunoise in a flat tray. Allow to stiffen. Cut out the desired shapes and warm them in an oven at 120 °C for 15 minutes.
› Cook the pig's skin until it is completely cooked through. Dry for a few hours in the dryer. Cut into pieces and fry in the deep fryer, so that the skin 'explodes' and puffs out. Pat dry and chop into a fine crumble.
› Take the langoustines out of their shells and carefully remove the intestinal tract with a sharp knife or pair of tweezers. Heat a little olive oil in a non-stick pan and fry the langoustines on both sides for 1 minute. Remove the pan from the heat and allow to rest for 2 minutes. Season with pepper and salt. The langoustines must have a nice, glazed look.
› Blanch the peas in salt water until they are completely cooked through. Allow to cool and then puree the peas with the stock and the mint to form a smooth mixture. Pass through a sieve and heat up with the cream. Season with salt and pepper.

› Cut the rosettes loose from the cauliflower and chop them finely. Cook them in some brown butter and season with pepper and salt. Simmer the remaining pieces of the cauliflower in the stock with the cream, pepper, salt and nutmeg. When ready, pass through a sieve but keep the cooking juices separately. Puree the cauliflower in a kitchen robot, adding a little juice, if necessary. Season with pepper and salt.

› Boil the potatoes thoroughly and pour away the water. Mash them with some butter, until they form a coulis. Flavour with salt and curry. Spread the mixture on a tray to a depth of 3 centimetres. Steam for 8 minutes at 100 °C and then bake for 10 minutes at 160 °C. Dry for 15 minutes at 120 °C.

› Place a warm wedge of pig's cheek on the plate and sprinkle with the pig skin crumble. Add the following other ingredients at random: the langoustine, the cauliflower rosettes, the blocks of goose liver terrine and Iberico ham, and the crispy potato. Intersperse with dots of pea cream, cauliflower cream, cauliflower tartar, and the pig's cheek sauce. Garnish with affilla cress.

Ox cheek with open ravioli, Paris mushrooms, rucola, langoustine and tarragon

For 4 people

1.2 kg ox cheek
butter
2 onions
1 sprig thyme
2 cloves garlic
2 tablespoons mustard
250 ml Westmalle 'dubbel' (brown abbey beer)
800 ml brown stock
pepper and salt

For the rucola-mushroom mixture:
450 g Paris mushrooms
butter
2 tablespoons sour cream
150 g rucola, finely chopped
pepper and salt
1 teaspoon candied lemon
1 teaspoon conserved tomato

For the langoustines:
4 langoustines (size 7 to 9)
1 tablespoon olive oil
pepper and salt

For the Béarnaise sauce:
3 egg yolks
2 egg cups tarragon vinegar
3 egg cups water
pepper, freshly ground
salt
90 g unsalted butter, at room temperature
2 tablespoons tarragon, finely chopped

For the decoration:
4 cooked wonton skins
8 spring onions, cooked in salted water with butter
some rucola leaves
some parmesan flakes
pink pepper, bruised

› Clean the ox cheeks. Colour them in a heat-resistant, cast iron pot (Staub-type). Remove the cheeks and set them to one side. Melt a knob of butter in the pot and add the onion. Cook until soft, and then add the meat and the aromatics. Pour in the beer and the stock. Bring to the boil and skim. Put the pot in the oven and cook for 2 hours and 30 minutes at 180 °C. Allow the meat to rest for at least 2 hours in the juice, so that it can absorb the liquid. Pass the juice through a sieve and degrease it. Return it to the heat and reduce by a half. Slice the ox cheek into thick wedges and cut it into roundels, using a kitchen ring of the required size. Fry the roundels in brown butter. Season with pepper and salt.
› Cut the mushroom into fine slices and fry in a knob of butter. When cooked, add the sour cream and stir. Then add the rucola, salt, pepper, candied lemon and conserved tomato.
› Take the langoustines out of their shells and carefully remove the intestinal tract with a sharp knife or pair of tweezers. Heat a little olive oil in a non-stick pan and fry the langoustines on both sides for 1 minute. Remove the pan from the heat and allow to rest for 2 minutes. Season with pepper and salt. The langoustines must have a nice, glazed look.
› Mix together the egg yolks, tarragon vinegar, water, pepper and salt. Place on a medium heat and beat for 5 minutes until a light and frothy mixture results. Remove from the heat when the mixture begins to bind and add the knobs of butter. Stir well. Finish by adding the tarragon.
› Put a roundel of ox cheek at the bottom of a serving ring, then a layer of the mushroom and rucola mixture, and then a second ox cheek roundel on top. Coat with the Béarnaise sauce. Put the serving ring onto a deep plate and then remove the ring. Cover the ox cheek 'tower' with a cooked wonton skin. Add to this structure a fried langoustine and two spring onions (cooked in salt water with butter), and decorate with some extra rucola, the parmesan cheese and the pink pepper. Serve the sauce for the cheeks separately.

Arnold Hanbuckers & Karen Keygnaert

∫ A'qi ∿

At the age of sixty-five, Arnold Hanbuckers started a new restaurant, together with Karen Keygnaet, who has been his right-hand man - or rather woman! - for more than 20 years. Arnold is now entrusting the restaurant entirely to Karen, assisted by a team of young associates. During his long career, Hanbuckers gained a reputation as an intelligent, ultra-critical and highly individualist chef who constantly searched for the essence of good cuisine. In every aspect.

A new restaurant

More than half a century of cooking in four different restaurants: that, in a nutshell, is the career of Arnold Hanbuckers. The first of the four was 'De Sultan' in Ieper, where he cooked for eleven years. Next came 'Ter Heyde' in Bruges, where he clocked up another eleven years. He then moved to 'De Herborist', which he ran for sixteen years. And since 2009 there has been 'A'qi'. His reputation was really built in 'De Herborist', where he cooked with well-known and not so well-known vegetables, seasoned with rare herbs and flowers. He left the restaurant after a family disagreement and it is now in the hands of his son, Alex. A number of his kitchen staff left with him, including his faithful right-hand woman, Karen Keygnaert. "I felt that I just couldn't leave the men and women with whom I had worked for so long to their fate. They gave me the drive and inspiration to start up a new business. To begin a restaurant you need good health, money and expertise. I had all three – and so I decided to give it one last shot." Motivation of this kind can give a person immense drive, and this is something that Hanbuckers has never lacked. But life in the world of high-class professional cooking is hard and your health is something that you can never take for granted. At the end of 2013, Hanbuckers decided that the time had come to call it a day. And so he has passed on his restaurant to Karen Keygnaert. "I am going to run the business on exactly the same basis," she says. "With honest, no nonsense cooking, quality products and a style that will be familiar to our large group of regular customers. I will be doing this together with Tomas Puype, who has already been working with us for ten years."

Respect and authenticity

Karen Keygnaert and chef Hanbuckers have been hand in glove for more than 20 years. They often supplement each other's comments. Her love of cooking persuaded her to give up her original plans to become an architect. She started in 'De Herborist' as a complete novice and since then has been cooking for twenty years at Hanbuckers' side. She is now his confidante, sounding board and helpmate. "She supplies the details, the artistic touch," says Arnold. "The finishing, garnishing and presentation," adds Karen. A desire to constantly innovate is built into the genes of both of them. Karen: "We are always on the look-out for new products that are unfamiliar to us, but we are also keen to try out new and original methods with existing products, such as kale. But it is important that the kale should still taste of kale. Respect the product and do it full justice. Try and accentuate its flavours by adding another ingredient. Try to enhance rather than diminish."

This is clearly a touchy point for both of them: the authenticity of a cuisine and (in their opinion) the impoverishment of Belgian cuisine in recent years. Arnold: 'I eat out five times a week and what I get on my plate – even in Michelin star restaurants – sometimes borders on the unbelievable. I will name just a few of the most common mistakes: the violation of products and preparations through a lack of basic knowledge; the presentation of dishes with just a few lines of foam, a couple of pieces of greenery and a microscopically small main ingredient; the use of self-picked wild herbs without the necessary botanical knowledge; and the serving of raw ingredients which can sometimes be poisonous without cooking." Karen: "You can add to this an almost sheep-like desire to copy. Chefs see something when they are abroad and then copy it blindly. There is certainly nothing wrong with using new influences, but we should try to do our own thing with them. Your cuisine must remain authentic. Many young chefs do not yet have sufficient mastery of the essentials to make something exciting and creative with these new ideas. It is a bit like contemporary Spanish cuisine. In the 1970s Spanish cooking was nowhere. Just twenty years later, it is now regarded by many as the best in the world. From zero to hero. But its growth has been like a tree which grows too fast: it has plenty of attractive branches and leaves above ground level, but too few firm roots in the soil. When the storm winds blow, it will crash to the ground. In contrast, French cooking has strong roots, because it is based on solid gastronomic foundations as a result of the consistent use of good products and good practices to a consistently high standard. And don't be fooled: French cuisine is still evolving and improving steadily. In the long run, it will outlast its Spanish rival."

The cuisine at 'A'qi' is a complex one, which uses a mixture of good Belgian and foreign ingredients. However, the three signature dishes are all based on Belgian products: North Sea shrimps, veal and (with a slight

> *Try and accentuate flavours by adding another ingredient.*

A: Arnold Hanbuckers; K: Karen Keygnaert

➜ **Who or what influenced your choice of profession?**
A: I come from a family of hoteliers and restaurateurs.
K: It is a creative profession which requires intense commitment every day.

➜ **What was your first culinary experience or memory?**
A: The first time I ate at 'Rostang' in Antibes. At that time, it was a top restaurant under Jacques Maximin, with a completely new vision of cooking.
K: During my training period with Arnold he invited me to dine at 'Oud Sluis'. It was the first time that I had ever eaten food of that standard, and it was an unforgettable experience.

➜ **What can really make you mad in the kitchen?**
A: Suppliers who do not deliver products that meet my standards of quality.
K: If everyone in the kitchen needs me all at the same time, so that I cannot concentrate on my cooking.

➜ **What is your most important personal quality?**
A: Determination.
K: A practical and problem-solving approach.

➜ **What would you like to have more time for?**
A: My private life.
K: For family, friends and other interests.

➜ **For you, what is the epitome of luxury?**
A & K (in unison): More time!

➜ **What is your favourite vegetable?**
A: Every vegetable.
K: Artichoke is my absolute favourite; it's just a pity that it takes so much preparation.

➜ **What are you favourite aromas and smells in the kitchen?**
A: Fresh coriander.
K: The smell of meat turning lightly crisp as it fries in butter.

➜ **What is your favourite dish?**
A & K: Everything that is good and made with feeling.

➜ **Which small object could you not do without in the kitchen?**
A & K: A dish cloth.

➜ **Which chef has inspired you the most?**
A: Jacques Maximin.
K: Arnold Hanbuckers.

➜ **What type of cuisine do you not like?**
A: Italian; I don't like pasta.
K: Heavy farmhouse-style cooking.

➜ **What was the last celebrated restaurant that you visited and what was your opinion?**
A: 'Bristol' in Paris: top!
K: 'L'Arpège' in Paris: it's amazing what that man can do with vegetables.

➜ **Who is your perfect table companion?**
A: My wife.
K: My friend and other friends who enjoy good food. People who do not enjoy food are generally not good company.

➜ **What is your favourite aperitif?**
A: A good dry sherry, but on a warm day I prefer a nice, cool Hoegaarden (a white beer).
K: For a gastronomic meal, I usually take a glass of champagne to keep my palate fresh, but on a pleasant terrace on a sunny day a Campari and orange will do very nicely.

leap across the border into The Netherlands) lobster from the Oosterschelde (the Scheldt estuary). Arnold: "We would be limiting ourselves unnecessarily if we only worked with Belgian products. They only get a place on our menu card if the quality is good enough. Most of our other ingredients come from abroad. In recent years, we have come increasingly into contact with quality products from Japan, which has given our recipes a slightly more oriental flavour."

A real kitchen is the best place to learn

Arnold Hanbuckers is known for preferring to work with people who have not followed training at a hotel school. People like Karen Keygnaert. "This is because their vision of cooking has not been contaminated by preconceived ideas, so that they can approach problems in an original manner," writes Arnold in his book *Auberge Herborist*, that was published in 2002. And his own personal vision is still uncontaminated. "In the hotel schools, they should try to see every class as a kitchen. For the first year, the students should do nothing but clean and prepare the products; in the second year, they should be allowed to progress to the mise-en-place; only in the third year should they start to cook. In subsequent years, their knowledge of cooking techniques can be broadened and refined, until at the end of the sixth year they are finally ready to work in a restaurant. This is how we work in practice. Graduates from the hotel school often know nothing; you need to re-teach them everything. They are not properly prepared for the realities of a hard working life in the restaurant business. Many of them quit when they realise that they have to work evenings and during the weekend. In much the same way, the so-called reality programmes on television give a distorted view of our sector. To become a good cook takes years of graft and experience; it doesn't happen in just a couple of months in front of the cameras. High salary costs and social insurance contributions are also having a damaging effect on Belgian cuisine. In relative terms, large companies pay a fraction of the taxes demanded from small, local entrepreneurs, such as restaurant holders. But we have been targeted as the new victims to be sucked dry by the state. It is gradually becoming more and more difficult, if not impossible, to keep on running an effective business."

A'qi
Gistelse steenweg 686, 8200 Sint-Andries
050/30 05 99
www.restaurantaqi.be

North Sea shrimps with a rock shrimp mousse and tomato jam

For the rock shrimp mousse:
200 g rock shrimps
100 g mascarpone
pepper and salt

For the tomato jelly:
4 large, fresh tomatoes
1 finely chopped clove of garlic
1 finely chopped onion
olive oil
pimento d'Espelette
vegetable gelatine

For the dried tomato water:
10 large, fresh tomatoes
vegetable gelatine

For the wasabi cream:
wasabi powder (according to taste)
10 cl water
10 cl cream
1/2 teaspoon xantana

For the black sesame biscuits:
50 g butter
2 tablespoons of flour
1 tablespoon of egg white
1 tablespoon of sugar
4 tablespoons of black sesame seeds

2 large cauliflowers
150 g hand-peeled North Sea shrimps
some stalks of chives

› Blend the rock shrimps and the mascarpone and season with salt and pepper.
› Peel the tomatoes and cut the flesh into chunks. Lightly cook the garlic and the onion in little oil, add the tomatoes and allow the mixture to simmer on a low heat, until it reduces to a thick tomato sauce. Season with the pimento d'Espelette and bind with the vegetable gelatine (36 g per litre). Empty the jelly onto a platter.
› Cut the tomatoes for the tomato water into rough blocks and let them harden in the freezer. When hard, take them out again and allow them to thaw. Carefully collect the juice which escapes, but without pressing the tomatoes. Bind the juice with the vegetable gelatine (36 g per litre) and pour into a container. Allow to stiffen. Cut the hardened block into fine slices and place them to dry on plastic film.
› Mix all the ingredients for the wasabi cream to the required consistency with hand-held mixer.
› Make a dough with the butter, flower, egg white and sugar. Mix the dough with the sesame seeds; two-thirds seeds to one-third dough. Place little mounds of dough on a silicone baking mat. Roll out with plastic film. Bake in an oven at 180 °C until the biscuits are crisp.
› Chop the heart of a large cauliflower into a julienne and blanch it in boiling water until it is al dente.
› Cut a series of circles out of the tomato jelly. Place a kitchen ring of the same diameter on top of them and spoon in the shrimp mousse. Press firmly into place. Carefully remove the kitchen ring. Sprinkle several peeled shrimps on top of the mousse and arrange. Dress with the slice of dried tomato water and the chives. Add the cauliflower julienne, the biscuits and the wasabi cream. Spoon some of the remaining tomato jelly onto the plate.

Decoration in **1, 2, 3**

1. Spoon the shrimp mousse into the kitchen ring.
2. Blanch the cauliflower julienne.
3. Mix the black sesame seeds and the dough in a ratio of two-thirds seeds to one-third dough.
4. Roll fine slices of tomato jelly around a few stalks of chives.
5. Pipe the wasabi cream onto the plate.
6. Cut thin segments of a peeled tomato and dip them in olive oil.
7. Place them on top of the shrimps.

Oosterschelde lobster with herring eggs and cucumber

2 Oosterschelde lobsters (each weighing 1 kg)

For the tomato jam:
5 large, fresh tomatoes
250 g cherry tomatoes
olive oil
salt
crystal sugar
butter
1 finely chopped onion
juice of 1 lemon

For the pink grapefruit jelly:
4 pink grapefruits
vegetable gelatine

For the green ginger sauce:
250 g pickled ginger flakes
1 teaspoon of dried matcha powder
1/3 teaspoon xantana

2 hard-boiled eggs
50 g wasabi seeds
4 full teaspoons of herring eggs
100 dried ling roes, cut into curls
12 squares of crisply baked filo pastry
12 slices of cucumber
12 red spinach leaves

› Cook the lobster, remove the shell and cut the meat of the tail into thick slices.
› Peel the large tomatoes and cut them into chunks. Mix with the cherry tomatoes (halved but not peeled). Sprinkle with the olive oil, salt and sugar. Place for 15 minutes in an oven at 180 °C. Allow the mixture to drain and then stew it in a large pot with a little butter, the onion and the lemon juice.
› Press the grapefruits and bind the juice with the vegetable gelatine (36 g per litre). Pour onto a tray to a thickness of 0.5 cm. Allow to set and then cut into rectangular slices.
› Mix the pickled ginger and its juices with a spoonful of dried matcha powder. Bind with the xantana.
› Chop the white of the hard-boiled eggs into a brunoise. Mash the yolks with some olive oil and use a pair of spoons to form quenelles. Roll them in the wasabi seeds.
› Dress the plate with a rectangle of tomato jam and place a layer of grapefruit jelly on top of it. Add layers of lobster slices and herring eggs. Place curled pieces of ling roe on the layer of herring eggs. Place a pastry square on the layer of lobster and cover with the brunoise of egg white and the egg yolk quenelles with wasabi seeds.
› Decorate with slices of rolled cucumber, filled with the green ginger sauce, and garnish with a leaf of red spinach.

Veal tartar with lamb sweetbreads, red beetroot and onion rings

For the veal tartar:
400 g veal
50 g parmesan
olive oil
salt
pimento d'Espelette

For the vegetable brunoise:
1 carrot
1 courgette (just the exterior, with skin)
1 mango
100 g red quinoa

For the red beetroot jelly:
4 red beetroots
vegetable gelatine
4 passion fruits

For the curcuma sauce:
1 fresh curcuma root
10 cl chicken stock
1 pinch of xantana

1 onion, cut into rings
airbag (finely ground pig skin from
Sosa; breadcrumbs are an alternative)
250 g fried lamb sweetbreads
white pimpernel leaves
balsamic vinegar syrup

› Place the veal in the freezer until it is nicely stiffened, then cut the meat into a fine brunoise. Mix the brunoise with the parmesan and the olive oil. Season with salt and pimento d'Espelette.
› Chop the vegetables and fruit into a brunoise and mix with the quinoa.
› Peel the red beetroot, cut them into chunks and remove the juice in a juice centrifuge (if you do not have a centrifuge, use 25 cl of ready-made biological beet juice). Bind with the vegetable gelatine (36 g per litre; i.e. in this case 9 g). Pour the beet juice onto a tray and let it harden. When stiff, cut and roll fine slices.
› Cut the passion fruits in half and press out the juice from the flesh. Bind the juice with the vegetable gelatine (36 g per litre) and let it stiffen. Cut out a number of balls with a small parisienne scoop.
› Mix the curcuma root with the chicken stock. Pass through a sieve and bind with the xantana.
› Coat the finely cut onion rings with airbag (finely ground pig skin) and deep fry them until they are crispy.
› Fill small rectangular dressing tins with the veal tartar and the vegetable brunoise. Place the lamb sweetbreads and the onion rings on top. Add the red beetroot rolls, topped with balls of passion fruit jelly and the curcuma sauce. Garnish with the white pimpernel leaves and a few sprinkled drops of syrup of balsamic vinegar.

Christophe Hardiquest

ℐ *Bon Bon* ℘

Christophe Hardiquest lives with the seasons and has a passion for authentic products. His knowledge of ingredients is phenomenal and his sense of taste is legendary. It was not without good reason that he was crowned as 'Chef of the Year' by GaultMillau.

Inspired by the past but focused on the present

After his initial training at the hotel school in Namur, Christophe Hardiquest worked in Brussels restaurants and hotels such as 'L'Amandier', 'Sea Grill', 'Villa Lorraine', the Conrad Hotel and 'Voyage à travers les sens'. He made further detours to Roland Debuyst's 'L'Orangeraie' and 'La Crémaillère' in New York. In the spring of 2011 he exchanged his cosy but small bistro-restaurant in Ukkel for a more specious and luxurious location in Sint-Pieters-Woluwe.

Four chefs have played an important role in the professional life of Christophe Hardiquest. "Olivier Roellinger truly amazed me with his knowledge of herbs, and Alain Passard with the precision and simplicity of his dishes. Then there are the two chefs who truly moulded my approach to cooking: Yves Mattagne, a master with fish and shellfish, and Pascal Simon, the former chef at the Conrad Hotel, whose understanding of products is unparalleled. I seek the inspiration for my recipes in travel, reading and the ingredients themselves. I also collect old cookbooks, the oldest dating from 1723. I select products that were used then and adjust their use to reflect modern expectations. I am not too proud to serve duck 'à l'orange' or blanquette of veal in a totally new manner, lighter and presented differently, while still preserving the original taste. By the same to-ken, the baking of goose liver in clay is a technique that has existed for more than three hundred years. I invent nothing new; I simply put existing techniques, however old, to my own uses. Modern tech-niques interest me as well, since I am curious by nature. But these new methods must be able to convince me of their worth within the framework of my overall cooking concept. As far as I am concerned, product, cooking time and taste are still the most important things."

Artisan chef

His move to a new location has done nothing to change the philosophy of Christophe Hardiquest. He is still the same 'artisan chef' who has mastered his craft to an exceptional degree. He only works with products of the very highest quality, such as milk calves from Corrèze, lamb from Sisteron, langoustines from Guilvinec, but also North Sea shrimps and sole, spring chickens from Aalst and Geuze beer from Brussels, as well as less fashionable ingredients such as oxtail, brawn and rare vegetable varieties that have long been forgotten by most other chefs. Ninety-five percent of his vegetables are biologically grown and most come from the six hectare market garden plot specially set up by his brother-in-law in Dour. "Although we use French products, wherever possible we want the Belgian 'terroir' to shine through in our recipes. For example, we make fantastic recipes with Belgian 'Kriek' and 'Geuze' beer, in combination with endives and local game. The casseroling process with the beer results in an endive that almost tastes like pear! We also make a beer caramel and a 'Geuze' sabayon. You will not find this anywhere else; you can only eat it here. As far as I am concerned, one of the main tasks of a Belgian chef is to promote the products of his own region and country. And we do not need to purchase these products from large multi-national suppliers who are only concerned with mass production and profit, but from small-scale producers who work with passion and are concerned, above all, with flavour. For the moment, there are too few Belgian 'terroir' products of the required quality. But by encouraging our domestic producers to focus

Although we use French products, wherever possible we want the Belgian 'terroir' to shine through in our recipes.

In a nutshell

→ **Who or what influenced your choice of profession?**
My grandmother.

→ **What was your first culinary experience or memory?**
Rhubarb pie and vanilla custard.

→ **What can really make you mad in the kitchen?**
When there is no respect.

→ **What is your most important personal quality?**
Generosity.

→ **What would you like to have more time for?**
To learn to play the guitar.

→ **What are you best at in the kitchen?**
Product knowledge.

→ **What do you most enjoy doing in the kitchen?**
Everything.

→ **What is your favourite vegetable?**
Jerusalem artichoke.

→ **What is your favourite type or cut of meat?**
Cheeks.

→ **What type(s) of fish do you like to work with?**
The smaller, fattier types, such as herring.

→ **What are your preferred herbs for fish and meat dishes?**
Garlic.

→ **What is your favourite dish?**
Meat balls in tomato sauce.

→ **Which small object could you not do without in the kitchen?**
Pincers to pick up my ingredients.

→ **What type of cuisine do you not like?**
Fusion cuisine.

→ **What was the last celebrated restaurant that you visited and what was your opinion?**
'Le Meurice' in Paris. Pure genius.

→ **What is your worst ever professional experience?**
Forgetting a table.

→ **Who is your perfect table companion?**
People who enjoy life.

→ **What is your favourite aperitif?**
Campari with tonic.

→ **What do you most enjoy eating on your day off?**
Pasta.

→ **What are your favourite book and your favourite cooking book?**
Het Parfum by Patrick Süskind.

on higher standards, we can turn the tide. We are only at the very beginning of this process, but it is the only way to build up a clear identity. I am very impressed by the philosophy of Kobe Desramaults of 'In De Wulf'. He loves his local 'terroir' and is opening the way for others. But it is important that we should not all try to do the same. I am afraid for the standardisation of our cuisine. What you eat at my restaurant should not be the same as what you can eat at Kobe's, or Yves Mattagne's or Gert De Mangeleer's. Every chef must have his own individual personality. Following the Spanish wave and the Scandinavian wave, are we to expect a Belgian wave in the near future? It

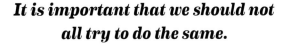

It is important that we should not all try to do the same.

is a possibility. We all have a basis in French cuisine, but cooking in France is currently at a low ebb. The present generation of French chefs seem unable to escape from their own arrogance. But there are a considerable number of up-and-coming young Belgian chefs who have plenty of talent and the right attitude to succeed. I am convinced that in the near future Belgian gastronomic cuisine will be able to establish its own strong identity. At the very least, it is something that we are all working towards – myself included."

Bon Bon
Avenue de Tervuren 453, 1150 Brussel
02/346 66 15
www.bon-bon.be

Tartar of langoustines with a jasmine jelly

For 4 people

For the jasmine jelly:
4 dl water
1 piece kombu (sea weed)
10 g dried bonito (Katsuo Bushi)
25 g jasmine tea
6 gelatine slices/litre
20 g sake
5 g soya sauce

4 langoustines
40 g Belgian caviar 'Oscietra'
olive oil
fleur de sel
fresh jasmine flowers

› Heat the water to 85 °C. Allow the kombu, bonito and jasmine tea to soak for 15 minutes, having first covered the pan with plastic foil. Pass the resulting liquid through a sieve. Reheat to 80 °C and dissolve the gelatine in the liquid. Freshen with the saki and flavour with the soya sauce.
› Pour this jelly mixture into the bottom of four plates and let it set in the fridge.
› Remove the shells from the langoustines and remove the innards. Cut the langoustines in two and then chop them into fine pieces, to form a tartar.
› Remove the plates from the fridge 10 minutes before serving. Place on each plate a quenelle of 10 grams of caviar.
› Season the langoustine tartar with olive oil and fleur de sel and place it around the caviar.
› Decorate with some jasmine flowers.

Sea bass on a bed of oysters

2 kg cockles
2 l white wine
3 bulbs garlic
thyme
3 ginger shoots
1 l cream 40 %
1 sea bass 2/3
16 oysters (Perle Blanche)
200 g coarse sea salt
2 egg whites
4 nori leaves (seaweed)

For the sauce:
butter
lemon juice

› Clean the cockles thoroughly and cook them in the white wine. Collect the cooking juices, having first tossed lightly several times, so that any sand remains at the bottom of the pan. Reduce the juices by three quarters, together with ten cloves of garlic, three finely chopped ginger shoots and the cream.
› Clean the sea bass and remove the skin. Keep this separately.
› Open the oysters and clean them in their own juice.
› Cut the cockles into tiny pieces. Put them in a pan with the coarse sea salt and the egg yolks.
› Chop the oysters into fine pieces and place them on top of the sea bass. Cover with the fish skin and the nori leaves and sprinkle with finely chopped oyster shell.
› Pre-heat the oven to 200 °C. Cook for 1 minute per 100 gram.
› Make the sauce using the cockle juice. Heat the juice lightly, thicken with butter and finish with lemon juice. Pass through a fine sieve and mix with some of the oysters.

Goose liver in clay

For 4 people

For the onion conserve:
240 g raw onion, finely chopped
1 dl olive oil
2 cloves garlic, finely chopped
salt
0.3 dl sherry vinegar

280 g goose liver
50 g juniper berries, dried and ground
2 kg red clay
pepper
fleur de sel
4 salted biscuits
4 salad bouquets (curly lettuce, shiso, herbs)

› Make an onion conserve with the onion, olive oil, garlic and salt. Allow to stew gently on a light heat for two hours, and finish by adding the sherry vinegar.
› Smoke the goose liver with the juniper berries. Allow to cool and keep in the fridge.
› Roll out the clay and divide into two equal slabs. Place a sheet of suphurised paper on one of the slabs. Season the goose liver with the fleur de sel and put it on the sulphurised paper. Cover with a second sheet of sulphurised paper to isolate the goose liver from the clay. Cover with the second slab of clay and press the sides together, so that the entire parcel of clay is hermetically sealed.
› Pre-heat the oven to 200 °C and bake the goose liver in the clay for 20 minutes. When ready, break the clay open, cut the goose liver in slices and season.
› Arrange the slices on a plate with the onion conserve, a salted biscuit and a bouquet of salad.

The preparation in 1, 2, 3

Roll out the clay.

Put the finely ground powder of juniper berries in the smoking pan.

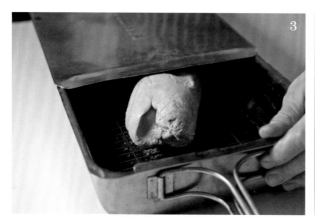

Place the goose liver in the smoking pan.

Warm smoke the goose liver.

Place a sheet of sulphurised paper on the clay.

Season the goose liver with pepper and salt.

Place a second sheet of suphurised paper on the goose liver and cover with the second block of clay.

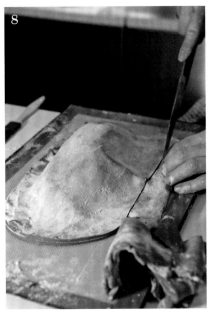

Cut off any overhanging edges.

Seal hermetically with the fingers.

Sergio Herman

∫ *The Jane* ∖

It was surprise when Sergio Herman announced that he was planning to close his three-star restaurant 'Oud Sluis' at the end of 2013. Or maybe it wasn't. After all, he had been saying for years that he planned to stop. "At Oud Sluis I had reached the limit of what I could achieve, both literally and figuratively. For years I have been trying to refine flavours down to their purest essence, to make my dishes as perfect as possible. I feel that I am now at the peak of my powers at 'Oud Sluis'," he commented in interview an. Yet while 'Oud Sluis' might be stopping, Sergio is not. In the coming years, he intends to focus on his other restaurants: 'Pure C' in Cadzand and 'The Jane' in Antwerp. It is here that he hopes to find that higher level that he is still searching for.

How did a rebellious lad from Zeeland become one of the most hyped chefs in The Netherlands and, perhaps even more so, in Flanders? It probably had something to do with his own early culinary upbringing. Sergio grew up in 'Oud Sluis', the fish restaurant run by his parents. "When I was in secondary school, sometimes, my parents came to collect me at 12 o'clock on Fridays and then we would drive off to a restaurant somewhere. We did all the top places in Bruges and Brussels; we went to Roger Souvereyns at 'het Scholteshof' in Stevoort or 'Interscaldis' in Kruiningen, when Maartje Boudeling was still working there. It was the same on holidays in the south of France; we ate at all the toppers: Roger Vergé, Alain Chapelle, 'La Bonne Auberge'

> **When I was in secondary school, we used to have Friday afternoons off. Sometimes, my parents came to collect me at 12 o'clock and then we would drive off to a restaurant somewhere.**

in Antibes. I liked good food and I liked the atmosphere in the restaurants. But following in my dad's footsteps? No, that idea never really appealed to me. At first, the real problem was that I couldn't really decide what I wanted to do. On top of that, I was a bit 'playful' - and that's putting it mildly! After my second year in the MAVO, my parents sent me to a technical school in Bruges. But that didn't work out, either. I finally ended up at hotel school 'Ter Groene Poorte' in Bruges. I wasn't really one of the better pupils, certainly not on the practical side. During the weekends I worked at home in my parents' restaurant, and as part of my studies I was taken on as a trainee at 'Kaatje bij de Sluis' in Blokzijl. From then on, things started to go better. I gradually gained more confidence, and by the end of the summer I was the best in the class at the practical lessons. After I graduated from the hotel school, I worked for nine months for Cas Spijkers, which at that time was definitely 'the-place-to-be' for young cooks like myself. But in 1990 I went back to work at my dad's place, because he was starting to have trouble with his shoulder. I really wanted to go abroad: perhaps a training job in a top restaurant or two, learning new languages, discovering other ways of cooking. I still regret that I never had the chance to do all that. But you know how it is: if you're needed at home... Between us, we gradually began to introduce a more innovative style of cooking. From being a classic mussel restaurant, we evolved into a speciality restaurant. In 1995 we were awarded our first Michelin star, in 1999 our second and in 2005 our third."

Slawinski, Gagnaire and Boxy

He is in no doubt about his greatest source of inspiration. "I owe an awful lot to my dad. He was always hard on me. But he taught me all about taste and also gave me his own determination to succeed. The strength that I now have, the will to keep on fighting and to keep on believing in myself: I got all that from him. The first chef who really blew me away was Willy Slawinski. I was just 18 when I visited his restaurant. He was a visionary, a true pioneer. His recipes were so refreshing and so innovative, flavoured with herbs and spices that I had never even heard of! He really took things to another dimension. Later, I was charmed by Pierre Gagnaire when he was still in St. Etienne, in a restaurant that was completely decorated in white, with jazz music in the background and beautifully presented dishes. Then there was Stefan Boxy, who ran a restaurant with his brother in Kortrijk. For me, that was the best restaurant in Belgium at that time: hugely underrated, but brilliantly revolutionary in its ideas, with plenty of biologically-grown fruit and vegetables. If I look back, I now realize that they were not only all great trend-setting cooks, but were also people who could talk knowledgeably and with passion about fashion, design and art. They certainly opened my eyes, and showed me that I still had a lot to learn, which would only be possible if I continued to question every aspect of what I was doing in the kitchen. It is thanks to them that I started colouring outside the lines. Or rather, colouring my own lines. Each of my dishes undergoes a long process of trial and error before it finally ends up on the customer's plate. Everything is thought through in details, from preparation to presentation. The flavours, the plates, how you dress them, what you put under them, what you serve with them: these are all parts of a complete whole, a total package. I know I make things difficult for myself, but I need that to survive. Otherwise, I wouldn't be able to stand here every day with the same 100% enthusiasm. But that is the reason why 'Oud Sluis' is something special. We are fully booked months in advance. I never dreamed that we would make it to where we are today. But enough is enough. I have been here for 25 years. Now I want to try something different. I want to keep on growing, not only as a chef, but also as a person. And I want to do it with the same loyal and faithful

staff, who mean so much to me. They have always been good to me, and now I want to do something in return. Over the years, I have had plenty of people in my kitchen who have risen far above average in the cooking world, people like Filip Claeys, Kobe Desramaults, Pieter Lonneville and Ken Verscheuren, to name but a few. I am really proud that they have each gone on to follow their own unique way - and have made such a success of it. Back then, I was too young and had not yet evolved far enough as a cook to do something in collaboration with others. But now the time is ripe. Look at 'Pure C', for example, where Circo Bakker is the chef. And I have entrusted 'The Jane' to my right-hand man, Nick Bril. I have now reached the point where I need to let go - and delegate! In future, I simply want to be busy with my own creativity - and that doesn't just mean cooking; it also means interiors and details. Keeping people sharp behind the scenes, supporting them, inspiring them, helping them to focus: that is going to be my job from now on."

A changing mentality

Does Sergio see an essential difference between Belgian and Dutch cuisine? "The Belgians have an eating culture. The Zeelanders have something similar, perhaps because they live just across the border. The Belgians opt for quality, for excellent products. But also for quality of life. Whether they are cooking for their family at home or going out to eat in a restaurant, they put their heart and soul into it. That's built into their genes. It's not quite like that in The Netherlands. People here can cook as well, but you can't really compare it with Belgium. You do it with much more skill and flair. Even so, I am a bit worried about the future. The catering industry in general is under huge pressure from the high levels of tax and social insurance, levels that are much higher than in The Netherlands. This is putting the break on development in the sector. To make matters worse, the mentality is also changing. Today's generation of promising cooks is less prepared to put in the necessary hard work than in the past. That is worrying. The top layer of great chefs will become thinner and thinner. But there will still be plenty of other alternatives, where people can still eat well and have a good time. I see this in 'Pure C'. The customers think it's great, both in terms of entourage and experience. I wanted to create a restaurant where I would want to go and eat myself - and I think I have succeeded. And it's the same with 'The Jane'. Hopefully, it will become a classic, just like we are turning 'Pure C' into a classic. They are restaurants that serve great food in a great setting with a great atmosphere, and all at an acceptable price: that is the future of our business."

> **They are restaurants that serve great food in a great setting with a great atmosphere, and all at an acceptable price: that is the future of our business."**

The Jane
Militair Hospitaal, Marialei- Lange
Leemstraat - Boomgaardstraat
2018 Antwerpen
www.thejaneantwerp.com

In a nutshell

→ **Who or what influenced your choice of profession?**
My father.

→ **What was your first culinary experience or memory?**
Roger Verger in 'Moulin du Mougins', together with my parents. I was about six years old. I ate scallops, stuffed courgette with truffle, and goose liver. I loved it all!

→ **What can really make you mad in the kitchen?**
If people are sloppy or keep on making the same mistakes. That really gets on my nerves! I have become calmer as I get older, but once I lose control of my temper, I really let fly - with both barrels!

→ **What is your most important personal quality?**
Determination, stubbornly persisting to the end.

→ **What would you like to have more time for?**
My children.

→ **What other job would you like to do?**
It would have to be something artistic. I have always been fascinated by design, photography and art, all of which make the world a more attractive place to live in.

→ **For you, what is the epitome of luxury?**
Free time and the luxury of every once in a while being able to read a book or a magazine in peace and quiet, all by myself.

→ **What do you most like doing in the kitchen?**
Looking for unusual combinations, developing new flavours, perfecting my dishes.

→ **What do you least like doing in the kitchen?**
Mise-en-place. I used to do it a lot, but not any longer, because my role now involves much more than just standing around in the kitchen.

→ **Who is your perfect table companion?**
Firstly, my wife; secondly, my wife and children; and thirdly, my good friends. In the past, I sometimes went out eating alone, and I really enjoyed that as well.

→ **What do you like eating at home on your day off?**
Something pure, like a nice piece of fish with vegetables and a light vinaigrette.

→ **What small object could you not do without in the kitchen?**
A Molen knife and a Bamix. And a tea-towel over my shoulder; that always gives me a comforting feeling.

→ **What type of cuisine do you not like?**
I am open for all type of cooking; there is nothing I don't like or am not prepared to try.

Crab/dashi/ hamachi/ buttermilk/ salty-tasting herbs

For 4 people

For the dashi jelly:
10 cl cream
100 g Granny Smith apples, peeled and without core
5.4 cl dashi vinegar
20 cl chicken stock
1.5 cl lemon vinegar
4.5 g agaragar
salt and pepper

For the buttermilk foam:
50 cl buttermilk
5.6 g salt
8.3 g sugar
0.5 cl lemon juice
0.7 g xanthana (xanthan gum)
3.4 cl cream
3 slices of gelatine

For the buttermilk vinaigrette:
5 cl buttermilk
14 g egg white
0.2 g xanthana
0.5 cl lemon vinegar

40 g Granny Smith apple, peeled and without core
2 cl fermented scallop juice
2 cl olive oil
3 cl grape seed oil
salt and pepper
juice and grated zest of
1 lemon

For the dashi/yuzu/vanilla foam:
50 g dashi
1.62 cl yuzu juice
1.25 cl water
1/8 of a vanilla stick
1.5 g albumin
26.25 g egg white powder

For the oyster chips:
75 g sushi rice
32.5 cl water
200 g oysters without juice (fully drained)
25 g trisol
60 g rice meal
3 g salt
4.5 g silver dust

For the crab tartar:
1 crab
1 l water
1 carrot
3 stalks of green celery
salt and pepper
thyme and rosemary

For the lemon raw cream:
1 kg cream or sour cream
3 slices of gelatine
salt
50 g lemon jelly

For the lemon jelly with apple:
15 cl lemon juice
10 cl lime juice
10 cl calamansi juice
5 cl ginger juice
50 cl sugar water
13 g agaragar
11 g gellan gum

For the watercress oil:
1. 5 clumps of watercress
20 spinach leaves
1 l grape seed oil

salt
1 teaspoon lime juice

For the hamachi carpaccio:
1 hamachi fillet

Other ingredients:
4 white strawberries, cut into six pieces
1 swede, in 0.3 cm slices from which circlets are cut
Oscietra Royal Belgian caviar (for the finishing)

For the herbs:
2 pieces of each:
Japanese parsley
sea needle
prick-madam (sedum reflexum)
bronze fennel
rucola cress
lemon marigold flowers
bladder campion flowers (silene vulgaris)

Dashi jelly:
› Stir together the cream, Granny Smith apple, dashi vinegar, chicken stock and lemon vinegar and pass through a fine sieve. Bring the sieved mixture to the boil and pass through the sieve again. Pour part of this jam into a silicone mat with crab-shaped moulds. Pour the remaining part onto a metal tray with a depth of 0.5 cm. Allow to cool. Use a small cutter ring to cut circlets out of the resultant jelly.

Buttermilk foam:
› Mix the buttermilk with the xanthana. Soak the gelatine in cold water. Heat the cream, lime juice, salt and sugar to 50 °C. Add the soaked gelatine. Pour this mixture through a sieve and add to the buttermilk. Pour the resulting mixture into a kitchen sprayer. Pressurize the sprayer. Place the sprayer in a bowl of ice-cold water and keep in the fridge for 2 hours. Fill the silicone mat with round moulds with the spray-mix and place in the freezer to harden. When frozen, press gently out of the silicone moulds.

Buttermilk vinaigrette:

› Stir together the egg white, buttermilk, xanthana, lemon vinegar, Granny Smith apples and scallop juice. Add this mixture little by little to the olive oil until a light emulsion is obtained. Pass through a fine sieve and season according to preference.

For the dashi/yuzu/vanilla meringue:

› Mix together the dashi, yuzu juice, water, albumin and egg white powder in a Kitchenaid at position 4 for 30 minutes or in a kitchen robot at medium-high speed. Pipe small roundels of the resulting mixture onto a silpat and place in an oven at 90 °C for 3 hours. Allow to cool and then remove the hardened roundels from the silpat.

Oyster chips:

› Boil the rice in water until all the water has evaporated. Put the rice in a Thermomix and mix together with all the other ingredients for 15 minutes at 90 °C. Pass the resulting mixture through a sieve and spread it evenly over a silpat. Bake for 25 minutes in an oven at 120 °C.

Crab tartar:

› Bring all the ingredients to the boil and add the crab. Boil for 2 minutes. Remove the pan from the heat and allow the crab to cool for 8 minutes in the cooking juices. Remove the crab and allow it to cool further in the fridge. When fully cooled, clean the crab.

Lemon raw cream:

› Heat 100 g of the raw cream to 50 °C. Soak the gelatine in cold water and then add it to the cream. Stir in the rest of the ingredients.

Lemon jelly:

› Stir together all the juices with the sugar water and heat gradually. Add the agaragar and the gellan. Stir thoroughly. Pass the resulting mixture through a sieve and keep it in a cool place. Once cooled, mix in a Thermomix or kitchen robot.

Watercress oil:

› Place all the ingredients in a Thermomix and mix for 3 minutes at position 8.

Hamachi:

› Cut thin slices (0.5 cm) and keep in the freezer. Cut out circles of flesh with a cutter.

Finishing:

› Place the circlet of dashi jelly in the middle of the plate. Using the same cutter that was used for the hamachi carpaccio, cut a circle out of the middle of the dashi jelly. Place the carpaccio in the resulting 'hole' in the jelly. Season with olive oil, salt and pepper. Dress around the carpaccio with the buttermilk vinaigrette, lemon jelly, watercress oil, lemon raw cream, white strawberries and swede. Position the herbs in between these dressings. Spray the buttermilk foam onto the hamachi carpaccio and place the crab tartar on top of it. Finally, add a crab-shaped piece of the dashi jelly.
› Finish with the oyster chips and the dashi/yuzu/vanilla meringues.
› Add a little Oscietra Royal Belgium caviar.

Choco-cherries

For 4 people

For the dulcey chocolate mousse:
50 cl cream
60 g egg yolks
108 g sugar
3.2 cl water
3 slices of gelatine
150 g Valrhona dulcey chocolate
125 g dark chocolate
12.5 cl cream

For the cherry and yoghurt sorbet:
16.5 cl cherry coulis
32.5 cl yoghurt
60 g glucose powder
30 g invert sugar

For the metallic cherry gel:
30 cl cherry coulis
20 cl cherry beer
25 g sugar
4.5 g agaragar
5 g metallic powder

For the cherry crisps:
200 g cherry puree
2 g xanthana
40 g sugar
50 g decorating sugar
10 g glucose

For the chocolate clusters:
100 g dulcey chocolate
50 g almonds
50 g pistachio nuts
50 g cherry crunch (freeze-dried)
50 g raw cacao

For the cherry feuilletine:
300 g dark chocolate paste
30 g cherry crunch (freeze-dried)
20g cacao butter
40 g rice-pops
70 g feuilletine

For the Roner rhubarb:
4 sticks of rhubarb
2 stalks of sweet woodruff
5 cl cherry coulis

7 cl cherry beer
4 cl cranberry juice

For the cherry and almond cream:
10 cl lime juice
4 cl cherry coulis
1.5 cl almond milk
75 g butter
4 eggs
90 g sugar

For the rhubarb sorbet:
100 g green rhubarb juice (centrifuged rhubarb juice)
50 cl green rhubarb coulis (rhubarb reduced with sugar)
4 cl lemon juice
50 g invert sugar
3 g stabilizer
100 g glucose powder

For the rhubarb cream:
45 cl cream
106 g egg yolk
80 g sugar
12 slices of gelatine

90 g green rhubarb coulis
1.2 cl lime juice

For the rhubarb juice:
10 cl rhubarb juice from cooked rhubarb
8 cl cherry beer
1.5 cl lime juice
5 cl pomegranate juice

For the cherry mascarpone:
400 g mascarpone
9 cl cherry coulis
25 g sugar
7 cl lemon juice
1 slice of gelatine, soaked

For the garnish:
basil oil
agastache
oxalis
sweet woodruff
chocochips
raw rhubarb
fresh cherries

Dulcey chocolate mousse:
› Whip the cream until light and frothy. Soak the slices of gelatine in cold water. Boil the sugar and water to 121°C. Beat the egg yolks until they are light and frothy. Melt the dulcey chocolate and the dark chocolate. Bring the 12.5 cl of cream to the boil. Stir the cream into the melted chocolate. Squeeze the water out of the gelatine slices and dissolve them in the chocolate-cream mixture to obtain a ganache. Carefully add the sugar water and the light-beaten egg yolk. Beat with a whisk until cool/cold and then add in the ganache. Work the whipped cream into this mixture and continue stirring until a nice mousse is obtained.

Cherry and yoghurt sorbet:
› Heat the yoghurt with the invert sugar and glucose powder. Stir in the cherry coulis. Pass the resulting mixture through a sieve and place in the freezer to harden.

Metallic cherry gel:
› Bring all the ingredients apart from the metallic powder to the boil for 2 minutes. Pour the resulting mixture into a bowl and allow to cool. When cooled, transfer the mixture to a mixer and mix together with the metallic powder until a smooth gel is obtained. Press the gel through a fine sieve.

Cherry crisps:
› Stir all the ingredients together and mix them in a Thermomix at 70 °C for 15 minutes. Pass the resulting mixture through a sieve. Allow to rest for 24 hours in the fridge. Brush the mixture thinly onto silicone mats. Allow to dry for 6 hours in an oven at 90 °C.

Chocolate clusters:
› Roast an equal quantity of all the nuts in a grease-free pan until they are golden brown. Chop finely. Mix with the caramel chocolate (pre-melted in a bain-marie), raw cacao and cherry crunch. Place a sheet of greased paper on a tray. Place small heaps of the mixture on the tray and allow to cool in the fridge.

Cherry feuilletine:
› Melt the chocolate in a microwave oven. Stir all the other ingredients into the melted chocolate. Roll this mixture out between two sheets of baking paper. Allow to harden. When hard, cut out circular pieces with a cutter.

Roner rhubarb:
› Mix together the cherry coulis, cherry beer and the cranberry juice. Peel the sticks of rhubarb, cut them into pieces and place them in a vacuum bag with the sweet woodruff. Cook in the Roner at 65 °C for 12 minutes or steam for 12 minutes in a steam-oven at 65 °C. Cool immediately in ice-cold water. Cut the rhubarb into uniform, rectangular pieces about 3mm thick.

Cherry and almond cream:
› Mix the lime juice with the butter, cherry coulis, almond milk and sugar in a Thermomix at position 2 (100 °C). In the meantime, break the eggs into a bowl and stir until the whites and the yolks are thoroughly mixed. Add this egg mix to the mass when it has reached boiling point. Set the Thermomix to full speed for just a couple of seconds, before returning it to the position 2. Continue mixing until the cream becomes nice and thick. When this happens, briefly set the mixer back to full speed for another couple of second, but not too long - otherwise you will ruin the structure. Place the pot containing the cream immediately in some ice-cold water, until the cream has congealed nicely.

Rhubarb sorbet:
› Bring the 100 g green rhubarb juice slowly to the boil, together with the invert sugar, stabilizer and glucose powder. Next stir in the cherry coulis and the lemon juice. Pass the resulting mixture through a sieve and keep in the freezer.

Rhubarb cream:
› Heat the cream until boiling point. Beat together the sugar and the egg yolks until they form a white mass. Squeeze the water out of the gelatine slices and add them to the cream. Stir the egg-sugar mixture into the cream. Add lemon juice and rhubarb coulis. Allow to cool. Re-heat the cooled cream gently and pour onto a tray with a depth of 2 cm. Allow to harden. Use a cutter to cut out neat roundels.

Rhubarb juice:
› Stir all the ingredients together. Pass through a sieve and mix thoroughly.

Cherry mascarpone:
› Heat the cherry coulis until lukewarm. Squeeze the water out of the gelatine slices and dissolve them in the cherry coulis. Add in all the other ingredients and stir well, until a good, thick cream is obtained.

Finishing:
› Arrange all the different ingredients on or around each other on a plate. Dress with the juice, raw rhubarb and the garnish.

With hide and hair

For 4 people

For the aubergine cream:
250 g roasted aubergines
(6 aubergines)
pepper and salt
1/2 clove of black garlic
1/2 teaspoon of garam
masala
40 g egg white
2 cl chicken stock
10 cl olive oil
1 dash of Merlot vinegar
1 dash of sushi vinegar
juice of 1 lime
a dash of corn oil

For the black aubergine cream:
1/2 tablespoon of squid ink

For the artichoke cream:
4 large artichokes (steamed)
25 cl barigoule juice
5 cl cream
5 cl olive oil
125 g tapioca
1 tablespoon trisol

For the aubergine crisps:
1 aubergine
a dash of olive oil
a pinch of salt
a pinch of sugar

For the sage jelly:
500 g sage infusion (infusion
of chicken stock and sage)
3 g agaragar
2 g gellan gum

For the pepper vinaigrette:
10 cl pepper sauce
1/2 teaspoon black pepper
1/2 teaspoon Nepal pepper

30 g egg white
sushi vinegar
juice of 1 lime
1 cl chicken stock
a pinch of xanthana
5 cl olive oil
5 cl pepper oil
watercress oil

For the mustard vinaigrette:
50 g Dijon mustard
20 g egg white
1 cl chicken stock
a pinch of xanthana
sushi vinegar
lime juice
salt and pepper
15 cl watercress oil
10 cl grape seed oil

For the tamarind vinaigrette:
20 g cut ginger
lime juice
2 cl dashi vinegar
2 cl vintage soja
30 g tamarind paste
2 cl lemon vinegar
1 clove of garlic, cut
a dash of sushi vinegar
2 cl aloe vera juice
30 cl Granverde lemon olive
oil

For the meat:
1 nice piece of filet steak per
person

For the tartar:
200 g beef tartar
150 g beetroot brunoise
mustard vinaigrette
basil oil
3 tablespoons of finely grated
Parmesan cheese
1 shallot, finely diced

3 tablespoons of parsley,
finely chopped
salt and pepper
dashi chips
black garlic

For finishing:
rye-bread crisps
herbs and flowers

For the rendang:
1/2 onion, finely diced
2 cloves of garlic, finely diced
1 small piece of ginger, finely
diced
1 piece of lime grass
1/2 red chilli pepper, finely
diced
1/2 teaspoon curcuma
1/2 teaspoon crushed
coriander seeds
1/2 teaspoon cumin seeds
15 g trassi (shrimp paste)
20 cl chicken stock
20 cl beef juice
10 kaffir leaves, finely diced
20 cl coconut milk
15 g tamarind paste
grated peel and juice of
1 lime

For the horn spoon:
1 piece of roasted bone
marrow
1 shallot
salad of orzo pasta and
shallot (dashi vinegar, basil
oil, salt and pepper)
mini-roundels of swede
rye-bread crisps
tamarind vinaigrette

For 3 dl beef sauce:
beef scraps
shallots

onions
carrots
garlic
mushrooms
thyme
rosemary
black pepper
port
red wine
brandy
veal stock
chicken stock

For finishing sauce:
1 knob of butter
grated zest of lime
1 tablespoon brunoise of
marinated black garlic
1 tablespoon parsley
1 sage leaf, finely chopped

For the vegetable garnish:
1 mini-violet artichoke
1 quenelle of aubergine
caviar
1 artichoke leaf, boiled for
8 minutes in barigoule juice
1 piece of Parmesan cheese
(for grating)
1 piece of pickled aubergine
1 mini-aubergine (grilled on
the barbecue)
selection of herbs and
flowers
pasta cannelloni with sage
jelly, rolled tightly

Aubergine cream:

› Cut 6 aubergines in half and incise the flesh of the fruit both horizontally and vertically. Season them with salt and pepper and place them on a tray. Sprinkle them with corn oil and roast for 35 minutes at 170 °C. Allow to cool and then remove the flesh with a spoon. Keep part of the flesh for the aubergine caviar and place the rest in a mixer together with the egg white, garlic, chicken stock and garam masala. Mix thoroughly until a smooth and creamy mass is obtained. Carefully add the olive oil. Mix everything again and finally add the Merlot vinegar, sushi vinegar and the lime juice. Pass the resulting cream through a sieve.

Black aubergine cream:

› Take part of the remaining aubergine flesh and mix this in a mixer with 1/2 a spoonful of squid ink.

Artichoke cream:

› Mix all the ingredients together in a Thermomix at 90 °C for 25 minutes. Allow the resulting mixture to stand overnight in the fridge. Remix until warm. Check if the cream is well seasoned and spread it out on silpats to a thickness of about 4 mm. Place the silpats in a warm oven for 45 minutes at 120 °C.

Aubergine crisps:

› Cut the aubergine into nice roundels of about 6mm. Spread these out on a silpat, brush with olive oil and season with a little salt and sugar. Bake in the oven at 140 °C for 20 minutes, until crisp with a light golden colour.

Sage jelly:

› Boil the sage infusion and the agaragar for just a few seconds. Allow the mixture to cool to 80 °C. Add the gellan, mix thoroughly and pass through a fine sieve onto a flat, metal tray. Allow to cool.

Pepper vinaigrette:

› Place the pepper sauce, black pepper, Nepalese pepper, egg white, sushi vinegar, lime juice, chicken stock and xanthana in a mixer and mix until a smooth mass is obtained. While continuing to mix, carefully add the olive oil and the pepper oil. Mix further until the mass becomes smooth and shiny, but not too thick. Marble the emulsion by adding the watercress oil.

Mustard vinaigrette:

› The preparation is identical to the pepper vinaigrette. Remember to keep 5 cl of the watercress oil to marble the vinaigrette at the end of the preparation.

Tamarind vinaigrette:

› Mix together all the ingredients except the lemon olive oil. Use this lemon olive oil to marble the vinaigrette at the end of the preparation.

Tartar:

› Marinate the meat in the mustard, basil oil, Parmesan cheese, shallots, chopped parsley, salt and pepper. Place in a mould and press firmly. Place the marinated beetroot on top. Press firmly again and finish with the beetroot tartar. Dress with the mustard vinaigrette, dashi chips and black garlic.

Rendang:

› Keep 3 end slices of the lightly fried fillets of steak for the rendang. Sauté the onion, garlic, ginger, lime grass, and red chilli pepper, together with the curcuma, coriander seeds, cumin and trassi, until everything is nice and soft. Then add the chicken stock, beef juice and chopped kaffir leaves. Allow to reduce until a reasonably thick mass is obtained and then add the coconut milk at the end. Re-heat, add the tamarind paste and the lime zest and juice. Pass everything through a sieve.

Horn spoon:

› Marinate the orzo pasta in the dashi vinegar and the basil oil, seasoned with salt and pepper. Make three equal heaps on the horn spoon. Add the shallot rings on top and place the bone marrow in between. Break 2 small pieces of the rye-bread crisps and place them on the bone marrow. Sprinkle with the vinaigrette.

Beef sauce:

› Pass the sauce through a sieve and finish with a knob of butter, grated zest of lime, 1 tablespoon of a brunoise of marinated black garlic, 1 tablespoon of parsley and 1 finely chopped sage leaf.

Finishing:

› Divide the meat between the plates. Add the artichoke cream, sage jelly, aubergine crisps, black aubergine cream, the vegetable garnish and the three different vinaigrettes. Dress with the herbs, flowers and rye-bread crunch. Spronkle with a little of the beef sauce. Spoon the rendang into a small pot and place the horn spoon on top of it. Serve the tartar separately.

The preparation in 1, 2, 3

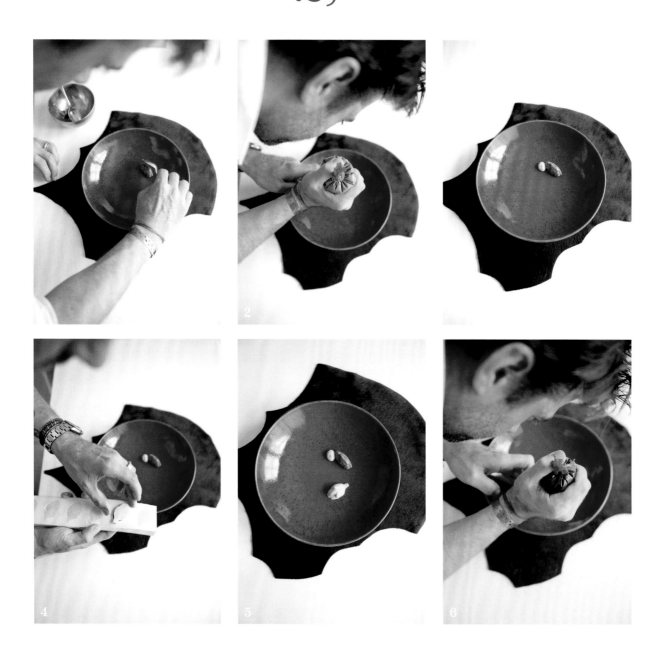

Piet Huysentruyt

∬ Likoké ⸩

According to Roger Souvereyns, Piet Huysentruyt was the best chef who ever worked for him at his restaurant 'Scholteshof'. Huysentruyt is both flattered and surprised by the comment. 'At school, I was always the worst pupil in the class!' says the man behind a series of successful television programmes like 'SOS Piet' and the seller of more books in Flanders than anyone in recent publishing history. Now he is back where he first started: cooking at the stove in his own restaurant. But this time in the south of France. And as unconventional as ever.

'During my training at the hotel school in Koksijde I wasn't exactly the easy-going, conformist type,' remembers Piet Huysentruyt in his typically honest and forthright fashion. 'When you are a student, you are supposed to carry things out exactly the way your teachers tell you. I always had a problem with that. The stock always had to be made 'their' way - and no other. Potatoes had to be cut like this, and not like that. I thought that I knew better. Not surprisingly, when the time came for my final exams I failed in grand style. Chef Eddie Van Maele was one of the jury, but he at least understood my way of thinking. Eddie has always been a bit of a free spirit himself, who never really got the recognition he deserved. At the school, I used to look up to him. And to Willy Slawinski, of course. For me, they were the standard-bearers of innovation. Perhaps they weren't always appreciated by the other cooks, because what they were doing was too new, too revolutionary.' After hotel school Piet Huysentruyt decided to stay in the cooking profession and was prepared to work extra hard to make his way. He started in the Brussels restaurant 'L'Ecailler du Palais Royal' under Attilio Basso. 'There I was drilled morning, noon and night, but I learnt a huge amount. If you have to clean ten crates of fish and shellfish every day, you soon find out the right way to do it! In a year and a half, I learnt about three-quarters of the things I now know about cooking. Basso was a demanding taskmaster. Certainly for his staff, but perhaps even more so for himself.' After Brussels, his career pathway took several different twists and turns. Via the network of director Notredame of hotel school 'Ter Duinen', in 1983 he found his way to restaurant 'Le PréCatalan' in the Bois de Boulogne near Paris. 'Today, it's a three-star restaurant. When I worked there they only had two. As far as I was concerned, I had been dropped in some kind of cooking factory. Many of the products, including their basic sauces, were delivered by their own catering service. I soon knew that there was very little I could learn. Besides, it was a financial disaster. I only earned 30,000 francs a month, but my one room garret in Paris - a bed, a cupboard and no hot water - cost me 25,000 francs. After three months, I was ready to leave. But director Notredame said that I had to stay: to leave so soon would damage the reputation of his school. But I have always had a strong stubborn streak - and so I left anyway.'

Basso, Pangaud and Souvereyns

Piet Huysentruyt set off in search of a new job in France. He was finally given a place in Boulogne-Billancourt by Gérard Pangaud, who at that time was the youngest two-star chef in the country. 'If I learnt three-quarters of my cooking knowledge from Attilio Basso, then I learnt the other quarter from Gérard Pangaud. He was a brilliant chef, who combined products that others wouldn't even dare think about. His creations formed the basis of my menu my own restaurant in Wortegem-Petegem. Pangaud's cuisine reminded me of Willy Slawinski. After that, I did a further year at 'La Cravache d'Or', a two-star restaurant in Brussels where Robert Kranenborg was the head chef.'

In 1985 Piet Huysentruyt began the final chapter of his culinary story before finally starting up his own business. He was given the opportunity to work with Roger Souvereyns in his famous two-star restaurant 'Scholteshof' in Stevoort. 'Until then, I had only been confronted with the rigid structure that so often seems to accompany 'star' cooking. The restaurants where I had worked had all been run with a kind of military precision. The atmosphere in the 'Scholteshof' was completely different. There was no structure. There was just Roger Souvereyns. Everyone called him 'boss' or 'patron', which I found strange. So I just called him 'chef', and he replied by telling me that I could use his first name. But that was strange as well! It was a hard school, but at least we were given the freedom to express our creativity. In cooking terms, I was actually able to be myself for the very first time, although Souvereyns continued to be extremely demanding. After three months, I wanted to take yet another step forward, this time to a three-star restaurant. I was given a place by Gérard Boyer in Reims. Souvereyns wasn't very happy about it but he let me go. A month later he came to see me and asked me to come back to Stevoort as chef. I agreed. There was always something compelling about Roger, but I never regretted my decision, because he gave me more or less carte blanche. He is still an outstanding chef. He can bring flavour to a dish like no one else can. His amazing sense of taste allows him to give a depth and intensity to his cooking that few can match. And he doesn't need all that many ingredients to do it. With just three different products he can create the most sublime end results. That is something that only the great natural talents can do.'

Contemporary and challenging

When he finally left the 'Scholteshof', Piet Huysentruyt briefly ran his own 'cook-in-your-home' business, before eventually opening his first restaurant in Wortegem-Petegem in 1995. He immediately demonstrated his culinary daring with a number of unusual combinations, which were far ahead of their time. Michelin soon recognized his talent with the award of a first star. His book *Eigentijds en eigenzinnig. De Vlaamse keuken heruitgevonden* (*Contemporary, characteristic and challenging: Flemish coking rediscovered*) delivers exactly what it promises, and is still very 'contemporary' more than 15 years after its publication. Signature dishes such as lamb with salicornia and mackerel, turbot with calf's brains, black pudding and apples are just two examples of his bold and innovative spirit. But his lobster with pig's trotters, red cabbage and oysters is the star dish with which he is perhaps most frequently associated. By this time, he had also made his acquaintance with the world of television. 'Up to then, cooking programmes had seldom been presented by chefs, which I had always found strange. When I was asked to do *Zondag Josdag* in 1995, I jumped at the chance. Before I knew it, one thing led to another!' He would later do more than a thousand episodes of *Lekker Thuis* for VTM, the leading commercial station in Belgium. His unconventional career still had its ups and downs, and after he lost his Michelin star Huysentruyt exchanged the cold of Wortegem-Petegem for the warmth of the Ardèche in France. In the meantime, he continued with his television work, making popular and successful programmes like *De Perfecte Keuken* and *SOS Piet*. A few years later he opened a restaurant in Les Vans, near his home. Hordes of Flemish tourists flocked to this new venture, many of them more keen on getting an autographed photo of the famous

'tv-chef' than appreciating the excellence of his food. This irritated Huysentruyt, gnawing away at his insides. His fascinating contribution to Belgian cooking through the years seemed to have been wiped away by his media career. In the public's mind, he was now 'The VTM-cook'. Had everyone forgotten how innovative and ground-breaking he had been at the start of his career? 'I have always liked working for television. I still do. It's just a shame that you tend to get 'pigeon-holed' by what you do on the box. People find it hard to look beyond the hype.' By 2010, he was tired of the whole celebrity circus and so he decided to close 'Le Lutin Gourmand'. He leased the building to a promising young cook and hoped that he would eventually buy it. But the deal fell through. Sometime later, Huysentruyt took the property off the market. He had a new concept at the back of his mind, but for the time being he was keeping the secret to himself. 'For two years I had to bite my tongue. I told no one. I wanted to make the announcement to the press myself, when the moment was right. This moment finally came on 15 June 2013, when Piet Huysentruyt opened his new restaurant 'Likoké'. Wouter Van der Vieren, the ex-chef at 'Clandestino' (Temse) and 'Wy' (Brussels) is in charge of the cooking. And the standards and the expectations are both high. The restaurant serves 'original dishes rooted in the soil of southern France'.

> **I have always liked working for television. I still do. It's just a shame that you tend to get 'pigeon-holed' by what you do on the box. People find it hard to look beyond the hype.**

Playtime!

Huysentruyt recently turned 50. He has also been diagnosed with diabetes and has overcome the effects of a mild stroke. Enough to give anyone pause for thought. He is a reasonably wealthy man. So why is he opening a new restaurant at his age? Why doesn't he just do the things he wants to do? 'But that is precisely what I am doing!' he laughs in reply. 'For me, this is playtime! If I look at the new dishes that Walter and myself have created, it makes me shiver with delight. A real wow-moment. Sometimes we only need to exchange a glance to know which direction a new recipe needs to take. We are both very emotional people. Our need to convince others is focused in our creativity. And if we get it right, it's enough to bring tears to our eyes. Like recently, when we finally found the flavour we had been looking for in a crayfish recipe. Or when Walter tried my salami - the best in the world - for the very first time. In fact, I am actually living out the dream of every cook: to open a nice little restaurant when you are fifty, with no financial worries to bother you. I paid for this all out of my own pocket. But I am still a businessman. I am not planning to lose money with this new venture. We have a staff of ten, half of them from the team in Walter's old restaurant. All from Flanders, because the French only

In a nutshell

→ **Who or what influenced your choice of profession?**
Just me.

→ **What was your first culinary experience or memory?**
My father's pilchards and scrambled brains on brown bread.

→ **What can really make you mad in the kitchen?**
Unprofessional behaviour.

→ **What is your most important personal quality?**
Determination.

→ **Of which of your personal characteristics are you least proud?**
I am not ashamed of any of my personal characteristics!

→ **How do you deal with set backs?**
Very well, thank you.

→ **What would you like to have more time for?**
Travelling.

→ **What other job would you like to do?**
I already have two jobs; a third one would be a bit over the top.

→ **For you, what is the epitome of luxury?**
Doing nothing.

→ **What do you like to give as a present to your friends?**
A super-duper party.

→ **What are you best at in the kitchen?**
Tricks.

→ **What do you least enjoy doing in the kitchen?**
Washing up and cleaning fish.

→ **What is your favourite vegetable?**
Potato.

→ **What is your favourite type or cut of meat?**
Onglet (top skirt of beef)

→ **What type(s) of fish do you like to work with?**
Line caught fish, such as sea bass.

→ **What are your preferred herbs for fish and meat dishes?**
Fleur-de-sel.

→ **What are you favourite aromas and smells in the kitchen?**
Casseroles.

→ **What is your favourite dish?**
Pasta with truffles.

→ **Which small object could you not do without in the kitchen?**
A ball-point pen.

→ **Which chef has inspired you the most?**
I rely on my own inspiration.

→ **What type of cuisine do you not like?**
I like all types of cuisine.

→ **What was the last celebrated restaurant that you visited and what was your opinion?**
Marc Meneau, at 'L'Esperance' in Vézelay. I have never felt so humiliated by a chef. My first ever letter to Michelin was the result.

→ **What is your worst ever professional experience?**
The day that Jan Verheyen took away my programme *Lekker Thuis*.

→ **Who is your perfect table companion?**
Everyone is welcome at my table.

→ **What is your favourite aperitif?**
White wine (Viognier).

→ **What do you most enjoy eating on your day off?**
As simply as possible.

want - or are only allowed - to work 33 hours a week. All these people need to be paid, which means that business side of things needs to be a success. If it isn't, I will have to think again. But looking at the way things are now, I am confident that everything will turn out fine.'

With the opening of 'Likoké', Piet Huysentruyt is looking to close the circle. To begin with, the restaurant is actually a tribute to his father. Likoké was the nickname given to his dad by the natives when he was running a coffee plantation in the Congo. At the same time, the new dishes also refer back to Huysentruyt's own past, and more particularly his restaurant in Wortegem-Petegem. 'This is my cuisine of 25 years ago, but brought up-to-date by Wouter and myself. They are not the same recipes, of course, but the basis is the same: the basis that made me famous - or should that be notorious? We are still using pig's trotters, pig's ears and an unconventional mixture of other ingredients - just like back in the good old days!'

Nature

Nature plays a prominent role in the new restaurant. The tables are made from rough wooden planks, the 'artistic' wooden plates have been specially crafted by a local wood-artist and the Belgian furniture-artist Catherine Op de Beeck has mounted a series of driftwood sculptures in the kitchen area. Huysentruyt wants to develop his restaurant as a base for cultural activities in the region: a truffle hunt, visits to a local olive mill, wine-tastings at local vineyards, etc. 'There is a ruined building nearby. If I can get planning permission, I want to turn it into a small hotel. The idea is that I will pick up people from the airports and stations in the region, and then bring them here for gastronomic weekends. In terms of food and cost, we will be setting a higher threshold. Even so, everyone is welcome. There is already a menu from as little as 70 euros. Besides, people will be willing to save up to come. Why? Because they like me. I have become what I am today thanks to all those people who liked watching me on TV. They can still come and ask me for a photograph and a signature. And I will be happy to give them. Since I turned fifty and, above all, since I had my stroke, I have become much calmer, more zen. In the past, I used to do everything myself. Now I have surrounded myself with good people, who can do everything for me. It's still quite hard, physically, but I haven't enjoyed myself so much in years. And let's not forget the most important thing: I have finally become a chef again...'

Likoké
7, Route de Païolive
F-07140 Les Vans
(33) 627 83 98 57
www.likoke.be

Sea bass with cherries, udder and goose-liver

For 4 people

640 g fillets of wild sea bass
(160 g per person)

For the cherry juice:
150 g cherries
butter
1 shallot, finely diced
10 g sugar
1dl white wine
4 dl vegetable stock
1 tablespoon cherry vinegar
pepper and salt

For the beetroot jam:
1 cooked beetroot
2.5 dl beetroot juice
3 g kappa
5 cl cherry vinegar
pinch of guar gum

For the cherry topping:
100 g unstoned cherries
7.5 cl water
3 cl cherry vinegar
3 cl white wine vinegar
30 g sugar

1 teaspoon coriander seeds
3 pieces star aniseed
1 teaspoon Jamaica pepper

For the udder and goose liver:
60 g goose liver
40 g boiled udder
pepper and salt
peanut oil

For the yoghurt-spice mix:
20 g coriander seeds
5 g cardamom

5 g Penja pepper
5 g Timut pepper
10 g Talauma pepper
10 g Tasmanian pepper
4 tablespoons yoghurt

For the decoration:
flowers and herbs (bronze fennel, marjoram flowers, etc., depending on the season)

For the cherry juice:
› Steam the unstoned cherries with the finely diced shallot in the butter. Add the sugar and continue to stew briefly. Dilute with the white wine and the vegetable stock. Allow the sauce to boil gently for 10 minutes. Mix thoroughly and pour through a sieve. Finish by adding salt, pepper and the cherry vinegar.

For the beetroot jam:
› Mix all the ingredients in a Thermomix at 80°C. Allow the resulting mixture to thicken. Mix again until a smooth jam is obtained.

For the cherry topping:
› Heat all the other ingredients for the topping and pour this mixture over the cherries. Keep a dozen or so whole cherries for the decoration. Cut all the remaining cherries in two.

For the udder and goose liver:
› Season the goose liver and put it in a vacuum bag. Cook the liver for 8 minutes in the Roner or in a bain-marie at 65°C. Refresh the liver - still in the vacuum bag - with some ice-cold water. Press the liver flat in a tray and allow to stiffen. Cut into small triangles. Cut the boiled udder into triangles of the same size. Fry the udder pieces lightly on both sides in the peanut oil. Place the goose-liver triangles on top of the udder.

For the yoghurt and spice mix:
› Mix together all the spices and heat them briefly in an ungreased pan. Allow to cool and then grind the spices finely with a mortar and pestle. Pass the spices through a sieve and use them to season the yoghurt according to your own preference.

› Grill the sea bass briefly on both sides on a grill plate or in a grill pan. Cook further in an oven at 60°C, until ready to serve.
› Decorate with some seasonal flowers and herbs.

Salat is not a salat

For 4 people

1 handful of rocket lettuce
1 handful of radish shoots
1 handful of pea shoots
1 handful of sorrel
1 handful of curly lettuce
1 handful of East Indian
leaves and flowers
1 handful of fresh peas
1 handful of broad beans

For the coconut oil slices:
20 cl coconut oil
4 cl olive oil (fermented)

green coulis according to
preference
1 slice of gelatine

**For the elderberry flower
vinaigrette:**
1.5 dl Chardonnay vinegar
0.5 dl sushi vinegar
1 laurel leaf
2 stalks of thyme
1 clove of garlic
8 twists of the pepper mill
1 pinch of salt
20 cl water
juice of 1/2 a lime

2 handfuls of elderberry
flowers

2 boiled violet artichokes
1 slice of smoked bacon
2 fresh anchovies
2 slices of black bread
olive oil
salt

For the mint mayonnaise:
10 cl grape seed oil
20 g egg white
0.8 cl sushi-apple vinegar
0.8 cl Chardonnay vinegar

1 cl lemon juice
0.5 g guar gum
15 mint leaves
pepper and salt

For the frozen snow:
25 cl milk
1 handful of mint
2 slices of gelatine
15 cl yoghurt
2 g anti-oxidant
1 g guar gum
40 g egg white
2 dl buttermilk
juice of 1/2 a lemon

› Wash all the salads and shoots. Boil the peas and the broad beans and shell them. Mix them into the salad and place in a wooden bowl.

For the coconut oil slices:
› Heat all the ingredients apart from the gelatine until they form a homogenous mass. Now add the gelatine. Pour the mixture onto a silpat or a silicone mat and allow to harden. Cut out circular slices with a cutting ring and arrange them on top of the salad.

For the elderberry flower vinaigrette:
› Boil all the ingredients thoroughly, pass the resulting mixture through a sieve and pour it over the elderberry flowers. Allow to soak for at least two days. Heat the vinaigrette before dressing and pour it over the coconut slices.
› Cook the artichokes à blanc. When ready, marinate them briefly with a little of the elderberry flower vinaigrette and some olive oil.
› Fillet the anchovies, sprinkle them with salt and allow them to rest for 12 minutes, before cutting them into fine strips.
› Heat the oven to 160°C. Place the bread and the smoked bacon between two silpats and bake in the warm oven until golden brown.

For the mint mayonnaise:
› Mix all the ingredients with a hand-mixer and season with salt and pepper. Allow the mayonnaise to stand for 1 hour and then pass through a fine sieve.

For the frozen snow:
› Allow the mint to soak for half an hour in the milk. Pour the milk through a sieve. Add first the gelatine and then the rest of the ingredients. Stir until a homogenous mass is obtained. Pour this mass into a sprayer, pressurize the sprayer and spray out the contents into large lumps. Allow to harden and then break into smaller pieces.
› Dress the salad with the various garnishes.

The preparation in 1, 2, 3

Chocolate sausages

For 4 people

8 large dried morel mushrooms
10 cl port
50 g mashed banana
1 dl cream
100 g '811' Callebaut chocolate
100 g Callebaut milk chocolate
25 g butter
5 drops of morel extract
dried morel powder
cacao powder

› Soak the morel mushrooms overnight in the port. Remove the mushrooms from the marinade and chop them finely. Mix the mushrooms with the banana. Bring the cream to the boil and add the chocolate. Finish by adding the butter and the morel extract.

› Pour this mixture into sausage-shaped moulds and allow to harden. Dress with the morel powder and the cacao powder before serving.

Moambe in my father's name

For 4 people

Basic preparation of classic moambe
20 g butter
1 broiler (cooking chicken, cut into eight pieces)
pepper and salt
1 onion
2 tomatoes
1 clove of garlic
1 tin of moambe sauce (palm nut paste in palm oil)
2 or 3 small peppers

2 dl water
1 tablespoon chicken stock

Moambe Likoké

Moambe jelly:
2 dl moambe sauce
2 g gelatine

Chicken:
1/2 chicken breast
2 g transglutaminate
(can be purchased online from www.Naturalspices.eu)

olive oil

Tapioca:
4 tablespoons tapioca
4 tablespoons palm oil

Paprika:
1/4 red paprika
1 tablespoon sugar

Pearl onions:
4 pearl onions
0.5 dl water
0.25 dl sushi vinegar

Roasted chicken skin:
Skin of 1 chicken
4 sot l'y laisse (chicken oysters)

Banana cream:
4 tablespoons sour cream
1/2 banana

Finishing:
2 sprigs of coriander

› Use a large, medium-deep pot. Melt the butter until just before the point when it turns brown. Season the chicken and cook it for 5 minutes on each side. Chop the onion and add it to the pan. Cut the tomatoes into eight pieces and add these also, together with the diced garlic, the moambe sauce and the peppers. Pour in the water. Be careful not to use too much water: the moambe sauce is thick when it is cold, but becomes fluid when heated. Using too much water means you will end up with a thin and runny sauce. Now add the chicken stock. Bring to the boil. Turn down the heat as soon as the boiling point is reached and allow the contents of the pot to simmer for a further one to one and a half hours. If the sauce is still too thick, this is the moment to add a little extra water.

Moambe Likoké
› Moambe jelly: Take 2 tablespoons of the moambe sauce and add 2 g of gelatine. Pour the resulting mass onto a tray to a depth of 1 cm and allow to stiffen. Cut out a strip of the stiffened sauce and bend it into a roughly circular shape that is not completely round.

Chicken:
› Remove half a chicken breast from the classic moambe preparation. Add 8 tablespoons of the sauce and 2 g of transglutaminate. Roll this mixture up in a piece of aluminium foil. Allow to hardenin the fridge for at least 6 hours, and then cut into slices. Fry the slices in olive oil and allow them to rest briefly in the excess sauce.

Tapioca:
› Boil the tapioca until cooked. Rinse thoroughly. Add 4 tablespoons of palm oil, so that the grains of tapioca turn orange.

Paprika:
› Peel the red paprika and cut it into a julienne. Cover the julienne with water. Add 1 tablespoon of sugar and allow this mixture to slowly candy on a low heat.

Pearl onions:

› Peel the onions and gently pull them apart. Singe the onion rings briefly with a blow torch. In the meantime, bring the water, sushi vinegar and sugar to the boil. Pour this warm mixture over the onions. Allow to stand.

Roasted chicken skin:

› Pre-heat the oven to 160 °C. Place the chicken skin between two silpats (silicon baking mats) and place a weight on top, so that the skin cannot curl during cooking. Roast in the oven until the skin turns a golden brown.

Chicken oysters:

› Fry the chicken oysters on all sides for 1 minute in a little olive oil and season with salt and pepper. Allow to rest briefly.

Banana cream:

› Mix the sour cream and the banana until they form a thickened cream.

› Arrange all the ingredients as shown in the photograph. Dress with the fresh sprigs of coriander.

Trout "800"

For 4 people

1 large trout from Villefort
8 g salt per kg fish
olive oil
8 jumbo crayfish
frying oil

Trout slabs:
150 g smoked trout
25 g horseradish, grated

10 cl consommé
6 cl sour cream
1 g guar gum
0.5 g antioxidant
3 cl water
3 slice gelatine

Fennel sauce:
2 fennel roots
1 apple
1 lime

1 cl apple-sushi vinegar
1,5 cl sea water
15 g fresh sansho pepper
3 pieces of star aniseed
0.5 g fennel seeds

Fennel:
1 mini-fennel
1 nori leaf
pork fat

Garnish:
5 cl Chardonnay vinegar
5 g agave
4 cl water
1 piece of peperoni
thyme, laurel, rosemary
1 piece of star aniseed
5 fennel seeds
10 g sansho pepper

› Fillet the trout but make sure that the belly is not cut through. Remove the bones and the skin. Salt the fillets, using 8 g of salt per kilo of fillet.
› Conserve the fillets in olive oil in a bain marie at 55 °C. Allow approximately 1 minute of cooking time for each 10 g of fish. Singe the belly with a blow torch until the belly flesh is 'mi-cuit' (semi-cooked).
› Deep fry the unpeeled crayfish tails for 10 seconds in hot frying oil. Place them immediately in ice-cold water. Peel the crayfish tails and marinate them in a reduced bisque (made from the crayfish claws).

For the trout slabs:
› Mix all the ingredients except the gelatine in a Thermomix at 60 °C. Add the gelatine once the mixture is thoroughly warmed. Pass the mixture through a sieve and pour into moulds. Allow to harden.

For the fennel sauce:
› Process the fennel roots and the apple in a kitchen centrifuge. Add the other ingredients and then heat until any impurities come to the surface. Remove these with a scoop and allow the purified mixture to drain in a piece of muslin.

For the garnish:
› Finely peel the mini-fennel with a scraper. Bring all the other ingredients for the garnish to the boil and pour these over the peeled fennel. Cut the nori leaf into very small squares. Arrange the other ingredients. Finally, cook the pork fat between two oven plates at 170 °C for 20 minutes. Season well.

› Dress and finish as shown in the photograph.

Wouter Keersmaekers

De Schone van Boskoop

He has been working behind the cooker in Restaurant 'De Schone van Boskoop' for more than twenty years. Before that, he learnt the skills of the trade at the restaurants of other famous chefs. During this period of largely classically-inspired training he transformed himself into a professional cook who likes to reach down to the very essence of things. But the 'things' which inspire him are just as likely to be early Savoy cabbage or calf sausages as some of the more traditional and 'noble' products used by his other colleagues.

Vegetables and offal

Wouter Keersmaekers opened 'De Schone van Boskoop' in 1993 and it was soon rated as one of the best restaurants in the country. Before that, he had spent periods in the kitchens of Johan Van Raes and Johan Segers. Two chefs in the classic tradition who cook close to their products, but who do not confine their cooking to elite delicacies. This interest for less familiar and less fashionable products has been a part of Keersmaekers' culinary DNA for the past twenty years. "In addition to learning cooking skills, my two mentors both taught me to have care and respect for products," he says. "Everything that is edible, digestible and healthy deserves our attention. I don't deliberately go in search of bizarre things, but just the ordinary and tasty things that have shaped our domestic cooking in Belgium throughout the years. Why shouldn't I serve veal sausages, when they are so delicious to eat? Or veal brawn? Or dishes with liver and kidneys? I don't force my guests to eat these things. There are plenty of other options on my menu. But I have gradually built up a group of customers who do like this kind of food. This has allowed me to give my cooking a slightly different look." Keersmaekers often refers to domestic cooking, which in his case also means the meals he was served at home in his youth. "I was lucky. The food in our house was always great. Both my mother and my grandmother had a fantastic sense of taste. Sure, we used to eat traditional things, but it wasn't uncommon to find a tajine on the table every now and then. My passion for a flavour-packed plate is something I got from them. I also remember that they were keen to ensure that our meals were varied and they gave plenty of attention to vegetables. This is probably where I inherited my own interest in vegetables. I have always respected nature's seasons, because of the freshness this ensures.

For this reason, I prefer to work with local vegetable growers in my region. Why should I import things from abroad when I can find top quality on my own front doorstep?"

Greater tension and identity

Wouter Keersmaekers' cuisine is still in full evolution. Following his early training in the classical tradition, he quickly began to look for new techniques to make his cooking lighter, but with a more varied and more intense range of flavours. "I didn't look too far. For example, I used a classic onion sauce as a basis for the creation of a similar type of sauce, but one in which a number of extra taste nuances give a better overall result. There is nothing wrong with traditional sauces, but as a chef I was not always happy to use them. I wanted something with more tension and identity. With the range of products available on the market today, we have a huge arsenal from which we can create greater intensity. For the contemporary version of onion sauce that I just mentioned, I use fermented garlic, prune vinegar and mirin (sweet Japanese rice wine). I am not looking specifically for exotic accents, but simply for accents that will give greater depth to the existing basic flavours." Keersmaekers has remained consistent throughout the years in terms of plate composition. The dishes which he presents to his customers must have meaning, so that any excessive and unnecessary decoration which detracts from this meaning is jettisoned. "I don't like plates that are too full and certainly not for a main course, some of which are nowadays dressed like desserts. Excessive decoration can sometimes cause you to miss the harmony of flavours that is the essential purpose of the dish. In addition, this kind of garnishing is time-consuming and requires a lot of manpower – and is therefore expensive. I would rather see my staff cleaning vegetables and cutting meat, than messing about for hours on end with plate dressing. Besides, you need to get your dressing done quickly; otherwise, your main ingredients will get cold, which is a shame for the product and for all the hard work you have done."

Improving knowledge

Like most top chefs, Wouter Keersmaekers likes to keep in touch with what is going on in the world of gastronomy. Gaining insights into the work of other chefs is, he feels, always an enriching experience. "I like to go and eat at the restaurants of the trend-setting chefs in Spain. They continue to be a source of inspiration – but being inspired is not the same thing as copying. I have also attended a number of short cooking workshops abroad. For

> **Both my mother and my grandmother had a fantastic sense of taste. Sure, we used to eat traditional things, but it wasn't uncommon to find a tajine on the table every now and then. My passion for a flavour-packed plate is something I got from them.**

example, I did one in London at the time when fusion was just coming into fashion. I never made use of any of the dishes that I learnt to cook there, but I did learn a lot in a short time about certain applications for herbs and species that I had never even heard of before. This kind of workshop deepens your knowledge and confronts you with other thoughts and ideas. It keeps you on your toes as a chef – and that can never be bad. I also like to go abroad occasionally with one or two of my colleagues, so that we can get to know the local cooking of a particular region. I can really enjoy simple country cooking. Farmhouse dishes and stews can tell you a lot about the culinary history of a region and help you to better understand their products. Besides, they are usually delicious and relatively accessible recipes, which you can eat more or less any day of the week."

De Schone van Boskoop
Appelkant 10, 2530 Boechout
03/454 19 31
www.deschonevanboskoop.be

In a nutshell

→ **Who or what influenced your choice of profession?**
My mother and father.

→ **What was your first culinary experience or memory?**
'Le Chêne Madame' in Liege, with my mother and father when I was twelve.

→ **What can really make you mad in the kitchen?**
When previously agreed instructions are not followed.

→ **What is your most important personal quality?**
I do not bear grudges. What's done is done. I don't keep harping on about it.

→ **What would you like to have more time for?**
Life.

→ **What other job would you like to do?**
Butcher.

→ **For you, what is the epitome of luxury?**
When nothing 'must'... and everything 'can'...

→ **What do you most enjoy doing in the kitchen?**
Making delicatessen products, from pâtés to veal brawn.

→ **What is your favourite vegetable?**
White beans.

→ **What is your favourite type or cut of meat?**
The cuts that no one else takes.

→ **What type(s) of fish do you like to work with?**
Flat fish.

→ **What are your preferred herbs for fish and meat dishes?**
Lemon thyme.

→ **What is your favourite dish?**
Calf's liver.

→ **Which small object could you not do without in the kitchen?**
My Windmill knife.

→ **Which chef has inspired you the most?**
Willy Slawinski.

→ **What type of cuisine do you not like?**
Fast-food.

→ **What was the last celebrated restaurant that you visited and what was your opinion?**
'Mugaritz' (in the Spanish Basque country).

→ **What is your worst ever eating experience?**
A restaurant in Middelburg.

→ **Who is your perfect table companion?**
My best friends.

→ **What is your favourite aperitif?**
Champagne.

→ **What do you most enjoy eating on your day off?**
Beef stew and chips.

→ **What are your favourite book and your favourite cooking book?**
At the moment, *Nose to Tail Eating* from the St. John's Restaurant in London.

→ **For whom would you one day like to cook, and why?**
Mick Cave, because his music fascinates me.

→ **Which famous customer would you one day like to welcome, and why?**
Penelope Cruz, because I would love to meet her in the flesh.

→ **Which famous person from the past would you like to have welcomed as a customer?**
Brillat Saverin.

Scallops and king crab with cauliflower and buttermilk

2 dl buttermilk
50 g butter
1 tablespoon old mirin
1 g xantana
1 large cauliflower
salt
120 g crab meat
1 ½ tablespoons mayonnaise
1 teaspoon finely chopped chives
1 teaspoon finely chopped parsley
100 g purslane
0.5 dl chicken stock
1 knob of butter
1 teaspoon pro-cream
8 scallops
oil

› Heat the buttermilk to 80 °C. Mix with the butter, flavour with the mirin and bind with the xantana. Cook half of the cauliflower in salt water until it has softened. Drain and mash with a fork into a puree. Cut the other half cauliflower into rosettes and cook until they are al dente. Grate the stems with a micro-grater to form a crumble. Mix the crab meat with the mayonnaise and the finely chopped herbs. Mix the purslane with the chicken stock and the butter, then bind with the pro-cream. Fry the scallops in oil until the outsides are lightly crisp.

› Arrange a scallop and a quenelle of crab on each plate. Add a quenelle of cauliflower puree and dress with the cauliflower rosettes and crumble. Decorate with drops of the purslane cream and serve with the buttermilk.

Liver, kidney, heart and sweetbreads of young goat with a pickle cream, carrots and legumes

For 4 people

8 goat sweetbreads
1 goat heart
150 g chicken stock
150 g pickles
0.5 dl cream
1 teaspoon gelespessa (Sosa)
pepper and salt
100 g young peas
100 g broad beans
100 g mangetouts (snow peas)
1 knob of butter
1 young artichoke
2 carrots
1 small goat liver, cut into four pieces
4 goat kidneys
butter

› Blanch the sweetbreads briefly in boiling water. Allow them to cool, then peel them. Cut the heart into four pieces. Heat up the stock with the cream and the pickles. Mix the stock thoroughly, bind it with the gelespessa and season with salt and pepper. Blanch the legumes briefly, then cook further in a little butter. Boil the artichoke until it has softened sufficiently and then cut into four. Cook the carrots and cut into small blocks.

› Fry the liver, kidneys and heart in butter until they are 'rosé' (light pink inside). Divide the meat between the plates. Fry the sweetbreads until they are cooked through and add them to the plates. Garnish with the legume vegetables, the artichoke and the carrots. Serve with the pickle cream.

Roasted pig's head

1/2 pig's head
200 g kitchen salt
1 bundle of rosemary, finely chopped
1 tablespoon coarse sea salt
1 tablespoon red wine vinegar
1 dl dark stock
vegetables according to season and preference

› Wash the half pig's head. Cut off the ears and singe away the hair. Put the head in salted water and allow it to pickle for four days. Change the water after two days. After the fourth day, soak the head for a further day in ordinary water to desalinate the meat. Mix the rosemary with the sea salt and smear it over the head. Put the head in a vacuum bag and allow it to marinate in the fridge for two days. Thereafter, cook the head for 16 hours at 78 °C.

› Remove the cooked head from the vacuum bag and collect the juices separately. Brush the head with the wine vinegar and roast in the oven for 1 hour at 180 °C. Add the dark stock to the collected meat juices. Carve the meat off the head and serve with seasonal vegetables of your choice (for example, young turnips, celeriac, broad beans, etc.).

The preparation in 1, 2, 3

Take half a pig's head, cut off the ears and pickle it.

Idem.

Put the head in a vacuum sealed bag, with rosemary and coarse sea salt.

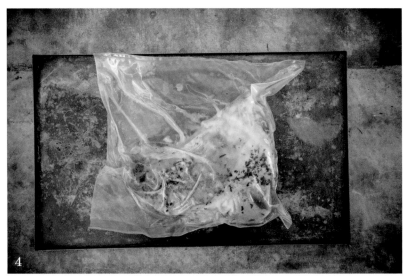

Cook the head for 16 hours at 78 °C.

Roast the head in the oven at 180 °C.

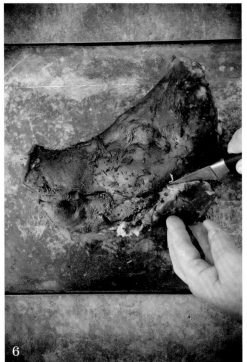

Carve the meat off the head.

Lieven Lootens

ʃ 't Aards Paradijs ᘛ

Lieven Lootens is a self-made cook, who found his dada
in creative vegetable cooking. It won him the title of
'Vegetable Chef of the Year'.

A self-taught cook with ambition

Lieven Lootens never followed cookery school or training of any kind. "I got my passion for gastronomy from my grandmother, who was a gifted cook. She used to cook every day in the castle of the baron, near where we live, and was also asked for all the big events and festivities. My mother inherited her talents, and she passed on an interest in food to me. But I didn't want to be a cook; I found it too limited. I was crazy about biology, chemistry and sport and was planning to study sport and sciences after school. I followed the lessons that interested me with enthusiasm, and for the other subjects I always managed to just scrape through. Until the fifth year. Then I blocked. I had had enough of school and decided to go and work in my parents' restaurant, 'Tony's Grill' on the Korenmarkt in Ghent. I busied myself with the general organisation and it seemed to work well. When I was nineteen I wanted to take over the business. By the time I was twenty, I had a business plan. However, my parents weren't ready to stop, and so suggested as an alternative that we should turn our family home into a restaurant. But I was driven by ambition and by a determination to cook better than they had done, and so I gave them an choice: either I take over the kitchen or I leave. And that's how I started here in 1993. Little by little, I began to cook

with more empathy and gradually refined my dishes. In the meantime, I have also renovated and extended the premises here single-handed. I wanted it to be better and more comfortable. We recently bought the neighbouring house, so that we now have more storage space. If I had followed hotel school, I might have found my own style much quicker and perhaps I might already have had a star. But I now have a popular and respected restaurant without a star – and I am happy enough with that."

I got my passion for gastronomy from my grandmother, who was a gifted cook.

Back to nature

"It is not about prestige or my own ego. I am not actively looking for praise from the cooking guides, although it's a welcome bonus if you get it. I want to gather people around me because of who I am and because they like my food, not because someone wants to push me into a particular box. I have always had this urge to be different, to be as original as possible. I have followed trends, sometimes to almost extreme lengths. During my 'molecular' period I cooked with liquid nitrogen pots in the dining room and used every kind of new technique to try and give my dishes a new twist. This frightened away some customers, but it also won me many new fans. At the beginning of 2010 I decided to throw myself wholeheartedly into vegetable cuisine. After years of high-tech cooking, it was now time to go back to authenticity. Back to nature, you might say. Even so, I look back with pleasure on my 'molecular' phase. It made me technically stronger and also taught me to better appreciate the classic cooking values. These values also suggest possibilities for a new way forward. We are now in a position to combine the new techniques with the traditional flavours of Belgian cooking to create a new and technically advanced Belgian cuisine. This will be our new identity. Our classic Belgian and Flemish cooking is solid, well-seasoned and full of stewed and melted aromas. These are tastes that everyone knows – and this is something we need to hold on to. We can strengthen this identity by using more local products. I try to put an emphasis on home-grown vegetables, such as salsify, parsnip and burdock root, and less common ingredients like icicle radish, rat's tail radish, sorrel root and nasturtium tubers."

A focus on vegetables

This conversion to vegetable cuisine took place following his curing from a form of gout by a diet based on vegetables, nuts and cereals. "It motivated me to put the focus more on vegetables and their possible combinations with meat, fish and poultry. This is more than just a fad or a moment of madness. Ever since I was young, I have been fascinated by nature. I went fruit-picking as a teenager, just so that I could make things with it at home. When I was older, I always used to go for a walk before service, just to see what was growing outside.

In a nutshell

➜ **Who or what influenced your choice of profession?**
The endless creativity that you can use in this profession.

➜ **What was your first culinary experience or memory?**
For every family birthday we used to go and eat on the next Sunday afternoon at the 'Blanke Top' in Cadzand. The magnificent view, the classic cooking and the respect that my grandparents had for the chef made it a wonderful experience, time after time.

➜ **What can really make you mad in the kitchen?**
If products are not treated with the proper respect.

➜ **What would you like to have more time for?**
Sport, singing and travel.

➜ **What other job would you like to do?**
Sculptor.

➜ **For you, what is the epitome of luxury?**
Freedom.

➜ **What are you best at in the kitchen?**
Keeping calm when things get hectic.

➜ **What do you most enjoy doing in the kitchen?**
Inventing new things.

➜ **What do you least enjoy doing in the kitchen?**
Having to repeat myself.

➜ **What is your favourite vegetable?**
Tomato.

➜ **What is your favourite type or cut of meat?**
Red Angus beef from the Meyer Farms (Montana, USA).

➜ **What type(s) of fish do you like to work with?**
Wild sea bass.

➜ **What are your preferred herbs for fish and meat dishes?**
Spanish tarragon.

➜ **What are you favourite aromas and smells in the kitchen?**
Lemon verbena.

➜ **What is your favourite dish?**
Lentil soup.

➜ **Which small object could you not do without in the kitchen?**
A tasting spoon.

➜ **Which chef has inspired you the most?**
Martin Berasategui (Bilbao).

➜ **What type of cuisine do you not like?**
German cuisine.

➜ **Who is your perfect table companion?**
Colleagues.

➜ **What is your favourite aperitif?**
Madeira, old and dry.

➜ **What do you most enjoy eating on your day off?**
Vegetable wok with plenty of spices.

➜ **Which famous customer would you one day like to welcome, and why?**
Prince, because he is slightly bonkers (in a nice kind of way!) and endlessly creative.

➜ **Which famous person from the past would you like to have welcomed as a customer?**
Grace Kelly, because she was refined and had exclusive taste.

Nowadays, I grow my own vegetables and herbs, and have an arrangement with three allotment holders in Merendree, who also grow for me. Wim Maes of Cook&Herb, a professional grower of special vegetables and herbs, is another important supplier. Now, more than ever, is the time to let nature have free rein in our food. This has an inspirational effect. Working with vegetables has given me a new dynamism. They offer so many interesting possibilities. They allow me to play more with flavours and textures: raw, marinated, boiled, fried or roasted. My dishes have even become a little more complex as a result. More adventurous too, but without losing their balance. Taste and temperature continue to be more important than presentation. But I have the feeling that I have gained in authenticity."

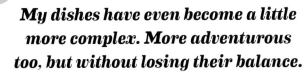

My dishes have even become a little more complex. More adventurous too, but without losing their balance.

Restaurant 't Aards Paradijs.
Merendreedorp 65, 9850 Nevele-Merendree
09/371 57 56
www.aardsparadijs.be

Asparagus trio, with langoustine and basil

1. Langoustine consommé and asparagus foam with a basil variant

For the consommé:
500 g heads and claws of langoustines
5 cl olive oil
10 cl cognac
4 shallots, finely chopped
2 carrots, finely chopped
2 leek whites (no leaf), finely chopped
40 cl white wine

1 l water
1 piece ginger
2 stalks lemon grass
2 g arrowroot
Jamaican pepper, ground
3 g salt
1 g chilli powder

For the asparagus foam:
25 cl reduced asparagus stock
4 asparagus, boiled
10 cl cream
3 g agaragar
1 g guar gum

› Fry the langoustine heads and claws in olive oil and mash them in the pan while they are still cooking. Continue stirring and add the cognac, then the shallot, carrot and leek. Continue to fry on a lower heat, until the mixture glazes. Add the white wine and some cold water, and allow to simmer on a low heat for 1 hour.
› Allow everything to cool, so that impurities can sink. Pass through a fine sieve. Put the resulting fluid in a pan on a low heat and add ginger and lemon grass. Cook gently for a further 15 minutes. Add the arrowroot, dissolved in a small quantity of water. Remove any surface scum with a sieve, check the seasoning and add pepper, salt and chilli powder.
› Prepare an asparagus stock by making an infusion with the asparagus peelings. Allow these to reduce to a quarter, in order to intensify the flavour. Keep in the fridge overnight, so that any bitterness is eliminated. Add the boiled asparagus and mix to a fine consistency. Add the cream, agaragar and guar gum and heat slowly to a temperature of 90 °C. Pour into an aerosol spray and keep warm under pressure until needed for use.
› Fill the glasses with the consommé and finish with the asparagus foam.

2. Tartar of asparagus with a langoustine carpaccio, basil mayonnaise, a crispy herb salad and marshmallows

For the asparagus milk:
peelings of 10 asparagus
30 cl milk

For the sour cream:
juice of 1/2 lemon
20 cl cream
pepper and salt

For the basil mayonnaise:
1 egg yolk
1 tablespoon mustard
10 cl basil oil (blanched basil, blended with olive oil and passed through a sieve)

8 langoustines 12-15 (500 g gross weight)

For the asparagus tartar:
4 asparagus
10 cl asparagus stock
10 cl langoustine stock or shellfish stock

1 g agaragar
1 g iota

For the herb salad:
2 cl raspberry vinaigrette
4 handfuls of micro-leaves or a fine young herb mix

For the marshmallows:
4 slices gelatine
50 g milk

200 g asparagus milk
pepper and salt
freshly ground ginger

› Cook the asparagus peelings slowly in the milk for 3 hours on a low heat.
› Fold the lemon juice into the cream, stir well and season with pepper and salt.
› Beat the egg yolk, mustard and basil oil to create a smooth and creamy mayonnaise.
› Shell the langoustines, roll them in plastic foil or pack them tightly in a square tray with sides and a depth of 7 centimetres. Freeze briefly and then cut crossways into slices of 0.5 centimetres thick.
› Chop the asparagus into a fine brunoise and place them on a tray in a form measuring 7 x 7 centimetres. Mix the langoustine stock and the asparagus stock and add the agaragar and the iota. Pour the fluid over the asparagus tartar and allow to cool.
› Place the langoustine slices on top of the asparagus brunoise.
› Stir the vinaigrette into the micro-leaves or herb mix and spread this herb salad over the tartar.
› Soak the gelatine and heat the milk to 40 °C. Allow the gelatine to dissolve in the fluid and beat into a foam. Constantly check the temperature, which must remain at 40 °C.
› Pour the ice-cold asparagus milk into the foaming fluid and mix continually at high speed for 10 minutes. Spread the mixture open and allow to stiffen. Shape the marshmallows out of the mixture, once it has become hard enough. Place a number of the marshmallows around the herb salad and dress with a few drops of sour cream and basil mayonnaise.

3. Dunes of langoustine flan with fried langoustines and asparagus

For the langoustine flan:
20 small langoustines
15 cl cream, beaten
2 egg whites, beaten
pepper, cayenne pepper and salt

For the asparagus foam:
25 cl asparagus stock
5 g maïzena (thickener)
50 g butter
15 cl whipped cream
2 g sucro

1 bag of fried kroepoek (prawn crackers)
8 large langoustines
olive oil
some lemon basil leaves

› Blend the small langoustines to a fine consistency. Add first the cream, then the egg white and lastly the herbs. Make quenelles from this mixture and steam them for 2 minutes at 90 °C.
› Bind the asparagus stock with the maïzena and a knob of cold butter. Beat in the whipped cream and then mix to a creamy mass with the sucro.
› Pulverise the kroepoek crackers into kroepoek sand in a blender.
› Fry the langoustine tails in olive oil.
› Arrange all the ingredients on a plate and sprinkle the quenelles with the kroepoek sand.
› Finish with the lemon basil leaves.

Blackberry sorbet with a jelly of quince, elder and blackberry, and desegmented blackberries

For the sorbet:
20 cl water
200 g sugar
100 g fresh blackberries

For the quince jelly:
2 quinces

For the elderberry coulis:
25 cl elderberry syrup
50 cl water
6 g iota

For the blackberry ganache:
50 g blackberry coulis, pure and sieved
5 g invert sugar
10 g butter
50 g dark chocolate (Callebaut Madagascar)

For the de-segmented blackberries:
blackberries
1 litre raspberry coulis
6 g iota

sugar leaves (sweetleaves)

› Boil the sugar and the blackberries in the water. Allow to cool. Puree the blackberries in the sugar water and pass through a sieve. Use this mixture to make a sorbet in the ice-cream machine.
› Peel the quinces. Cut them into pieces and allow them to reduce in a little water, until they reach the required thickness and colour.
› Mix the elderberry syrup and the water. Heat this mixture with the iota to 80 °C.
› Heat the blackberry coulis to 50 °C. Melt the butter and the invert sugar in this mixture and pour it over the chocolate. Stir with a spatula and work at temperature between 35 °C and 38 °C. Pour onto a tray and allow to crystallise for at least one night. Form into ganache balls.
› Put some blackberries into liquid nitrogen. Crack them in a tea-towel with a rolling pin, until the small round segments come apart. This same method will also work with deep-frozen blackberries. Make a gel by warming the raspberry coulis with the iota.
› Take round scoops of the blackberry sorbet and insert a blackcurrant ganache ball into each of them. Drop them into the liquid nitrogen. Dip them for 2 seconds in the raspberry gel and roll them immediately in the de-segmented blackberries. Serve these large 'blackberries' in a round dessert dish with a few drops of the different coulis and decorate with the sugar leaves.

Flemish pigeon with Pedro Ximénez, mushrooms, figs and red onion

4 figs
2 punnets of woodland mushroom
(chanterelles and white knight
mushrooms)
400 g butter
juice of 1 lemon
pepper and salt
10 cl Pedro Ximénez sherry (PX)
5 cl argan oil
10 cl date vinegar
2 farm-bred pigeons
5 cl Madeira
30 cl poultry stock from the carcasses
1 red onion

For the mushroom paper:
100 g butter
100 g mushroom puree
100 g egg white
100 g flour

› Cut the figs into slices 1 centimetre thick and place them in a warming cabinet or a pre-heated oven at 60 °C. Fry three-quarters of the mushrooms in a little butter with a few drops of lemon juice and the sherry. Season with salt and pepper.
› Finely chop the mushroom mixture in a blender, and add the butter to create a smooth cream.
› Cut the remaining quarter of the mushrooms into slices and marinate them in a vinaigrette of argan oil and 2 centilitres of date vinegar.
› Cut the legs off the pigeons. Also remove the back and the wings. Keep the front of the carcass with the breast fillets. The back is normally round in shape, so that the pigeon 'rolls' on the cutting board. By removing the back, the carcass can now rest flat. This allows easier cutting and also means that the breast fillets remain in a naturally relaxed position during the cooking process, which is important for the moistness, tenderness and taste of the cooked meat.
› Make a poultry stock from the wings and back, reducing with PX. Thicken with one or two knobs of butter and freshen with the Madeira.
› Make sherry butter by emulsifying 5 centilitres of PX in a warm pan with 200 grams of butter.
› Place the pigeons and the legs in separate vacuum bags. Cook at 55 °C: the legs for 3 hours and the breasts for 1 hour. Remove from the vacuum bags and grill for 1 minute in the Green Egg. Keep them warm in the sherry butter.
› Make mushroom paper by mixing together all the necessary ingredients. Brush the resulting mixture thinly over a sheet of baking paper and bake for 8 minutes at 160 °C.
› Brush the cream onto a plate in the form of a rectangle. Neatly arrange the pigeon fillet and the leg, with the vegetables and the figs around them, and coat with the sauce. Cover the entire composition with the mushroom paper and seal it, like an envelope.

The preparation in 1, 2, 3

> Remove the back and wings of the pigeons. Cut off the legs from the carcass.
> Keep the carcass with the breast fillets still attached.
> Sprinkle the carcasses with herbs such as thyme leaves and flowers, borage flowers and coarse salt. Place a knob of butter on each carcass.
> Place the pigeons in a vacuum bag and seal.
> Cook slowly until tender at 55°C in a roner or bain-marie.

David Martin

♪ La Paix ↘

In many ways, David Martin is a bit of an odd-man-out. This French chef, who was trained in both Paris and Brussels, breathed new life into the almost defunct Brasserie 'La Paix'. Together with his wife and in-laws, he plotted out a new course – but with great feeling and respect for the past – for this famous eating house which first opened its door as long ago as 1892. In the process, Martin created a highly individual culinary dynamic which has given the new 'La Paix' the status and identity of a contemporary icon.

An impressive track-record

Under the careful guidance of David Martin, Brasserie 'La Paix' has become one of the most talked about places to eat in the country. The brasserie – at the slaughterhouse in Anderlecht – had enjoyed a special reputation for many years. It was once one of the capital's most popular eating venues, but was threatening to lose its attractiveness to a modern public. Not that the public was staying away; but it was clear that major investment and new ideas were necessary to keep the business thriving. The time was ripe for a fresh wind in this legendary restaurant run by the Obbiet family – which, with the exception of Fridays, was only open at lunchtime. This fresh wind was to be found in the person of son-in-law David Martin. Martin was already well-known in Brussels for his work at the top restaurant 'Bruneau'. The Frenchman had started his cooking career at the tender age of fifteen and an impressive track-record had already brought him from the Landes to Paris. There he worked under the tutelage of (amongst others) Alain Passard, where he also had Pascal Barbot – who would later become a three-star chef at 'L'Astrance' – under his guidance. While in Paris, Martin also collaborated professionally with another three-star chef in the making: Yannick Alléno, who is currently cementing his impressive reputation at Restaurant 'Le Meurice'. When he was offered the position at 'La Paix', many culinary observers were surprised. Why would a chef with experience of some of Europe's top restaurants want to go and work in a brasserie? "The cuisine at 'La Paix' was one that both appealed to me and challenged me," says David Martin. He immediately saw the potential. With respect for the authentic, pure,

no-nonsense cooking for which 'La Paix' is famous, Martin slowly but surely made the kitchen his own. The clientele were not shocked by the antics of a new chef who was trying to 'prove himself'. On the contrary, Martin made changes one step at a time: a different accent here, a new element there. It was hardly noticeable, but it was effective. The fact that 'La Paix' is essentially known as a meat restaurant was no limitation for the Frenchman. Rather the opposite, in fact. "Right from the very first day I enjoyed working with their traditional meat recipes. And I still do. Why should I want to work with fish? I can express all my culinary ideas and skills just as well with meat dishes." Martin gradually brought a new refinement to these traditional standards, partly by a more careful selection of products and partly through the use of new techniques to supplement the old ones. What remained unchanged was the relatively sober character of the food on the plate. "I am not keen on too many visual embellishments. Why must food always be 'pretty' to look at? In fact, why does everything need to be 'pretty' nowadays? Why must women always try to be thin and beautiful? I have an eye for shape and form, just like any other good chef – but it is content that counts. When aesthetics

> **The cuisine at 'La Paix' was one that both appealed to me and challenged me.**

La Paix
Rue Ropsy-Chaudron 49,
1070 Brussel (Anderlecht)
02/523.09.58
www.lapaix1892.com

become an objective in their own right, so that they are sometimes regarded as being more important than character and flavour, then we are not doing full justice to our profession. Food must never be reduced to just a matter of 'how it looks'. Otherwise our kitchens – like society at large – threaten to become dominated by an increasingly soulless visual ethic."

An emphasis on flavour

While we are talking, David Martin shows us a piece of beautifully marbled beef. With a sense of pride, he allows us to smell the aroma of a well matured entrecôte. He looks for meat with character, such as that provided by the dappled red breed, delivered by master butcher Hendrik Dierendonck from Sint-Idesbald. "By allowing the meat to mature still further once it has arrived in Brussels, it develops a stronger identity. I give it extra flavour on a special Josper grill, fired with Argentinean charcoal and vineyard wood. Then I serve it with just chips and mayonnaise. No unnecessary garnishing. If I added a bit of garnish, most of my customers would just leave it at the side of the plate!" But this desire for simplicity does not mean that Martin has lost sight of the visual aspect altogether. However, decorative elements remain firmly subordinated to the all-important matter of taste. He redefines a classic dish like asparagus with Maltese sauce by deepening the flavour in his own unique way and adding textures which create a different 'feel' in the mouth. "Yes, and in this way the dish also looks better than it used to, simply because of the approach I have employed. My basic idea is to give the dish an extra intensity. If this also makes it more visually attractive, so much the better. But that is just a by-product: it is never an objective in itself. I don't like too much detail in plate presentation. I want real food on my plates. I want my customers to work a little. Meat needs to be cut. I don't like people messing around with my food. I hate specially tuned cars and I hate stylized food. Food dishes should just look ordinary. Pleasing to the eye certainly, but not geometrically proportioned or overloaded with too many different elements, so that the unity of the plate is destroyed."

Tradition and innovation

David Martin wants to be recognised first and foremost as a chef who is in step with the times. "'I live in the here and now. 'La Paix' has a proud and historic past, and this is something that I respect. Its traditions are important, but I also keep a close watch on all the latest culinary developments. If a new technique interests me or if I can see a way to use it to our benefit, I will not hesitate to introduce it – after first testing it thoroughly. I also work with slow cooking at low temperatures and I use modern binding agents to make my cuisine lighter. But I am always on my guard against 'suivisme': the blind copying of someone else's ideas."

➜ **Who or what influenced your choice of profession?**
I made the choice when I was fourteen years old.
My grandfather, who was also a chef, influenced
my decision.

➜ **What can really make you mad in the kitchen?**
When people fail to concentrate properly, so that
the cuisson, slicing, choice of product or seasoning
are not what they should be. These are the
elements which contribute towards the success of
a dish.

➜ **What is your most important personal quality?**
Impulsiveness.

➜ **What would you like to have more time for?**
Music and car racing.

➜ **What other job would you like to do?**
Wine maker, furniture maker, metal worker,
musician.

➜ **For you, what is the epitome of luxury?**
Limitless time to be with my friends.

➜ **What do you most enjoy doing in the kitchen?**
Exchanging ideas with my team about a new dish.

➜ **What is your favourite vegetable?**
Potatoes.

➜ **What is your favourite type or cut of meat?**
Any cut that is well chosen and properly matured
with passion and professionalism.

➜ **What type(s) of fish do you like to work with?**
No doubt about it: fatty fish.

➜ **What are your preferred herbs for fish and meat
dishes?**
A mustard dressing with caramelised bio-lemon –
self-made!

➜ **What is your favourite dish?**
No dish in particular: the company and the
location are more important.

➜ **Which small object could you not do without in the
kitchen?**
My little butter spatula.

➜ **Which chef has inspired you the most?**
Again, no chefs in particular, but several chefs
with a strong personality and identity.

➜ **What type of cuisine do you not like?**
Any cuisine which lacks love, reflection or passion.

➜ **What was the last celebrated restaurant that you
visited and what was your opinion?**
Asador Etxebarri in the Spanish Basque country.
What a revelation and what a mastery of fire and
heat! There, something simple becomes something
complex. You are moved by the magic of the
experience, without the need for artificial aids or
a stunning décor. I will definitely go back again –
even if I have to walk to get there!

➜ **What is your worst ever professional experience?**
When I forgot to put salt in the bread as the pastry-
and-bread chef in a three-star restaurant.

➜ **What is your favourite aperitif?**
Campari.

➜ **What are your favourite book and your favourite
cooking book?**
Cuisine et confidence by Anthony Bourdain: finally
a book by a chef that cuts through the taboos.
Also *Le dictionnaire de la néophysiologie du goût*:
it has been in print for more than 140 years and
describes the origins and taste of every foodstuff
you can think of.

➜ **For whom would you one day like to cook, and why?**
Andy Warhol, in the hope that he might pay for his
bill with a painting!

➜ **Which famous person from the past would you like to
have welcomed as a customer?**
Rene Magritte, to discuss his sources of
inspiration.

Sandwich with butter, cheese and beef ham from the Flemish red-brown breed supplied by the Dierendonck butchers

For 4 people

500 g sourdough bread
1 litre concentrated farmhouse
chicken stock
3 egg yolks
20 cl vegetable stock
150 g salted butter
45 g yellow grain mustard seeds
10 g black grain mustard seeds
30 g sugar
1 bio-lemon
1 paprika
0.5 litre water
Comté cheese, 24 months old
8 slices of beef ham from the Flemish
red-brown breed
horseradish cream
fresh herbs according to preference

› Mix the bread with the chicken stock and spread the resulting mixture on a silicone baking mat. Bake the dough in an oven at 180 °C until it has a light, golden colour. Heat the egg yolks, vegetable stock and the salted butter in the thermomix at 75 °C. Heat the mustard seeds with the sugar, lemon and paprika, until nearly all the moisture has evaporated. Make sandwiches with the thin bread crusts, the butter cream, cheese, beef ham, conserved mustard seeds, horseradish cream and fresh herbs.

Presentation in **1, 2, 3**

› Squirt rosettes of butter cream onto the bread crusts.
› Put another bread crust on top.
› Add cheese, beef ham and conserved mustard seeds.
› Squirt some horse-radish cream onto the sandwich filling.
› Garnish with leaves from the fresh herbs of your choice.
› Finish by placing a final bread crust on top.

1

2

3

4

5

6

Bresse chicken with burnt aubergine and roasted cauliflower

For 4 people

For the chicken:
1 Bresse chicken
1 bio-lemon, cut into large segments
1 bundle sage
50 g Picholine olives
salted butter
some vineyard tendrils

2 aubergines from Sicily
pepper and salt
1 young cauliflower from Brittany
20 fresh laurel leaves
1 paprika
1 fresh bulb of garlic from the Gers
200 g salted butter
1 teaspoon powdered chicken skin
0.5 litre concentrated chicken stock

› Clean out the innards of the chicken and stuff the carcass with the lemon, sage, olives and salted butter. Tie up the legs with string and cook in a cast-iron pot for 40 minutes, with the lid on. During the last 5 minutes of cooking, add the vineyard tendrils to perfume the meat, this time without the lid. Remove from the heat and allow the chicken to rest for 10 minutes.

› Grill the aubergines on charcoal until the leaves turn dark brown. Season with pepper and salt and mix the aubergine to a fine cream. Put the cauliflower in a cooking pot. Prick the surface and insert the laurel leaves. Add the garlic (as a whole bulb?? BG) and the Spanish pepper. Coat with the softened salted butter and sprinkle with the powder of dried chicken skin. Cook for 1 hour at 200 °C.

› Serve the chicken with the aubergine cream and the cooking juices flavoured with the lemon, olives and concentrated chicken stock. Serve the cauliflower separately, as a whole.

Millefeuille of Basque pig's ears, sake and tamarind

For 4 people

8 pig's ears, from a Basque pig
3 litres vegetable stock
0.25 litre old sake
10 cl soya sauce
20 cl mirin
5 g dried tuna
1 g star aniseed
1 g nutmeg
150 g dried tamarind
30 g cacao
5 g pimentón de la Vera (powder of dried paprika)
seasonal vegetables, according to preference
ponzu

› Cook the pig's ears in the vegetable stock with the sake, soya sauce, mirin, tuna, star aniseed and nutmeg for $3\frac{1}{2}$ hours.
› When ready, remove the ears and allow them to drain. Reduce the remaining stock to a quarter. Put the ears on top of each other in a terrine and cover with the reduced stock. Keep for 24 hours in the fridge. Cook the tamarind without seeds, together with the cacao and the dried paprika powder, in 60 centilitres of cooking juices from the ears, until the consistency becomes malleable.
› Remove the ears from the terrine and slice them as finely as possible. Dress the plate with the tamarind.
› Serve with seasonal vegetables - in this case aubergines from Sicily – marinated in ponzu.

Yves Mattagne

↲ Sea Grill ↳

Yves Mattagne learnt his trade at the former Hilton Hotel in Brussels under Michel Theurel, where (amongst others) Michel Addons and Gert-Jan Raven also received their training. The setting of an international hotel as a place of work fascinated him right from his very first day. Perhaps for this reason, he is still active there, but since 2010 he has been working as an independent chef in what has become the Sea Grill Restaurant of the Radisson Blu Royal Hotel. This restaurant, which he single-handedly placed on the culinary map of Belgium, is generally recognised as one of the best places to eat fish in the entire country.

Internationally active

Yves Mattagne has watched the development of Belgian cuisine from a slightly different perspective in comparison with many of his colleagues. International hotels are his chosen working environment. For more than twenty years he has lent his considerable talent and expertise to a prestigious hotel-restaurant project: even today, the Sea Grill is still regarded as one of the capital's most respected eating establishments. Under his impulse, the restaurant was given a new élan in 2010 – the year in which he became its independent chef-owner. He transformed the grillroom, which had previously focused exclusively on the needs of businessmen, by giving it a contemporary fresh, urban-chic interior – and a new lease of life. As in the past, he continues to provide culinary advice for the restaurant activities of the Radisson hotel chain worldwide. And it is in this capacity that Mattagne has acquired vast international experience during the past two decades. The wide range of his experience, both as a restaurant manager and an organiser of events and festivities, means that he has helped to give shape and form to numerous new culinary ventures, both at home and abroad.

The globalisation of cooking

"The cuisine in our country has undergone huge changes in recent years. And I do not just mean through the introduction of new techniques, but also as a result of the availability of new products and flavours that were not previously well-known in this part of the world. Our cuisine – like cuisine everywhere – is being increasingly subjected to the effects of globalisation. Moreover, with the growth of foreign travel, both for business and for pleasure, many of our customers now have a greater experience of international food. They are more open for dishes that they have tried and enjoyed elsewhere. This does not mean that we all need to suddenly start cooking in an exotic manner. Nevertheless, in top gastronomy traditional Belgian cuisine has given way to a style of cooking that is more international both in terms of product and technique. Chefs such as Pierre Wynants or Pierre Romeyer cooked with an obviously Belgian spirit. Just look at the dishes which made them famous: mostly made with local products of the very best quality. True, sometimes with a French influence here or there, but the identity was essentially Belgian. I also prefer to work with local products if I can, but they must be top. Since I took over the Sea Grill, I have had more freedom to choose my own suppliers, which is a big advantage. For example, I have been able to find a supplier of really excellent chip potatoes. But in the final analysis, I am not really all that bothered where they come from. I just want the best potatoes, so that I can make the best chips. And it is the same

People in Belgium still enjoy eating. Without this broad basis of interest, it would not be possible to create a qualitative cuisine with strong support and a strong identity.

with tomatoes, courgettes and so on. My fish and shellfish are mainly delivered from Brittany, because that is the region where I most consistently find the best quality. I think that the average level of cooking and the number of good restaurants has increased considerably during the last twenty years. Top chefs have become more critical, because they are now cooking for a more internationally experienced public that has also become more critical. The chefs are no longer prepared to take risks and so they opt exclusively for products of the best quality. Of course, there is still a trend to work with local products, but this is only because the local suppliers are likewise prepared to make an extra effort to provide the quality required – otherwise they risk losing their best customers. Fortunately, they are better organised than in the past and so their products are now getting the attention they deserve."

Variations on a theme

In addition to international influences, Mattagne sees the more adaptive nature of cooking in our country as an important evolution. And he does not just mean the introduction of new techniques. "You don't need to embrace so-called molecular cuisine to be innovative. You can also innovate from within the framework of a more classical cuisine. In this respect, I am thinking of my variations on the classic Béarnaise sauce, which has given my cooking its own strong definition. By experimenting with variations on familiar themes, you can create a new identity of your own. My oysters with Béarnaise was a success right from the word 'go' and this inspired me work further on the same idea. As a result, I created a Béarnaise derivative with lobster and more recently another with caramelised sweet and sour onions and morel mushrooms. In fact, I now have a total of some fifteen Béarnaise-based sauces. My customers love them and keep on

In a nutshell

→ **Who or what influenced your choice of profession?**
My school holidays in a family hotel on the Belgian coast from my eighth birthday onwards.

→ **What was your first culinary experience or memory?**
During my first years as an assistant-cook at the Hilton Hotel in Brussels I had the opportunity to work at a banquet with Pierre Wynants, Pierre Romeyer and Freddy Vandecasserie, who for me at that time were the cooking 'immortals'. Later, I did another culinary event in the same hotel with Jacques Le Divellec, where I discovered a whole new way of cooking fish.

→ **What can really make you mad in the kitchen?**
When people don't work as a team or when I need to repeat myself.

→ **What is your most important personal quality?**
Uncompromising but friendly.

→ **What would you like to have more time for?**
My children.

→ **What other job would you like to do?**
Interior designer.

→ **For you, what is the epitome of luxury?**
Being happy.

→ **What are you best at in the kitchen?**
Making sauces, forming a team and being open for others.

→ **What do you most enjoy doing in the kitchen?**
Discovering new products, working with them and making new menus.

→ **What is your favourite vegetable?**
Endive and asparagus.

→ **What type(s) of fish do you like to work with?**
Sole and turbot.

→ **Which small object could you not do without in the kitchen?**
A spoon, for both tasting and for dressing plates.

→ **Which chef has inspired you the most?**
Jacques Le Divellec.

→ **Who is your perfect table companion?**
Someone who values food and the work it involves and who is prepared to speak their mind, irrespective of whether their comments are good or bad. All criticism is welcome – as long as it is constructive.

→ **What is your favourite aperitif?**
A good white wine.

→ **What do you most enjoy eating on your day off?**
It depends on the season, but meatloaf cooked to my grandmother's recipe is something that I really love.

→ **What are your favourite book and your favourite cooking book?**
In the past, the books published by Robert Laffont, which contained authentic recipes that were feasible. Those recipes were really focused on taste. Most of today's cook books are more focused on design than on flavour...

coming back for more. And that is why I have no intention of changing my approach. At the end of the day, this is what our profession is all about: cooking for the pleasure of our customers."

A broad and mixed public

While many hotel restaurants find it difficult to attract customers, the Sea Grill has never had this problem. It was a great success right from the very start. But in general, the threshold for eating out in a hotel is still relatively high. It is only in world centres such as London, Paris or New York that this suspicion does not exist. "We began with this same handicap, but I think that the idea of a fish restaurant targeted at businessmen was still the right choice. Fortunately, the quality of our food and the excellence of our table service have also attracted a number of leisure diners. It is this last group in particular that we hope to appeal to with our new interior. Eating out has become much more a form of entertainment than in the past. As a result, we today have a pleasing mix of businessmen staying in the hotel and couples who just come here to spend a quiet evening. The clientele for top gastronomy has become much broader, but the competition has also increased. These are both positive developments for the sector. Fortunately, people in Belgium still enjoy eating. Without this broad basis of interest, it would not be possible to create a qualitative cuisine with strong support and a strong identity. If the government could finally show some

> *The cuisine in our country has undergone huge changes in recent years. And I do not just mean through the introduction of new techniques, but also as a result of the availability of new products and flavours that were not previously well-known.*

understanding for the labour intensive nature of our profession, the sector would be able to grow even more. And this could only be to the benefit to our eating culture and to the country as a whole."

Sea Grill
Rue Fosse Aux Loups 47, 1000 Brussel
02/212 08 00
www.seagrill.be

Langoustine and foie gras with carrot, pimento, mango, passion fruit, caramel, peanut and spring onion

For 4 people

4 large langoustines

For the carrot cream:
500 g young carrots
2 red peppers
10 g ginger
1 splash of olive oil
1 knob of butter
pepper and salt

For the crispy lacquer:
100 g isomalt
1 tablespoon glucose
60 g peanuts, toasted

40 g black and white sesame seeds, toasted
1 tablespoon red wine vinegar
1 pinch of spice powder (cinnamon, star aniseed, black pepper, coriander seed)

For the yuzu-mirin sauce:
30 g ginger
10 g citronella (in stick form)
1 clove garlic
10 cl mirin
10 cl truffle juice
0.5 l brown chicken juice
10 cl light soya sauce
40 g miso
20 g yuzu

For the mango crispies:
200 g mango puree
27 g sugar
33 g isomalt
7 g glucose

4 young onions
butter
2 boksoi
olive oil
2 passion fruit
4 slices foie gras (each of ca. 30 g)
ghoa cress

› Remove the langoustines from their shells and rinse them in ice-cold water.
› Peel the carrots and cut them into small blocks. Wash and de-seed the red peppers and also cut them into small blocks. Put both the carrots and the peppers into a vacuum bag, together with the ginger and the olive oil. Cook in the steam oven for 40 minutes at 92 °C. When ready, mix in a blender, add a knob of butter and season with salt and pepper.
› For the crispy lacquer, melt the isomalt and the glucose in a steel pan. Then add the peanuts and the sesame seeds. Cook until the mixture turns a light, golden brown, and then dilute with the red wine vinegar. Finally, add the spice powder. Pour the mixture out onto a tray covered with grease-free paper and allow to cool and harden. When hard, break into large pieces with the aid of a blunt knife.
› For the yuzu-mirin sauce, heat together the ginger, citronella and garlic on a moderate stove. Dilute with the mirin and the truffle juice. Allow this mixture to reduce by half, then add the chicken juices and the soya sauce. Again, allow to reduce by half, then add the miso. Pass twice through a fine sieve and finally add the yuzu.
› For the mango crispies, put all the ingredients in a thermomix and heat them to 90 °C (on setting 4). Pour the mixture into rough squares on a baking mat and dry them in an oven ('easydry') for 24 hours at 62 °C. When dry, roll the squares around a metal cylinder 1 centimetre in diameter. Do this under the warming bridge, so that the squares remain warm and malleable.
› Cut the young onions into sticks of 3 centimetres and cook in a steel pan with a little butter until soft. Cut the green leaves of the boksoi into a diamond shape and heat these briefly in some olive oil. Spoon the flesh out of the passion fruit and keep separately.
› Colour the langoustines and the foie gras on both sides in a hot pan. Put some carrot puree on the right-hand side of the plate and spread it out across the full width. Put the langoustine and the foie gras on top of the carrot. Spoon some of the passion fruit and lacquer work between the ingredients. Add the spring onions and the boksoi and finish with the mango crispies and the ghoa cress. Serve the sauce separately.

Salmon and oysters with wakame, sake, yuzu, sesame seeds and blue ocean

For 4 people

1 fillet of wild salmon
1 cucumber
2 tablespoons onion, finely chopped
2 tablespoons celery, finely chopped
1 knob of butter
1 dl white wine
8 Venus shells

For the soya meringue:
25 cl soya sauce
25 cl water
120 g desi meringue
25 g ovoneve
80 g squid ink

For the oyster jelly:
8 oysters (e.g. royal oyster 'grand cru')
13 g vegetable gelatine

For the wasabi cream:
15 g cream
2 g wasabi
pepper and salt

For the sake and yuzu vinaigrette:
10 g ginger
1 leaf of bear's garlic, finely chopped
1/2 tablespoon sesame oil
150 g yuzu juice
120 g light soya sauce
120 g mirin, 3 years old
20 g sake
2 g squid ink
70 g tomato water (fine mix a number of tomatoes and allow to drain in a moist cloth)

For the decoration:
black pepper from the mill
white and black sesame seeds, roasted
2 g lemon caviar
12 stalks of crazy pea cress
12 blue ocean flowers
some dried wakame leaves, preserved in water
12 stalks of borage cress
12 gooseberry sea squirts

› Cut the salmon fillet away from the skin. Trim the edges into a neat shape, preserving the heart of the fillet. Cut the fillet into sashimi (thin slices) about 1 centimetre thick. Also cut the cucumber into long, thin slices, using a mandolin. Cut these cucumber slices into rectangles measuring 2 by 15 centimetres and roll them up lengthwise. Fry the onion and the celery in a little butter. Add the white wine, then add the shells as soon as the wine boils. Place the lid on the pot, so that the shells can open.

› For the meringue, mix the soya sauce, water, desi meringue and ovoneve in the kitchen robot. Add the squid ink and mix again. Pour the mixture into a plastic piping bag and pipe small round meringues onto the tray of the drying machine. Allow to dry for 24 hours.

› Remove the oysters from their shells and keep the juice for the jelly. Chop the oysters finely and pass the juice through a fine sieve. If necessary, add a little mineral water to the juice, so that there is 250 millilitres of fluid. Warm some of this fluid to 80 °C, add the gelatine and continue heating until the gelatine is dissolved. Then add the remaining oyster juice and the chopped oysters. Pour this mixture immediately into a rectangular receptacle to a height of 0.5 centimetre. Allow to cool in the fridge.

› Mix the cream with the wasabi and season with salt and pepper. Put the cream into a squeeze bottle.

› For the vinaigrette, cook the ginger and the bear's garlic on a moderate heat in the sesame seed oil, to release the aromas. Remove from the stove and dilute with the yuzu. Add the other ingredients with the exception of the tomato water; this should only be added immediately prior to dressing.

› Arrange the salmon sashimi (six per person) on top of each other on the plate (like roof tiles). Season with black pepper from the mill and some sesame seeds. Cut the oyster jelly into cubes of 0.5 by 0.5 centimetre. Squeeze a few dots of wasabi cream on the plate and dress with a little lemon caviar. Finish with the remaining herbs and the cucumber rolls. Serve the vinaigrette separately.

The preparation in 1, 2, 3

1

Roll up the rectangular strips of cucumber into a tight spiral.

2

Pour the mixture of chopped oysters, oyster juice and gelatine into a receptacle.

3

Cut the salmon fillet into sashimi.

4

Place the sashimi slices and a cube of oyster jelly on the plate.

Add two of the cucumber rolls.

Place some Venus shells on the plate and add dots of the wasabi cream.

Put a wakame leaf neatly on top of the salmon.

Decorate further with the remaining garnish.

Add a piece of soya meringue.

King crab and white Tremelo asparagus with watercress, morel mushrooms, chlorophyll of tarragon and verbena

For 4 people

4 raw king crab claws

4 asparagus from Tremelo (grown in full ground)
butter
salt

For the watercress puree:
2 bundles of watercress
salt
300 g shallot
600 g white wine
600 g cream

For the bear's garlic emulsion:
1 knob of butter
35 g onion, finely chopped
10 g garlic
60 g bear's garlic
1 dl white chicken stock
1 dl cream
25 g butter

For the chlorophyll of tarragon:
1 bundle of tarragon
3 g xantana

8 morel mushrooms
white chicken stock
butter

verbena leaves
affilia cress

› For the king crab 'dome', cut the legs with a bread knife under the first joint, beginning with the thickest part of the leg. Cut open the shell of the two parts and remove the meat. Cut the thickest part lengthwise in two, but not completely. Take a half-round plastic mould with a diameter of 5 centimetres and fill it with the finely chopped crab meat. Wrap the mould in plastic foil and place it in a shrinkable vacuum bag. Immerse the bag in boiling water until it shrinks around the mould and then cool immediately. Cook in the roner for 8 minutes at 80 °C.

› Clean the asparagus and place them in a vacuum bag with some butter and a little salt. Cook in the roner for 35 minutes at 85 °C.

› For the puree, blanch the watercress in boiling salt water and then cool immediately. Mix the watercress with a little water in the blender and pass through a fine sieve. Put the puree into a sieve in which a moist cloth has been placed. Allow the puree to drain, so that it becomes firm. Allow the shallots to reduce with the white wine. Add the cream and reduce further by two-thirds. Pass the resulting mixture through a fine sieve. Warm this shallot cream just before serving and then add the watercress puree, in a ratio of two-thirds puree to one-third cream. Pour or spoon into a squeeze bottle.

› For the bear's garlic emulsion, melt a knob of butter in a steel pan. Add the onions and the garlic and stew them lightly, without allowing them to colour. Add the bear's garlic and cook briefly, so that the aromas are released. Add the chicken stock and allow the mixture to simmer for a further 10 minutes. Then add the cream and simmer for another 10 minutes. Remove from the heat and pass through a fine sieve. Immediately prior to serving, add a knob of butter and mix with a hand mixer to create a foaming mass.

› For the tarragon chlorophyll, extract the sap from the tarragon leaves with a sap centrifuge. Bind the sap with the xantana and put the mixture into a squeeze bottle.

› Cook the morel mushrooms in some light chicken stock that has been thickened with a little butter.

› Place the 'dome' of king crab in the middle of the plate. Cut the asparagus into four equal pieces and arrange them on the plate, two standing and two lying. Put the morel mushrooms to the right of the plate. In between the ingredients, squirt some watercress puree and tarragon chlorophyll. Finish with the verbena and the affilia cress. Serve the emulsion separately.

Bert Meewis

∫ *Slagmolen* ∖

Bert Meewis does not like thinking in boxes. And certainly not where his cooking is concerned. He believes that standard terms such as 'classic' and 'contemporary' are becoming increasingly difficult to define in the culinary world of today. Meewis himself is a case in point. The cuisine at Restaurant 'Slagmolen' can quite easily be associated with the first of these concepts, but he also applies many modern techniques which raise his classically schooled approach to a much higher level of excellence.

Moving with the times

Bert Meewis readily admits it: he was rowing against the tide when he decided to open a restaurant which nowadays is about as classic as they come. The focus is on simplicity. An honest type of cooking which can be enjoyed day after day because of its sheer purity and reliability. A type of cooking that is true to itself and to the customers who eat it. "I started with a very classical basis, but through the years I have gradually evolved towards a more contemporary cuisine. In the past, I would have happily served a slice of foie gras with just some apple and a simple garnish: classic and traditional. It was what my customers wanted. To be honest, I still do much the same thing, but with a more elegant presentation, a lighter sauce and a flavour-enhancing garnish. Being 'classic' is not the same as being 'old-fashioned'. For me, 'classic' means staying as close as possible to the taste and form of the original product and being generous." His dishes have a contemporary complexity of flavours, but without losing their natural accessibility. Meewis wants his customers to be able to recognise what they are eating. The dishes described in the menu must be reflected in what can be seen on the plate. He is not keen on less well-known ingredients or elaborate technical 'special effects'. But this does not mean that he is ignorant of recent developments in the culinary world; on the contrary, he follows these closely. "I still keep my eyes open and my ear to the ground, and I still attend with pleasure the cooking demonstrations given by my colleagues. Just so I know what is happening. How can you have an opinion about something if you have never seen it or don't know what it is? However, I will only use these new concepts if I feel that they can add something to my style of cooking in terms of stronger

and better taste. I am not interested in 'being fashionable'. But this is not to say that I have simply dismissed all the many innovations of recent years. On the contrary, my kitchen has most of the same equipment that you would find is a so-called 'molecular' kitchen. These machines have technically enhanced the range of flavours available to chefs and for this reason have established for themselves a well-deserved place in every chef's arsenal. They also offer a chef a much more extensive range of practical possibilities. The impact of machines such as the roner, thermomix or pacojet is irreversible. But the extent to which you use these machines also influences the nature of your cooking. My dishes have also acquired a greater complexity of flavours. Even so, you need to remember that this not only requires inspiration and material, but also manpower. Fortunately, I have gradually been able to increase the size of my kitchen team. I know it sounds like a cliché, but without a tight and close-knit team around you, it is impossible to grow as a chef. Creating a new dish demands plenty of creative thinking in advance, but you still need enough capable, professional hands in the kitchen to turn your bright ideas into perfectly formed and perfectly flavoured food on a plate. Cooking is still – thankfully – an art."

The 'Scholteshof'

Bert Meewis first learnt this art under kitchen coryphées such as Marc Paesbrugghe ('Sir Anthony Van Dijck'), Ludo Tubée ('Belle Epoque'), Johan Segers ('Restaurant 't Fornuis') and Roger Souvereyns ('Scholteshof'). These chefs taught him that authentic cooking does not tolerate compromise. Something is either tasty or it is not. There is no grey area in between. "I worked for Souvereyns for four years. That was where I learned the most, because he was one of the few people of his generation who had a personal vision of cooking. And to be honest, I still see no true successor to Roger, neither at home or abroad. With his

'Scholteshof' he created a unique total experience. It was a magical place to work, and it is a crying shame that it was never awarded three stars. I think that most of the customers were attracted by that same magic, by the exceptional nature of the hospitality. Stylised, yet homely and familiar. People didn't come to the restaurant just for the food, but also for all the other elements that were created around it. At the present time, Michel Bras in France is the only other chef who comes close to creating this same kind of atmosphere. But Bras is much more cerebral, more zen. He requires his customers to make a spiritual effort to understand everything that he puts before them. As a result, his brand of magic unfolds step by step.

For me, 'classic' means staying as close as possible to the taste and form of the original product and being generous.

With Souvereyns, everything formed part of an integrated whole.
He almost literally grabbed his guests by the throat, with the purpose of stimulating their senses and exciting their emotions. In the
'Scholteshof' I was able to work very closely with the products. I did
a stint in most of the different kitchen posts. For one year I did nothing other than clean the products. But that is the basis of everything
and I learnt a huge amount during those twelve months: filleting fish,
boning meat, opening scallops... This gives you a real feeling for the
products, so that you are better able to understand what they mean,
where their possibilities are to be found and what limits they have."
As with many chefs who learnt their trade in the 'Scholteshof', the
memory of those days is still strong in Bert Meewis. As a restaurant,
the 'Slagmolen' echoes the same sense of unity and refinement. Less
opulent, perhaps, but with the same aim of welcoming visitors in
a pleasant atmosphere in which they will feel comfortable. A typical Limburg feeling? "It is not my intention that my guests should
leave here in a state of near-euphoria. I just want to serve them good,
honest food and make sure that they have a good time. I have about
thirty customers who come every week. For me, this is the best yard-
stick of success and shows that my cooking is still accessible. That
is exactly what I want – and it is only possible by remaining true to
your products."

Slagmolen
Molenweg 177, 3660 Opglabbeek
089/85 48 88
www.slagmolen.be

In a nutshell

→ **Who or what influenced your choice of profession?**
My mother was a good cook, who was always baking cakes. Because academia was not really my thing, the choice of a technical college (the hotel school in Koksijde) seemed a logical one.

→ **What was your first culinary experience or memory?**
My first communion party in Restaurant 'Kristoffel' in Bocholt.

→ **What can really make you mad in the kitchen?**
When someone is disrespectful of quality products or equipment.

→ **What is your most important personal quality?**
Honesty.

→ **What would you like to have more time for?**
For my family and friends.

→ **What other job would you like to do?**
Nothing comes close.

→ **For you, what is the epitome of luxury?**
Being happy and healthy with the people around me who I love.

→ **What do you like to give as a present to your friends?**
A good bottle of wine or champagne.

→ **What do you most enjoy doing in the kitchen?**
Preparing meat.

→ **What is your favourite vegetable?**
Asparagus or endive.

→ **What is your favourite type or cut of meat?**
Calf's kidney.

→ **What type(s) of fish do you like to work with?**
Turbot and sole.

→ **What are your preferred herbs for fish and meat dishes?**
Tarragon.

→ **What is your favourite dish?**
Grilled steak, fresh Béarnaise sauce and hand-cut chips.

→ **Which small object could you not do without in the kitchen?**
A whisk.

→ **Which chef has inspired you the most?**
Joël Robouchon.

→ **What type of cuisine do you not like?**
I can appreciate any type of cuisine, as long as it respects the products, whatever their origin.

→ **What was the last celebrated restaurant that you visited and what was your opinion?**
'Le Pré Catelan' in Paris. A lovely restaurant, with good service and fine food.

→ **Who is your perfect table companion?**
First and foremost, my wife and children. Then my family and friends.

→ **What is your favourite aperitif?**
Champagne or Ops Ale.

→ **What do you most enjoy eating on your day off?**
Spit-roasted chicken, fresh chips, fresh mayonnaise and a green salad.

→ **What are your favourite book and your favourite cooking book?**
I used to regularly consult a book by Eddy Van Maele, but in all honesty I am not a great reader.

→ **For whom would you one day like to cook, and why?**
I would like to cook for my children, their partners and my grandchildren, all seated at a big oval table. At the end of the meal, I hope the littlest one stands up and says: "Grandad, that was fantastic!"

Young Anjou pigeon with a port sauce

2 Anjou pigeons, each weighing
ca. 500 g
4 young carrots
1 green courgette
1 yellow courgette
1 handful of fresh peas
100 g chanterelle mushrooms
1 dl port
3 dl poultry stock
3 dl veal stock
thyme
laurel
1 clove of garlic
butter
potato puree
chopped parsley
pepper and salt

› Cut off the breast fillets and the legs from the pigeon carcass. Cook the breast fillets in a vacuum bag for 20 minutes at 65 °C and the legs for 2 hours at 58 °C in a roner. Allow to cool in ice-water. Clean the vegetables, blanch them briefly and allow to cool. Clean the chanterelle mushrooms and keep them apart. For the sauce, colour the pigeon carcasses in the oven. Add the port and dilute with the poultry consommé and the veal stock. Then add the finely chopped vegetables (mirepoix), together with the thyme, laurel and garlic. Reduce the mixture, pass it through a sieve and thicken with a knob of butter. Make the potato puree, season with salt and pepper and finish with parsley. Sear the pigeon fillets in a hot pan and allow them to rest on the stove for 5 minutes. Heat the vegetables in some butter and fry the chanterelles. Arrange all the ingredients neatly on the plate and serve the sauce separately.

Pyrenean lamb

1/2 'baron' of French milk lamb from
the Pyrenees
8 green asparagus
100 g morel mushrooms
butter
peas
potatoes
0.5 l poultry stock
100 g salted ham
2 dl white wine
mirepoix of vegetables
thyme
laurel
1 clove garlic
3 dl veal stock
3 dl poultry consommé

› Bone the baron (rear end) of lamb and separately cook the saddle, ribs and legs. Roast the saddle for 10 minutes in an oven at 200 °C. Colour the legs in a frying pan and then cook further for 12 minutes in an oven at 200 °C. Likewise colour the ribs in a frying pan, but then allow to rest on the stove. Peel the asparagus and boil until they are al dente. Wash the morel mushrooms carefully under the tap in lukewarm water and fry them in some butter. Make a pea puree. Peel and wash the potatoes and cut into shape. Cook them in a pot with the poultry stock and the salted ham. For the lamb juice, colour the lamb bones in the oven. Dilute with the white wine and add the vegetable mirepoix, thyme, laurel and garlic. Dilute further with the calf stock and the poultry consommé. Allow to reduce to the require thickness and then pass through a sieve. Carefully carve the different cuts of lamb. Arrange the meat neatly on a plate and dress with the morel mushrooms, some asparagus and the pea puree. Finish with the lamb juice.

The preparation in 1, 2, 3

› Place the lamb on the carving board with the stomach cavity underneath.
› Cut away the saddle and the legs from the rib cage.
› Cut the rib cage in two.
› Cut the meat away from the ribs.
› Separate the legs from each other.
› Remove the meat from the hind leg.
› Tie the loose-cut meat from the hind leg in a net.
› Cook the meat from the saddle, ribs and legs in a pan.

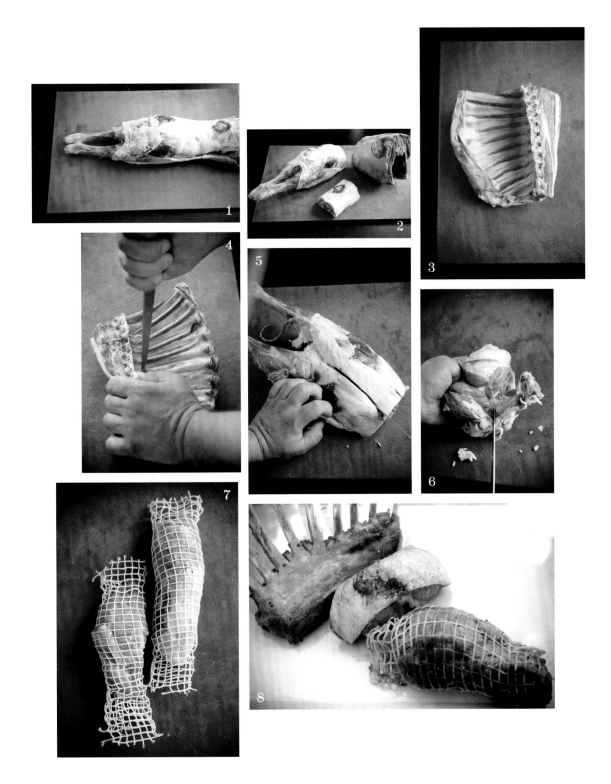

Dame blanche (White Lady)

1 l cream, 35 % fat
2 litres cream milk
6 vanilla sticks
24 egg yolks
600 g sugar

For the sauce:
25 cl milk
50 g callets (round pellets) of pure
chocolate (Callebaut 811)

For the decoration:
0.5 l cream
40 g fine sugar
some biscuits

› Allow the milk and the cream to reduce with the split vanilla sticks, from which the marrow has been removed. Beat the egg yolks with the fine sugar and the vanilla marrow until it results in a light white mass (ruban). Stir the milk-cream mixture into the ruban and allow this to heat through (without boiling) until it forms a thin custard (crème anglaise). Allow to stand overnight, so that the vanilla flavour can be fully absorbed.
› Heat the milk for the chocolate sauce. Add the callets when the milk boils and stir until the mixture begins to glisten.
› Half whip the cream with the fine sugar.
› Make the ice-cream with the crème anglaise mixture in the ice-cream machine and serve with the half-whipped cream, chocolate sauce and some suitable biscuits.

Lionel Rigolet

♪ *Comme Chez Soi* ♪

Lionel Rigolet is continuing the culture of gastronomic excellence associated with this most mythical of all Belgian restaurants. Since he took over the running, more and more younger people are finding a way to his door.

Love at first sight – with culinary consequences

Love can sometimes have far reaching consequences. Just ask Lionel Rigolet! In the hotel school in Namur he fell head over heels for Laurence Wynants, the daughter of Pierre Wynants. The feeling was mutual – and so began what would become an intense career together. When Lionel started looking for a job, Pierre Wynants suggested that he should come and work for him. He did, for a year and a half, and then went off to do his national service. He followed this up with training periods at the restaurants of a number of leading French chefs: Robuchon, Haeberlin, Girardet and Lenôtre. "I returned to 'Comme Chez Soi' just two days before my wedding," grins Lionel. "I first did a stint in all the different kitchen posts and then I began cooking at the side of my father-in-law. He told me all his secrets and taught me everything he knew. He regarded me as the son he had never had. If he talks about Laurence and me, he always refers to us as 'the children'. Of course, it has not always been easy. My father-in-law is very fixed in his ways and there were occasional disagreements, but I seized the chance that he offered me. At first, I simply copied his dishes. Little by little, I added ideas of my own. We would give a recipe a new twist or change the presentation slightly. We also built a brand new kitchen, an investment of a million euros."

Changing the guard

"At this point, my father-in-law thought that the time was right to step back out of the limelight and hand over the torch to me. I became head chef at 'Comme Chez Soi', although we continued to run the business together. Michelin saw this 'changing of the guard' as a reason to take away our third star, which we had had for the past twenty-seven years. For my father-in-law, this was a disaster. He was wounded and hurt. He had pictured the end of his career very differently. He had prepared the handover in great detail. I only took things over step by step. He advised me constantly. But to lose a star? No, that was something we had not expected. We were not happy with the decision, but there was nothing we could do about it. We just had to look forward and carry on. Since 2009 my father-in-law has also withdrawn from the running of the business side of things. Laurence and I are now responsible for everything and we have made a number of changes. For example, we now work more à la carte. This requires a different approach in the kitchen. To make this possible, we ask our guests to be patient during the longer preparation time that is necessary for the more complex dishes. This is not usually a problem. We have also reduced the number of couverts per service. From seventy to forty-five. I want to receive and serve my customers in the best possible circumstances. The reservation desk needs my permission if they want to accept more than forty couverts for a service. The regular rotation of dishes has been maintained. We change them four times a year, and the suggestions card is amended to reflect seasonal products. You can still find my

father-in-law's classics, such as sole with Riesling, sole 'Cardinal', fillet of beef with truffle, and his famous ham mousse. These are noted on the card as 'les incontournables' (literally meaning 'cannot be ignored'). All the other dishes are my own. I am not a modern chef, but nor am I a classical one. I look for a symbiosis between both schools of cooking. My recipes do not represent a radical break in style. I respect and maintain the traditions of our restaurant. I always take the flavour of the products and their cooking time as my starting points, to create a perfect marriage between taste, texture and structure. Of course I use some of the new techniques, but I would never risk switching fully to a high-tech, molecular cuisine. I will only apply new methods if they are appropriate to the personality of my own cuisine. I always assume that people will want to try out the dishes that they eat in a restaurant at home. I am not saying that my dishes are simple; the garnishing, for example, is very labour intensive. Even so, my dishes remain accessible and are based on tastes and products that can be recreated in any domestic kitchen. It is my task to perpetuate a gastronomic culture, the culture of 'Comme Chez Soi'. The new approach is certainly popular with the customers. Our turnover has increased and the average age of our customers has fallen. Young people used to think that our restaurant was stuffy and old-fashioned, but now we are sexy again! We notice that many youngsters – I am talking about people of fifteen to twenty years of age – want to come and celebrate their birthday here

> **I always take the flavour of the products and their cooking time as my starting points, to create a perfect marriage between taste, texture and structure.**

In a nutshell

➜ **Who or what influenced your choice of profession?**
My uncle, who was a traiteur cook. I used to help him during the summer holidays, when I was fifteen.

➜ **What can really make you mad in the kitchen?**
A lack of respect for ingredients. Or if food is wasted.

➜ **What is your most important personal quality?**
Perfectionism.

➜ **What would you like to have more time for?**
Sport.

➜ **What are you best at in the kitchen?**
Precision.

➜ **What do you most enjoy doing in the kitchen?**
Developing new dishes.

➜ **What is your favourite vegetable?**
Mushrooms and asparagus.

➜ **What is your favourite type or cut of meat?**
Entrecôte.

➜ **What type(s) of fish do you like to work with?**
Flat fish.

➜ **What are your preferred herbs for fish and meat dishes?**
For fish: different types of curry; for meat: Provence herbs

➜ **Which small object could you not do without in the kitchen?**
My weighing scales.

➜ **What is your worst ever professional experience?**
The loss of our third star.

➜ **Who is your perfect table companion?**
Customers and friends who share our passion for food.

➜ **What is your favourite aperitif?**
A glass of white wine.

➜ **What do you most enjoy eating on your day off?**
Simple things: penne all'arrabbiata, spit-roasted chicken, fried entrecôte with a salad.

with their parents. We also have customers who now come and eat weekly, because the range of dishes is more extensive. Similarly, we have a growing number of 'expert' diners, gastronomes who like to visit all the great houses – and that is always a nice compliment. And this before we even mention our many foreign visitors. We are still one of the most mythical places to eat in Brussels."

Refined, product-oriented and dynamic

In his own style, Lionel Rigolet is continuing the gastronomic culture he inherited from Pierre Wynants. And just like his father-in-law, he is a staunch defender of high-quality Belgian cuisine. "In Belgium we have very many young chefs who stand out above the crowd. If you compare them with what the French chefs of their generation are doing and how they are rated in the various restaurant guides, it is clear that their work is seriously undervalued. We have a very refined, product-oriented cuisine in this country. We can create an even stronger identity by working further around our own, home-grown products. The new generation of Belgian chefs understands this. Their focus on products is refreshing and has created a new dynamic. Rather than going abroad to train, I would recommend young cooks to start their careers in Belgium. We have enough interesting chefs of our own, each with an individual style. They are perfectly capable of training up our next crop of culinary super-stars. We are every bit as good as other countries: it is just that we are too modest to shout about it."

" *We can create an even stronger identity by working further around our own, home-grown products. The new generation of Belgian chefs understands this.* **"**

Comme Chez Soi
Place Rouppe 23, 1000 Bruxelles
02/512 29 21
www.commechezsoi.be

Fried Norwegian lobster with Ghent mustard and tarragon, a jam of sea urchin caviar and black rice with ginger

2 Norwegian lobster, whole, each
weighing 600 g
olive oil

For the rice mixture:
100 g black rice
2 cl olive oil
30 g shallot, finely chopped
8 g garlic, finely chopped
8 g fresh ginger, in a fine brunoise

1 dl dry white wine
3 dl poultry stock

For the shiitake mixture:
20 g shallot, finely chopped
15 g butter
100 g shiitakes, in a brunoise
40 g conserved tomatoes, in a brunoise
2 g grated lemon flakes, finely chopped
3 g tarragon leaves, finely chopped
2 g red chili peppers

For the sauce:
300 g lobster heads, finely mashed
2 cl olive oil
75 g shallot, finely chopped
15 g garlic, finely chopped
35 g fresh ginger, finely chopped

45 g Ghent mustard mixture
30 g currant jelly
9 cl dry white wine
3 dl poultry stock
80 g cream

For the sea urchin jam:
25 g sea urchin caviar
1 cl tomato juice
1 g xantana
lemon juice

› Blanch the lobsters for 2 minutes in well-seasoned water. Remove the tails and the heads. Allow to cool. Blanch the claws for a further 2 minutes. When everything has cooled, remove the outer shells. Keep the lobster heads to make the sauce.

› Cut the tails in two lengthwise and remove the intestinal tube. Season the meat from the tail and claws immediately prior to serving. Heat a little olive oil in a pan and fry on both sides. Do not overcook: the meat must still be moist.

› Blanch the rice four or five times, so that it deepens to an intense black colour. Allow it to drain and cool after each blanching. Heat some olive oil in pot and fry the shallot, garlic and ginger. Add the rice and allow to cook until nearly dry. Dilute with the white wine and poultry stock. Add seasoning as required and allow to simmer until the rice is done. Drain off the fluid and re-check the seasoning. Stir in any leavings from the carving of the lobster meat.

› Stew the shallots in a little melted butter, add the shiitakes, season as appropriate and fry at high temperature, but without colouring. Remove the pan from the heat, add the conserved tomatoes, grated lemon flakes, tarragon and chili pepper. Re-check the seasoning and stir well.

› Fry the mashed lobster heads in olive oil, but do not colour them excessively. Add the shallot, garlic and ginger. Cook through. Add the mustard and the currant jelly and dilute with the white wine and poultry stock. Cook for a further 45 minutes on a low heat. Pass all the ingredients through a sieve and press firmly. Put the resulting sauce back in a pot, add the cream and bring to the boil. Allow the mixture to reduce slightly, add seasoning as appropriate and keep warm.

› Mix the sea urchin caviar, the tomato juice and the xantana in a thermomix. Pass the resulting mixture through a fine sieve, add seasoning and a little lemon juice. Pour the mixture into a piping bag.

› Blanch the tarragon and the parsley for the herb oil. Shock the herbs in ice-cold water and press out any excess water. Mix the herbs in a thermomix with the olive oil with lemon. Season as required and pass through a fine sieve.

› Cut the Clearwater lobster into fine slices. Place on rectangular pieces of sulphurised paper, add seasoning, sprinkle with olive oil and cook them lightly in a salamander or under a grill.

› Draw a line of herb oil across the plate and place the slices of

Clearwater lobster on top of it. Garnish with a few drops of the sea urchin jam.

› Put a few more drops of the sea urchin jam between two slices of the tomato water jelly and decorate with a dried tarragon leaf.

› Fill a number of cylinders with the shiitake mixture, place a slice of tomato jelly on top, add a few drops of sea urchin jam and decorate with a flower.

› Fill a kitchen ring with the rice mixture. Place a lobster tail on top. Spoon on some of the mustard sauce and decorate with a piece of lobster claw.

For the herb oil:
6 g tarragon leaves
20 g parsley
40 g olive oil with lemon

100 g Clearwater lobster
olive oil
tomato water jelly
tarragon leaves, dried
flowers
salt and pepper from the mill

The preparation in **1, 2, 3**

Cut the lobster tails in two

and remove the intestinal tract.

Fry the mashed lobster heads in oil,

add the shallot, garlic and ginger, then the mustard and currant jelly,

and dilute with the white wine and poultry stock. Cook for 45 minutes on a low heat.

Pass all the ingredients for the sauce through a sieve and press firmly.

Blanch the rice four or five times, so that it deepens to an intense black colour.

Add the conserved tomatoes, grated lemon flakes, tarragon and chili pepper to the cooked shiitake brunoise.

Put a few drops of the sea urchin jam between two slices of the tomato water jelly and decorate with a dried tarragon leaf.

Fill a number of cylinders with the shiitake mixture,

and place a slice of tomato jelly on top.

Fill a kitchen ring with the rice mixture.

Dress with a lobster tail,

some of the mustard sauce and a piece of lobster claw.

Fine bouillon of shellfish, Gillardeau oysters and fried gurnard with salicornia

400 g gurnard fillets, without bones
salt and pepper
olive oil

For the infusion:
1.5 l water
300 g shrimp shells
25 g fresh ginger, finely chopped
50 g shallots, finely chopped
15 g garlic, finely chopped

For the consommé:
1 l of the infusion
20 g lemon verbena
10 g fresh ginger
3 g lime leaf

1 g talauma (Vietnamese spice; juniper berry is an alternative)
5 g grated lemon flakes

For the vegetable mixture:
20 g leek white, in a fine brunoise
30 g cucumber, in a fine brunoise
15 g shallot, finely chopped
15 g blanching celery, in a fine brunoise
3 g red Spanish peppers, in a fine brunoise
5 g garlic, in a fine brunoise
40 g whelks, cooked and finely chopped
35 g carrots, blanched and finely chopped
40 g Gillardeau oysters, finely chopped
salt and pepper

0.5 cl cabernet-sauvignon vinegar
2 cl olive oil
1 cl lemon juice

8 slices of cucumber
Isigny cream
8 salmon eggs
8 leaves sweet cicely
60 g salicornia, very lightly blanched
8 razor clams, cooked and cleaned
4 flowers from the oyster plant (blue ocean)
8 fine slices red Spanish pepper, deseeded
pea puree
8 cockles, cooked and cleaned

› Season the fillets of gurnard with salt and pepper and fry them briefly in a non-stick pan with a little olive oil. Fry the skin side first, then the other side. The meat must remain moist.
› Put the water, shrimp shells, ginger, shallot and garlic into a pot, stir well and bring to the boil. Allow the mixture to 'brew' for 30 minutes and then pass the infusion through a sieve.
› Pour the infusion into a pot and bring to the boil. Add the lemon verbena, ginger, lime leaf and talauma. Reduce the heat and allow to boil gently. Stir well with a whisk. Simmer for 30 minutes and then pour into a filter cloth. Add the grated lemon flakes to the resulting fluid, season as required and allow to cool.
› Mix together the leek, cucumber, shallot, blanching celery, Spanish pepper, garlic, whelks, carrot and oysters in a pot. Season with salt and pepper, and add the vinegar, olive oil and lemon juice. Stir thoroughly. Re-check the seasoning. Allow to drain, then divide the mixture between a number of kitchen rings. Press firmly into place.
› Cut the cucumber in fine slices, season them and roll them up. Add a little seasoned Isigny cream and decorate with a salmon egg and a sweet cicely leaf
› Place the vegetable mixture in the centre of the plate and remove the kitchen ring. Add the salicornia, then the gurnard, then the razor clams. Decorate with a blue oyster flower. Position two cucumber rolls at two corners of the plate. Place two slices of Spanish pepper in the other corners. Add a little pea puree and dress with a cockle that has been lightly warmed in the consommé. Serve the consommé separately.

Carpaccio of Basque veal, veal brawn and veal cheeks with piccalilli and smoked herrings' eggs

400 g rib of calf from the Basque region, cleaned thoroughly

For the vinaigrette:
25 g egg yolks
20 g whole egg
10 g Ghent mustard
0.5 cl lemon juice
25 g anchovy juice (garum)
10 cl arachide oil
1.5 cl water
salt and pepper

For the pickle jelly (piccalilli):
4 cl cleared vegetable stock

40 g pickles (Comme Chez Soi)
1.6 g agaragar

For the jellied calf's brawn and calf's cheek:
15 g shallot, finely chopped
1 g garlic, finely chopped
olive oil
10 g Bellota ham, in brunoise
10 g raw ham, in brunoise
1 g lemon thyme
25 g cooked calf's brawn, in brunoise
25 g cooked calf's cheek, (18 hours at 75 °C)
10 g conserved tomatoes, in brunoise

2 cl dry white wine
6 cl poultry stock
0.6 g agaragar
1.3 g basil, in brunoise

fleur de sel
Pondicherry pepper
30 g smoked herrings' eggs
20 g French beans, blanched and cut into pieces
25 g artichoke, cooked and cut into batons
16 purslane leaves
40 g Bellota ham, shaped into little rosettes
8 puff pastry triangles

› Wrap the rib of veal in plastic foil and allow to stiffen in the freezer. When sufficiently hard, cut thin slices of 0.5 centimetre thickness with a slicing machine. Put the slices on a rectangle of sulphurised paper measuring 9 by 14 centimetres. Cover with plastic foil and place in the fridge.
› Pour the egg yolks, whole egg, mustard, lemon juice, anchovy juice, arachide oil, water, salt and pepper into a mixer bowl. Mix with a hand mixer until a creamy vinaigrette results. Season as appropriate and put away in the fridge.
› Pour the clear vegetable stock and the pickles into a blender and blend as finely as possible. Pass the mixture through a fine sieve and into a pot. Season as required, add the agaragar and bring to the boil. Boil for 1 minute and then pour the mixture onto a tray to a depth of 0.5 centimetre. Allow to stiffen in the fridge and then cut out rectangles measuring 2 by 6 centimetres.
› Stew the shallots and the garlic in a little olive oil. Add the two sorts of ham, the lemon thyme, the conserved tomatoes and the calf's brawn and cheeks. Stir well and cook for 2 minutes. Dilute with a little white wine and allow the mixture to reduce slightly. Add the poultry stock and the agaragar, season as required, and bring to the boil for 1 minute. Finally, add the basil. Pour onto a tray to a depth of 2 centimetres. Make the surface even and allow to cool in the fridge. When firm, cut out rectangles measuring 2 by 6 centimetres.
› Sprinkle both sides of the veal carpaccio with the anchovy vinaigrette. Arrange the slices neatly on the plate and sprinkle with fleur de sel and freshly-ground Pondicherry pepper. Garnish with smoked herrings' eggs, French beans and the artichoke batons. Place the calf's brawn in the centre of the composition and add a slice of piccalilli jelly. Decorate with the purslane leaves, Bellota ham rosettes and the puff pastry triangles.

Johan Segers

∬ 't Fornuis ⨑

Johan Segers opened his restaurant ''t Fornuis' in 1977. Prior to this, he had gained experience in the famous eating houses of the day in Antwerp, such as 'Vatelli', 'Cicogne d'Alsace', 'Criterium' and 'Jacob Van Galicië'. With the keys to ''t Fornuis' already in his pocket, he completed his culinary education with some further months of training at two French three-star restaurants, run by the brothers Troisgros and Jean-Michel Lorraine.

Fixed menu versus à la carte

"In the hotel school and the restaurants where I worked, French cuisine was held in high esteem. As young cooks, we had it drilled into us that we had to go to France if we wanted to learn all the skills of our trade. This was something of a disappointing experience for me. One of the plus points of French cuisine is its strong regional awareness and its preference for local products. However, at the Troisgrois, for example, very little was served à la carte. Ninety percent of their business was based on fixed menus. This meant very repetitive cooking for the kitchen staff. In addition, many of the ingredients were prepared in advance or even partially warmed beforehand. From an organisational perspective, everything was perfect, but also very French – in other words, with plenty of song and dance. The Antwerp restaurants were mainly à la carte, but this meant that the order slips were sometimes as big as a newspaper! Apart from a love of quality products, I learnt very little in France."

Different from all the rest

Right from the very beginning in 1977, Johan Segers embraced the new wave of nouvelle cuisine that was then sweeping across the world of gastronomy. "I wanted to be different from all the other restaurants in Antwerp. 'De Perouse' (the Flandria boat restaurant that had two Michelin stars at that time) had been serving excellent smoked salmon for decades. So I decided to serve marinated salmon. They had served gratinated scallops in their shell since time immemorial. I served them raw with three peppers. Nouvelle cuisine made it possible to combine fish with vegetables, something that

was very much taboo in the classical tradition. In the old days, langoustines were cooked through and through. I served them half cooked or raw in a tartar. Whereas most restaurants dressed the plates at table – even if this involved carving a whole pheasant in the dining area – I served my meals ready dressed from the kitchen. To my way of thinking, these were all obvious improvements. If you are forced to cook your pheasant whole – because your guests need to see it – the legs will be perfect but the breast will be dry and overdone. By splitting the two and plating them in the kitchen you can ensure that each part of the meat is properly cooked. And while the older generation of chefs used to like to hide behind their stoves, from day one I insisted on taking the orders myself. This all sounds self-evident nowadays, but it was very innovative at the time. Of course, I had to make some adjustments later. As a new boy, I wanted to make an impression but I took some things a bit too far. However, I soon found the best way to make a synthesis between classic and modern. And that is the way that I am still following, individualist that I am! I am happy that I have never given myself over to fads and fashions. Likewise, I have never listened to the predictions and preachings of guides such as Michelin and GaultMillau. I may have played along with them here and there, but without ever compromising my own values. And if you lose a star along the way? So be it. I like to win – but I am also a good loser."

The French are always saying that they have the best food products in the world. We have them, as well – so let's not be too modest about it! Put them on a pedestal.

No ordinary ingredients

For the menus in this book, Johan Segers has opted for ingredients that are less in vogue. "Such as garpike, a fish that swims along our coasts from the end of spring until the beginning of summer, and May cabbage, the sweet young leaves of the common cabbage. But I have also gone for 'waste' products – products that I have always worked with – such as calf's brain, calf's tongue, chicken stomachs and chicken livers. One of the very first dishes on my menu back in 1977 was pig's bladder filled with braised lamb's kidneys and lime leaves. Pork is another favourite of mine. A pig is one of the nicest and tastiest creatures there is! But where can you still find good pork? Nowadays, it make little difference whether a farmer gives his pigs space and feeds them well or pens them in boxes and force feeds them with concentrates: at the end of the day, he is still paid next to nothing for his product. And the same is true of good beef or flavoursome poultry. The better you care for your animals, the better the quality of the meat will be. Everyone is always talking about foodpairing. Well, for me foodpairing is a fish swimming around the sea with its mouth open or a cow being fed what it really needs. But the farmers are not prepared to listen to arguments of this kind. They have got it into their heads that it no longer makes any difference how they treat their animals. I was recently in the quayside fish market at Nieuwpoort and it struck me that only older people work there. The youngsters are not interested in the job anymore, because it simply doesn't pay enough. And this while the North Sea is still packed with so many excellent varieties of fish, such as turbot, cod and monkfish, but also plaice, whiting, megrim and our very own grey shrimps. It saddens me to see our fishmongers selling tilapia and Nile bass at almost give-away prices, while fish from our home waters is being destroyed on the quayside because no one is prepared to buy it. To my way of thinking, this is a crime: destroying good food can never be right. Of course, it is positive that the world of cooking continues to evolve, but it is a pity that we so often look abroad for new products and ideas, rather than focusing on the riches that we already have at home. We lack pride. For this reason, I hope that we will soon rediscover our regional awareness. We need to pump new life into our traditions. Not for conservative reasons, but to encourage creative renewal. The French are always saying that they have the best food products in the world. We have them, as well – so let's not be too modest about it! Put them on a pedestal!"

't Fornuis
Reyndersstraat 24, 2000 Antwerpen
03/233.62.70

In a nutshell

→ **What was your first culinary experience or memory?**
My communion parties during my childhood.

→ **What can really make you mad in the kitchen?**
If food is wasted.

→ **What would you like to have more time for?**
More contact with producers.

→ **What other job would you like to do?**
Sculptor.

→ **For you, what is the epitome of luxury?**
Being completely self-sufficient.

→ **What are you best at in the kitchen?**
Cleaning.

→ **What do you most enjoy doing in the kitchen?**
Boning.

→ **What do you least enjoy doing in the kitchen?**
I enjoy doing everything.

→ **What is your favourite vegetable?**
Potatoes.

→ **What is your favourite type or cut of meat?**
Calf's brains.

→ **What type(s) of fish do you like to work with?**
Herring.

→ **What are your preferred herbs for fish and meat dishes?**
Pepper.

→ **What are you favourite aromas and smells in the kitchen?**
Oven-fresh bread.

→ **What is your favourite dish?**
Casseroles.

→ **Which small object could you not do without in the kitchen?**
A Windmill knife.

→ **What is your favourite aperitif?**
A good glass of beer.

→ **What do you most enjoy eating on your day off?**
Sandwiches.

→ **What are your favourite book and your favourite cooking book?**
Het Parfum by Süskind and *Larousse Gastronomique*.

Fried garpike with May cabbage

120 g May cabbage (= ca. 200 g
boiled cabbage)
salt
800 g garpike
pepper
flour
2 tablespoons butter (to fry the fish)
5 tablespoons cream
2 egg yolks
1 tablespoon mustard
2 tablespoons whipped cream
butter
nutmeg

› Cut the cabbage into strips and blanch in boiling salted water. Wait until the cabbage is al dente. Drain and then cool in cold water.

› Remove the fins from the garpike and wash the blood out of the belly. Cut the fish into pieces, each about 10 cm long. Dry the pieces and season with salt and pepper. Dip them in the flour and fry briefly on both sides in a little butter. Remove the pan from the heat and allow to cool. Remove all the bright green bones from the fish pieces.

› For the glazing sauce, heat the cream until it reduces by three-quarters. Remove the pan from the heat and add the egg yolks to the cream as binding. Add the mustard and season with pepper and salt. Fold in the whipped cream. Pass the sauce through a fine sieve.

› Stew the May cabbage in a little butter and season with pepper, salt and nutmeg. Keep some of the cabbage apart and deep fry this briefly in hot chip oil.

› Spoon the sauce onto a plate, according to your preference. Put the plate under a hot grill, until the sauce turns golden brown. Arrange the May cabbage in the middle of the plate and place the garpike fillets on top. Decorate with the deep-fried cabbage strips.

Fresh pasta with chanterelle mushrooms, chicken liver, stomach and heart, and fresh morel mushrooms

4 chanterelle mushrooms
4 conserved chicken stomachs
12 conserved chicken hearts
coarse sea salt
3 sprigs thyme
3 laurel leaves
1 tin of goose fat (1 litre)
salt
1 bouquet garni (bouquet of thyme, laurel and parsley)
200 g fresh pasta
breadcrumbs
chip fat
8 tablespoons chicken stock
1 knob butter
pepper
120 g fresh morel mushroom
4 chicken livers

› Rinse the chanterelles, chicken stomachs and chicken hearts in water and remove all blood and any other impurities.
› First conserve the stomachs and hearts. Dry them and work them thoroughly in a mixture of coarse sea salt, thyme and laurel. Allow to stand for 12 hours in the fridge. Remove from the fridge and rise in cold running water, to remove all vestiges of the salt.
› Cook the stomachs and hearts gently in the goose fat (with an added splash of water) on a low heat for 3-4 hours.
› Bring the chanterelles to the boil in salted water. Remove the scum and add the bouquet of herbs. Allow to cook further on a low heat for 2 hours. When the chanterelles are cooked through, remove the outer membrane by rubbing gently.
› Boil the pasta in salted water until al dente.
› Cover the chanterelles in breadcrumbs and deep fry them in hot chip oil.
› Slice the conserved stomachs and hearts. Add a little chicken stock and a knob of butter, and season with pepper (but not with salt!). Clean the morel mushrooms and add them to the mixture. Bring to the boil for just a few moments, flavour as appropriate and then stir into the cooked pasta.
› Fry the chicken livers at the last minute.
› Fold them into the pasta and add some of the crisp-fried chanterelles.

Calf's tongue with a brain sauce

1 calf's tongue
1 calf's brain
salt
2 bouquets marmite (a vegetable
bundle consisting of tied leek, celery,
carrot, laurel, thyme onion and juniper
berries)
black peppercorns
vinegar
pepper
1 shallot
3 tablespoons mayonnaise
1 dl cream
sea salt

4 gherkins
16 fine leaves curly lettuce
black salt

› Immerse the tongue and the brains oversight in salt water to remove any impurities. Remove and rinse.
› Bring the calf's tongue to the boil in a new pan of salted water. When the water boils, remove the tongue and rinse it. Set it back in the water, and add the bouquet marmite, salt and a few peppercorns. Allow to cook gently for 3 hours on a low heat. Allow to cool at room temperature and remove the skin and any bones from the tongue.
› Remove the membrane from the brains by rinsing them under running water. Fill a pot with water and add the second bouquet marmite. Allow to simmer for 30 minutes on a low heat. Remove the vegetables and add a good splash of vinegar. Season with salt and pepper. Now add the brains, bring to the boil and then remove the pot from the stove. Let the brains cool in the stock until it is completely cold.
› Finely chop the shallot and stir it into the cream and the mayonnaise. Add this to cold brains, which have been lightly mashed with a fork, together with a little sea salt. Flavour with a splash of vinegar.
› Spoon this sauce onto the plate and cover with thin slices of calf's tongue. Dress with a finely chopped gherkin brunoise, some leaves of curly lettuce, pepper from the pepper mill and a sprinkling of black salt.

The preparation in 1, 2, 3

Put the bouquet marmite in a pan of water and allow to simmer for 30 minutes on a low heat.

Remove the brain membrane by rinsing them under cold, running water.

Rinse the calf's tongue after its first cooking.

Both the calf's tongue and the calf's brains are cooked with a bouquet marmite.

Mash the cold brains with a fork and add the mayonnaise cream, shallot, sea salt and a splash of vinegar.

Cut fine slices of calf's tongue
with a slicing machine.

Place the slices on top of the
mashed brain sauce.

Dress the plate with a gherkin brunoise, some
curly lettuce leaves, pepper and black salt.

Thierry Theys

ʃ Nuance ʅ

Some young chefs have the ability to climb to the culinary highlands at an early age. One such chef is Thierry Theys, who got off to a flying start with his Restaurant 'Nuance'. His fresh and original dishes were popular right from the very first day he opened. In less than five years, this young twenty-something has joined the ranks of Belgium's leading chefs, at least according to the good food guides. For Thierry, the foundations of his success are built on will-power and determination. And not just in the kitchen – running a restaurant is a complex business!

Versatility as a trump card

Thierry Theys exudes calmness to an unusual degree. Talking to us during the busy moments of a service or chatting once the storm of orders has passed: it all seems to make no difference to the young maestro. Professional cooking is all about good preparation and knowing exactly what you need to do at any given moment. This basic philosophy has been explained with far more words in many management text books, but for Thierry Theys it is simplicity itself. It is also the key to his success. "I knew from an early age that I wanted to work in a kitchen. My parents had a butcher's shop and that was probably a source of inspiration. I certainly learnt a lot about how to run a small, self-employed business. The prospect of long days never bothered me, and the idea of running a restaurant where people came to eat my food day after day seemed like a fantastic challenge. And it was much more than just a matter of cooking. I had seen how my parents spent many hours after their shop had closed on orders, maintenance, paperwork and preparation for the next day. It was hard work, but that didn't matter. The important thing was that the shop did well. That made them happy, and their happiness made an impression on me. It also gave me an insight into the many different facets of running a business of whatever kind. It was soon clear to me that running a restaurant would be just as complex. This is something that many chefs forget. I do my paperwork on my closing day and find (fortunately) that even that side of the business interests me. It also allows me to keep in touch with the financial side of things. Of course, it's great when guests and reviewers say that they have eaten well at your restaurant, but the figures still need to add up at the end of the year. Naturally, we have an accountant who keeps a close watch on the books, but a chef also need to keep his eye on the ball, so that his costs don't run out of control. Just being interested in the cooking is not enough to run a restaurant successfully. You need to have a view of the overall picture. This can act as an added stimulation, but it also means a lot of administration, which can be a burden at times. Even so, it is something that you simply have to do."

> *I knew from an early age that I wanted to work in a kitchen. My parents had a butcher's shop and that was probably a source of inspiration.*

A unique training school

Thierry Theys received his culinary training at the hotel school in Koksijde. A training which he praises above all for the attention it devoted to work attitude and character. "Of course, the main focus is on what happens in the kitchen and the dining area. We were given an excellent basic knowledge about the catering industry. But running a restaurant requires much more than the mastery

of a number of kitchen techniques. It demands discipline and perseverance. Two concepts that the instructors at Koksijde quite rightly concentrated on." Armed with this basic technical background and the right mental approach, Thierry Theys next spent a number of years in Paris and Monaco, where – as he himself says – he learnt the real skills of the trade in the star-rated restaurants of Alain Ducasse. "In Paris the cuisine was more technical, whereas in Monaco it was much more Mediterranean, with more 'southern' accents. But in both kitchens we worked every day with the very finest products. This is the kind of top quality that you can seldom buy in our country. The French producers reserve their best products for the best chefs in Paris. They cream off the market. There is hardly enough to satisfy their needs and they are forced to pay the highest prices. What is left over is for the rest of France and the rest of Europe. I was glad to have the opportunity to hone my product knowledge in such a product-rich environment. For example, I learnt how the best scallops and the best spider crabs look and (above all) taste. It was a unique training school."

> *People often say that a chef's taste palate only achieves its final definition when he is thirty-five or so. But surely this is no reason not to open your own restaurant at an earlier age?*

Knowledge, experience and inspiration

Before Thierry Theys opened 'Nuance' in Duffel, he also worked for a time at 'La Cabane' in Edegem, 'De Oosthoek' in Knokke and 'Beluga' in Maastricht. It was a good and varied track-record, which armed him with the weapons he needed to quickly take the next step: his own restaurant. "Some people found it too early, because they think that a young chef doesn't have the necessary experience to make a success of a new business. When you have finished your basic training at the hotel school, I think you need to

In a nutshell

➜ **Who or what influenced your choice of profession?**
No one, really. It was a conscious decision that I made by myself.

➜ **What can really make you mad in the kitchen?**
Disorder.

➜ **What is your most important personal quality?**
Honest and straightforward.

➜ **How do you deal with set backs?**
They motivate me to try and do better next time.

➜ **What would you like to have more time for?**
Family and friends.

➜ **What other job would you like to do?**
Baker.

➜ **For you, what is the epitome of luxury?**
Remaining healthy; it is a cliché, but like most clichés it is based in truth.

➜ **What do you like to give as a present to your friends?**
Wine or champagne.

➜ **What are you best at in the kitchen?**
That's not really for me to say!

➜ **What do you most enjoy doing in the kitchen?**
Everything, really.

➜ **What is your favourite vegetable?**
Artichoke, asparagus, truffles, ceps, morel mushrooms.

➜ **What is your favourite type or cut of meat?**
Côte à l'os and beef hind quarter (spider steak).

➜ **What type(s) of fish do you like to work with?**
Scallops, langoustines, sole and sea bass.

➜ **What are you favourite aromas and smells in the kitchen?**
Truffle.

➜ **What is your favourite dish?**
Pasta vognole with garlic.

➜ **Which small object could you not do without in the kitchen?**
Tweezers.

➜ **Which chef has inspired you the most?**
Alain Ducasse.

➜ **What type of cuisine do you not like?**
Anything that is not fresh.

➜ **What was the last celebrated restaurant that you visited and what was your opinion?**
'Hof van Cleve': absolute top.

➜ **What is your worst ever professional experience?**
Having to send my guests home because the power failed.

➜ **Who is your perfect table companion?**
My wife.

➜ **What is your favourite aperitif?**
Champagne Selosse rosé.

➜ **What do you most enjoy eating on your day off?**
Pasta.

➜ **What are your favourite book and your favourite cooking book?**
Culinary Art Chronicle.

➜ **For whom would you one day like to cook, and why?**
My late grandmother, because she had a heart of gold.

➜ **In which city would you like to live and work?**
Duffel.

consider very carefully where you want to work and what you can learn in those restaurants. It is not the number of years that count, but the quality of the knowledge and experience you acquire. In my opinion, variety is important. Many new chefs spend a relatively long period working for the same head chef before they open their own restaurants. There is nothing wrong with that per se, but it increases the likelihood that you will take over the style or signature of your mentor. This can even lead to a kind of culinary blindness, which is perfectly understandable – but it may take years before you can shake off this legacy and establish your own identity in your cooking. Of course, I was also influenced by what I saw and did. However, I seek my inspiration above all in the products of a limited number of suppliers with whom I work closely. For example, during the season I visit the Sanguisorba vegetable farm twice a week, where many less well-known vegetables and herbs are grown. This may inspire me to create a new garnish that I can combine with fish or meat. In this way, you can also develop a wider taste palate. Mine is still very much in the development stage, and I already know that in a few years it will be completely different. People often say that a chef's taste palate only achieves its final definition when he is thirty-five or so. But surely this is no reason not to open your own restaurant at an earlier age?"

Nuance
Kiliaanstraat 6-8, 2570 Duffel
015/63 42 65
www.resto-nuance.be

Oosterschelde lobster with flowers and tomato

For 4 people

For the romesco cream:
12 prunella tomatoes
olive oil
1 pinch sugar
salt and pepper
1 sprig thyme
1 sprig rosemary
1 sprig lemon verbena (or lemon mint)
3 cloves garlic
30 g white almonds, peeled
15 ml cabernet-sauvignon vinegar

2 lobsters (ca. 750 g)

For the chiboust of parmesan:
125 g soya milk
125 g parmesan
2 ½ slices gelatine
125 g egg white
25 g sugar
100 g cream, clotted

For the tomato assortment:
4 yellow cherry tomatoes
4 red cherry tomatoes
1 green zebra tomato
1 large tomato (coeur de boeuf)
olive oil
pepper and salt

For the tomato vinaigrette:
3 green tomatoes
3 tablespoons finely chopped fresh herbs, according to season and preference
1 dl olive oil
chardonnay vinegar
pepper and salt

For the decoration:
radishes, finely sliced
verbena
sorrel leaves
Greek basil
broad bean flowers
marigolds

› Cut the tomatoes into four and put the segments on an oven tray. Sprinkle with olive oil and sugar. Season with pepper and salt and place the thyme, rosemary, verbena and garlic randomly between the segments. Put the tray into the oven for 30 minutes at 120 °C. Take the shrivelled tomatoes out of the oven and mix them in a mixer. Add the almonds and dilute with the vinegar. Press this tomato cream through a sieve and store until needed for use.
› Cook the lobster: 3 to 4 minutes for the tail and an extra 2 minutes for the claws. Cool in ice water and remove the meat from the shell.
› Boil the soya milk and pour this onto the cheese. Mix to a smooth and creamy consistency. Dissolve the pre-soaked gelatine in the mixture and allow to cool to room temperature. Beat the sugar and the egg white and fold this into the cheese mix with a spatula. Do the same with the clotted cream. Pour out and allow to stiffen.
› Peel the cherry tomatoes and cut the other tomatoes into segments. Sprinkle them with olive oil and season with salt and pepper. Also season the herbs and flowers, if required.
› For the vinaigrette, mix the green tomatoes with the herbs of your choice, bind with olive oil and chardonnay vinegar and season with pepper and salt. Pass the vinaigrette through a sieve and keep in a cool place.
› Serve the lobster lukewarm, dress the other ingredients and decorate with radishes and herbs, as shown in the photograph.

The preparation in 1, 2, 3

> Tie up the lobster.
> Cook the lobster.
> Cool the cherry tomatoes in ice-cold water before peeling them.
> Cool the lobster in ice-cold water.
> Remove the lobster meat from the shell.
> Sprinkle the cherry tomatoes with olive oil and season them.
> Cut the lobster.
> Place the lobster and the tomatoes on the plates.
> Finish with the parmesan chiboust.
> Decorate with finely sliced radish, fresh herbs and flowers.

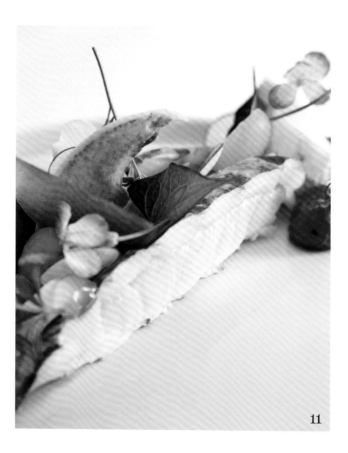

11

Turbot with truffle and cauliflower

For 4 people

4 portions of turbot, each of 175 g
olive oil
butter

For the cauliflower cream:
1/2 cauliflower
salt
100 ml cream
pepper
50 g butter

For the cauliflower couscous:
1/2 cauliflower

salt and pepper
50 ml rice vinegar
juice of 1 lime

For the croquettes:
1 kg mashing potatoes
200 g butter
1 egg yolk
pepper and salt
1 large truffle
200 g flour
2 beaten egg whites
250 g breadcrumbs

For the leek:
2 sticks young leek
pepper and salt
butter

For the juice:
1 shallot
truffle leavings
1 splash of white wine
250 ml chicken stock
100 g hazelnut butter (melted, skimmed and stiffened in advance)
pepper and salt
lime juice

› Fry the turbot in olive oil with a knob of butter. Keep the flesh moist.
› Cook the half cauliflower in well salted water. When cooked through, allow to drain. Mix to a fine sauce in the blender by adding a splash of cream and a knob of butter, and season with salt and pepper. Keep until needed for use.
› For the cauliflower couscous, finely chop the raw half cauliflower in the blender. Blanch briefly in boiling salted water. Allow to cool. Season with salt and pepper, rice vinegar and lime juice.
› Peel the potatoes and boil until cooked through. Make a smooth and creamy puree with a little butter, an egg yolk and the herbs. Fold in the freshly grated truffle with a spatula. Shape into small balls and put into the freezer. Coat with breadcrumbs in the classic manner; first by dipping the potato balls in flour, then in the egg white and finally in the breadcrumbs.
› Cut the leek into rings and cook them in a small amount of water with pepper, salt and butter.
› For the juice, lightly fry the shallot and the truffle leavings. Dilute with the white wine and the chicken stock. Allow to reduce by half. Pass through a sieve and add the hazelnut butter. Finish with pepper, salt and lime juice.
› Dress and decorate the plates as shown in the photograph.

Strawberry and vanilla

For 4 people

For the vanilla mousse:
125 g egg yolk
125 g sugar
200 g milk
200 g cream
1 vanilla stick, sliced opened (soaked
in the warmed milk with cream)
4 slices gelatine

For the strawberry mousse:
125 g egg yolk
100 g sugar
100 g milk
100 g cream
4 slices gelatine
225 g half-whipped cream
200 g strawberry puree
juice of limes

For the almond biscuit with vanilla:
125 g almond powder
20 g flour
112 g egg white
105 g sugar
2 vanilla sticks, with the marrow
scraped out

For the strawberry sorbet:
15 g flowering tea
300 ml sugar water (1/2 water,
1/2 sugar)
1 litre fresh strawberry puree, sieved

For the decoration:
different types of strawberry (Mara des
Bois, Gariguette, pineapple strawberry,
raspberry strawberry, woodland
strawberry)

› Beat up the egg yolk and the sugar to make a ruban. Warm the milk with the cream and the vanilla. Pour the two mixtures together and allow them to bind to a temperature of 83 °C. Add the slices of pre-soaked gelatine. Stir well and allow the resultant vanilla mousse to cool at room temperature.

› Beat up the egg yolk and the sugar to make a ruban. Warm the milk with the cream and the vanilla. Pour the two mixtures together and allow them to bind to a temperature of 83 °C. Add the slices of pre-soaked gelatine. Stir well and allow the resultant mousse to cool at room temperature. Add the cream, strawberry puree and lime juice. Stir well and pour into moulds in the desired form.

› Mix together the almond powder and the flour. Beat up the egg white, sugar and vanilla to make a meringue mixture. Fold the almond mixture into the meringue mixture with a spatula. Bake for 10 minutes at 180 °C.

› Allow the tea to brew in lukewarm sugar water. Pass through a sieve and add to the strawberry puree. Use this mixture to make a sorbet in the ice-cream machine.

› Dress the plates as shown in the photograph. If desired, decorate further with a selection of red fruits and a classic crumble.

Roger Van Damme

∫ Het Gebaar ∖

Roger Van Damme is a bit of an odd-man-out in the world of gastronomy. He started his career as a 'patissier' – a pastry cook – but made his way up the culinary ladder to become a star-rated chef: it was an unusual route to follow. Hungry for knowledge, the young master-baker visited Spain on numerous occasions to exchange ideas with kindred spirits, such as Albert Adrià. In addition to his undoubted initial brilliance with desserts and pastries, he gradually developed a repertoire and a reputation for a refined, technically complex and perfectly seasoned cuisine. Many of his original, decorative plate compositions have become textbook standards, and he now belongs to the very cream of Belgian cuisine – a cuisine which he has helped to shape and form in recent years to a significant degree.

Roger 'patissier'

Roger Van Damme followed his initial training in Bruges, where he shared the classroom and kitchen with his great friend (and three-star chef in the making) Sergio Herman. The choice of the hotel school was no accident: he had been surrounded by food since his childhood. Cooking and baking were daily activities in the Van Damme household. Roger thought that it might be a good way to make a living. "My father was a cook and a passionate maker of finely presented buffets. When I was just five, I remember staring wide-eyed at his beautiful decorative work. My grandfather was also a master-baker, who even wrote a number of cookbooks." Perhaps inevitably, Roger was also quickly bitten by the cooking bug: you might even say that his future career was written in the stars. "Even so, my initial preference for patisserie was more a coincidence than anything else. Relatively few chefs are interested in making desserts. To begin with, it really is a skill apart. Moreover, it is a skill that many chefs think is 'less important' than making starters and main courses. This is where the majority devote most of their time and energy. It is almost as if they want to score with the first two acts of the cooking 'drama', so that they have no passion or imagination left for the finale!" In traditional kitchen teams, which still devote considerable attention to desserts, it is usually a chef-patissier who takes charge. The preparation of a complex

dessert with varied flavours not only requires great concentration but also a high degree of technical skill. "Patisserie is a law unto itself. It has its own rules and demands a different more precise approach. Even so, it is perfectly possible to become competent in both savoury and sweet cooking, but only if you are prepared to learn their respective methods and techniques."

A logical evolution towards savoury dishes

Roger Van Damme evolved from being a pastry chef to become a technically brilliant and dynamically creative star-rated chef de cuisine. Partly out of interest, partly out of necessity. "I think that it is easier to make the transition from pastry chef to all-round chef rather than the other way around. During your training as a patissier you learn that discipline and accuracy are indispensable if you want to achieve the desired result. For example, you need to weigh almost every ingredient with precision. Improvising with desserts is not a good idea and usually leads to disaster. Sure, you can test things out during an experimental phase, but not in the middle of a service. But this does not mean that I value the work of a pastry chef more highly than the work of a 'chef de cuisine'. In general, the all-round chefs have a greater and deeper knowledge of products. As a patissier, you only work with a limited number of ingredients: flour, sugar, milk, cream, eggs, chocolate, fruit. It was this limitation that made me keen to learn more about the other aspects of quality cooking. These other aspects offer you greater variety, which makes the work more interesting – and challenging. The sheer number of different types of fish and meat automatically result in more tension in your cooking. There are just so many opportunities and possibilities. Besides, from a purely commercial point of view I needed to do more than bake cakes and mix ice-cream to make a decent living. For this reason my first menu in my first restaurant offered a wide selection of savoury dishes and snacks, in the hope of attracting a broad lunchtime public. Without those salads, carpaccios and club sandwiches I would not have been able to survive financially in the beginning."

Spanish connections – and local ones

For his sources of inspiration, Roger Van Damme still gives credit to a number of the fellow-chefs who have influenced him most in the past. "Out of pure curiosity, I analysed many of the classic desserts, breaking them down into their component parts, trying to better understand and refine them. Some of these components, such as cream and meringue, I later used as garnishing for other dishes. I was interested in improving their flavours and textures – but I was not the only one. In this respect, the remarkable Spanish chef Quique Dacosta has always been my greatest source of inspiration. Dacosta was one of the first chefs to work seriously with landscape decoration

In a nutshell

→ **Who or what influenced your choice of profession?**
When I was five, I used to love baking. My father was also often busy at home, preparing cold buffets for friends and acquaintances. He had a great eye for detail and presentation, and that is something that has always stayed with me.

→ **What was your first culinary experience or memory?**
A book by the brothers Michel and Albert Roux. It was the first cookbook I ever had. That book has a great emotional value for me, since the person who gave it to me has recently died.

→ **What can really make you mad in the kitchen?**
When staff ruin good products through lack of attention or poor work.

→ **What is your most important personal quality?**
I am never satisfied; or to put it more positively, I always want to do better.

→ **What would you like to have more time for?**
For my children, although at the moment I think I strike a reasonably good balance between family and work.

→ **What other job would you like to do?**
Director of a cooking programme for television. They have feeling for food and try to present it in the best possible light. And that is also the essence of a chef's job.

→ **What do you most enjoy doing in the kitchen?**
Making new creations, but every aspect of kitchen work has its fun side.

→ **What is your favourite vegetable?**
Lemon grass.

→ **What is your favourite type or cut of meat?**
Loin of Holstein beef.

→ **What type(s) of fish do you like to work with?**
North Sea sole or line-caught sea bass

→ **What are your preferred herbs for fish and meat dishes?**
Vadouvan.

→ **What is your favourite dish?**
Pancakes.

→ **Which small object could you not do without in the kitchen?**
A thermo-mixer.

→ **Which chef has inspired you the most?**
So many! Everyone has their own speciality, from which you can always learn.

→ **What was the last celebrated restaurant that you visited and what was your opinion?**
'Hof van Cleve'. Very good, a total experience that was 100% in order!

→ **Who is your perfect table companion?**
My wife (with or without the children)!

→ **What is your favourite aperitif?**
Our house aperitif: mojito royale.

→ **What do you most enjoy eating on your day off?**
Chips with a warm curry sauce or mayonnaise, or a fresh salad with anchovies, mozzarella, parmesan and tomatoes, prepared by my wife Cindy.

→ **What are your favourite book and your favourite cooking book?**
I like looking at books and there are a number that I consult regularly, but I am most proud of my own desserts book.

→ **Which famous customer would you one day like to welcome, and why?**
Celine Dion or Lionel Messi, both the very best in their field.

→ **Which famous person from the past would you like to have welcomed as a customer?**
Marie-Rose Morel. She had a very clear philosophy of life and I admire the way she looked after her sons during her fatal illness. A very strong-minded woman!

> # *Patisserie is a law unto itself. It has its own rules and demands a different more precise approach.*

on his plates. This always fascinated me and I learnt a huge amount from him. I came to know Albert Adrià as an exceptional creative spirit, who was constantly seeking to develop new forms and ideas, such as the use of crispy leaves, sponges and other edible structures. Together, these two Spaniards created a striking and innovative new range of decorative, flavour-packed 'accessories' which allow today's chefs, including myself, to make unusual and attractive plate compositions. And I am particularly grateful to Albert Adrià that I can still take all my questions to him. Back in Belgium, I have also learnt much about chocolate from world champion confectioner Gunther Van Essche, who works for the celebrated Antwerp chocolate house 'Del Rey'. He is unbelievably professional, and still devotes a large part of his time to creative experimentation. These three men helped to open my eyes and stimulated my desire for innovation and renewal. Together, they helped to shape my final style."

A source of inspiration for others

With his extreme sense of refinement and his natural talent for decoration, Roger Van Damme has in turn inspired many young Belgian cooks. His visually powerful ideas about plate composition and his ability to combine finely nuanced flavours are popular with today's up and coming generation of chefs. "It doesn't bother me that some chefs like to adopt my ideas. As long as they add something to them and use them to help create a genuine signature of their own. I also learnt some of my techniques from other chefs and it is thanks in part to them that I have been able to progress so far in this wonderful profession. But this, to me, is the most normal thing in the world. You learn from others, adjust what you learn, and apply it in different ways. It is a continually evolving process, but one in which innovation for innovation's sake must never become the goal. Innovation must simply support and help you in your main task: the cooking and serving of good food. This is why I still invest quite a lot of time in the further refinement of some of the truly classic Belgian dishes, such as pancakes. I have changed the recipe in a way that has almost made it my own. That is what I am most proud of and that is why it is on my menu. Besides, nothing gives me more pleasure than being able to cook 'the ultimate pancake' for my children. Although I hope that 'Het Gebaar' is something more than just a creperie!"

Het Gebaar
Leopoldstraat 24, 2000 Antwerpen
03/232 37 10
www.rogervandamme.com

Quenelle of vanilla mousse, an apple compote tartlet, pistachio sponge cake, crunch and vanilla cream

For the quenelle of vanilla mousse:

15 g cream powder
45 g egg yolks
250 g milk
50 g cream
1 vanilla stick, with the marrow removed
40 g sugar
1 slice of gelatine, soaked in cold water
1 splash of lemon vinegar
220 g cream, whipped with 25 g sugar

For the apple compote tartlet:

(for the caramel)
250 g sugar
210 g water
65 g glucose
(for the apple compote)
25 g lemon juice
25 g orange juice
60 g sugar
50 g caramel (see basic recipe above)
2 g xantana
600 g apples (Granny Smith)
300 g apples (Jonagold)
1 pinch cinnamon powder

For the pistachio sponge cake:

125 g sugar
125 g pistachio nuts, finely ground
25 g flour
15 g olive oil
100 g egg yolk
165 g egg white

For the crunch:

100 g soft butter
100 g almond powder
100 g light brown sugar

› For the vanilla mousse, whisk the cream powder and the egg yolk in a bowl, until smooth. Bring the milk, cream, vanilla and sugar to the boil. Pour a third of this boiling mixture onto the egg yolk. Mix well with a whisk and then pour back into the hot mixture. Cook further to a temperature of 85 °C. Weigh off 200 grams of this confectioner's cream. Squeeze the excess moisture out of the gelatine slice and add this to the still warm mass, beating well with a whisk. Add a splash of lemon vinegar. Pour the mixture into a bowl and allow to cool to a maximum temperature of 35 °C. Fold in the cream whipped with sugar. Put the mousse into the fridge and allow to stiffen for a minimum of 3 hours. Immediately prior to serving, make quenelles of the mousse, using two dry spoons that have been previously warmed in hot water.

› Boil the sugar and glucose in 85 grams of water until they form a light caramel. Boil the rest of the water (125 grams) separately and add at the moment when the caramel colours as desired. Allow this mixture to boil further to 118 °C.

› Make syrup from both types of fruit juice by bringing them to the boil with sugar. Add the warm caramel and stir thoroughly to create a single mass. Mix the xantana in a little water with a hand mixer. Peel the apples and cut them into small chunks. Stir 600 grams of apple chunks (half Granny Smith, half Jonagold) into the caramel syrup, and add the cinnamon and the xantana. Mix well and pour onto a baking tray covered with baking paper. Allow to caramelise for 20 minutes in a warm oven at 230 °C, stirring occasionally. Remove from the oven and mix with the remaining apple chunks (Granny Smith). Allow to cool fully and re-warm shortly before serving.

› Cold mix the ingredients for the pistachio sponge cake in a thermomix at setting 10, following the order of ingredients listed above. Cover the bowl and allow the mixture to rest overnight in the fridge. Pass the mixture through a sieve and spoon it into an aerosol spray. Pressurise the spray with three gas capsules. Shake well. Fill a polystyrene cup one third full with the mixture. Cook for 30 seconds in the microwave. Turn the cup upside down and allow to cool. Pull off pieces of the pistachio cake for the decoration.

› Pre-heat an oven to 150 °C. Mix together all the ingredients for the crunch in a bowl and kneed them with a flat dough

hook to form a malleable dough. Roll the dough out evenly with a rolling pin over two baking mats to a thickness of 1.5 centimetres. Put the baking mats on a baking tray and place the tray in the oven. Bake for 10 minutes. Take the tray out of the oven and remove the baking mats. Allow the dough to cool, so that it becomes hard. Crumble the cold crunch, either by hand or in a blender. Keep separately in a biscuit barrel.
› Warm the cream, egg yolk, vanilla and sugar in a pot to a temperature of 85 °C (or in the thermomix on setting 5). Remove the pot from the heat and add the gelatine slice, having first squeezed out any excess water. Mix with a hand mixer (or briefly in the thermomix on setting 10). Pour the fluid cream into a piping bag and allow to stiffen slightly in the fridge.
› Arrange all the elements neatly on a plate and finish with chocolate decorations, stevia leaves, apple rolls and lemon zest.

1 g salt
100 g flour

For the vanilla cream:
250 g cream
150 g egg yolk
1 vanilla stick, with the marrow removed
85 g sugar
1/2 slice of gelatine, soaked in water

For the decoration:
chocolate decoration
stevia (sweetleaf)
rolls of apple
lemon zest

Chocolate composition: mousse, crunchy, creamy, crispy, pastille and cremeux balls of lime, sprayed with chocolate

For the circle of chocolate mousse:
120 g milk
1 slice of gelatine
110 g Caraïbe chocolate
280 g whipped cream

For the quenelles (large and small) of light chocolate mousse:
140 g sugar
140 g egg yolk
90 g water
420 g plain chocolate
190 g cream, fluid
650 g cream, clotted

For the crunch:
125 g sugar
125 g almond powder
75 g flour
30 g cacao powder
100 g soft butter
5 g salt

For the chocolate cream:
250 g milk
15 g maïzena (thickener)
50 g cream
40 g sugar
45 g egg yolk
100 g plain chocolate, finely chopped
50 g soft butter

For the chocolate crisp:
175 g glucose
250 g plain chocolate
175 g isomalt sugar
100 g cacao paste

› Warm the milk and add the gelatine. Add the chocolate, place in the thermomix and mix to a smooth consistency. Pour into a bowl and add the cream at 45 °C.

› Cook the sugar, egg yolk and water to 85 °C in a pot, stirring constantly (or mix in the thermomix on setting 5). The result is known as 'pâté à bombe'. Using a spatula, spoon this mixture into the bowl of a kitchen robot. Beat at high speed until the mixture has the consistency of mayonnaise.

› In the meantime, melt the chocolate in the microwave. Then warm the fluid cream, also in the microwave, until it nearly reaches boiling point. Pour the hot cream carefully onto the chocolate and mix briefly, but without forming an emulsion. Add the still warm pâté à bombe to the chocolate cream. Check the temperature of this mixture: when it reaches 45 °C fold in the whipped cream. If the temperature is too low, re-heat briefly in the microwave. Pour into a dish and keep in the fridge. Use a spoon to form attractive quenelles from this mousse.

› Pre-heat an oven to 150 °C. Mix together all the ingredients for the crunch in a bowl of a kitchen robot and knead with a flat dough hook to form a malleable dough. Roll the dough out evenly with a rolling pin over two baking mats to a thickness of 1.5 centimetres. Put the baking mats on a baking tray and place the tray in the oven. Bake for 10 minutes. Take the tray out of the oven and remove the baking mats. Allow the dough to cool, so that it becomes hard. Crumble the cold crunch, either by hand or in a blender. Keep separately in a biscuit barrel.

› Make a paste with a third of the milk and the maïzena. Put the remaining milk, the cream and the sugar into a steel pan and bring to the boil. In the meantime, beat the egg yolk into the paste with a whisk. When the milk-cream mixture reaches boiling point, pour in the egg yolk-maïzena mixture and stir thoroughly. Stir constantly with the whisk, until the mass reaches a temperature of 85 °C. Remove from the heat and stir in the chocolate. Gradually mix in the butter a piece at a time. Pour the chocolate cream into a piping bag and allow to stiffen in the fridge.

› Heat the glucose and 50 grams of chocolate to 155 °C. Add the isomalt sugar and the remaining chocolate and cook to a temperature of 140 °C. Finally, fold in the chocolate paste with a wooden spoon. Pour the mixture onto a silicone baking mat and allow it to harden. Break it into pieces and powder the pieces in the blender. Pre-heat an oven to 150 °C. Sprinkle the powder through a sieve onto a silicone mat. Put the mat into the oven for 3 minutes. Remove and allow to cool slightly, so that you can break off a number of crispy pieces. If the substance cools too much, put it back into the oven for 1 minute, so that you can repeat the process.

› Melt the chocolate. Mix the Progianduja into the melted chocolate with a spatula. Crunch the crispies briefly in the thermomix, before finally adding the yoghurt powder, the zest and the crackling sugar. Mix thoroughly and half fill a number of silicone ball-moulds with this mixture. Put them in the freezer.

› Put the sugar in the water and bring to the boil. Take the pot off the heat and add the lemon grass and the grated lime. Cover the pot with plastic foil and allow to stand for 5 minutes. Pass the mixture through a sieve and weigh out 100 grams of the resulting fluid. Heat this base sauce with the lemon puree, sugar and egg yolk in a pot to 85 °C (or in the thermomix on setting 5). Add the slice of gelatine, having first squeezed out any excess moisture. Remove the pot from the heat and mix briefly with a hand mixer (or in the thermomix on setting 10). Allow the resulting mixture to cool in a separate pan to 37 °C. Gradually beat in the butter a piece at a time, using a hand mixer (or in the thermomix on setting 4), so that a smooth emulsion is formed. Pour this substance into a piping bag and fill a number of silicone ball- moulds. Freeze these balls in the freezer. When ready to serve, remove from the silicone moulds and spray them with plain chocolate. Allow them to thaw gradually in the fridge.

› Arrange all the elements neatly on a plate and finish with olive oil, gold decoration and chocolate decoration.

For the chocolate pastille:
300 g Caraïbe chocolate
300 g Black Progianduja (Sosa)
2 tablespoons yoghurt-crispy (Sosa)
2 tablespoons passion-crispy (Sosa)
2 tablespoons banana-crispy (Sosa)
1/2 tablespoon yoghurt powder (Sosa)
zest of an orange (candied)
2 tablespoons crackling sugar

For the cremeux balls of lime, sprayed with chocolate:
(for the basic sauce)
200 g water
55 g sugar
2 stems lemon grass, finely chopped
grated peel of 2 limes
(for the balls)
100 g base sauce (see basic recipe above)
30 g lime puree
45 g sugar
70 g egg yolk
1 slice of gelatine, soaked in cold water
100 g butter
plain chocolate (for the spraying)

For the decoration:
olive oil
gold decoration
chocolate decoration

Tuile, cremeux balls with lime and hibiscus, raspberry coulis, quenelles of mousse with woodland fruits, violet jelly, yoghurt cream and a raspberry mousse in a ball of chocolate

For the tuile (cookies):
115 g egg white
130 g flour
100 g icing sugar
65 g sugar
30 g cream
the contents of 1/2 vanilla stick
20 g soft butter

For the cremeux balls with lime and hibiscus:
(for the basic sauce)
200 g water
55 g sugar
2 stems lemon grass, finely chopped
20 g dried hibiscus
grated peel of 2 limes
(for the balls)
100 g base sauce (see basic recipe above)
30 g lime puree
45 g sugar
70 g egg yolk
1 slice of gelatine, soaked in cold water
100 g butter
1 drop of red colorant

For the raspberry coulis:
50 g water
50 g sugar
100 g raspberry puree
0.3 g xantana (Texturas)

› Mix all the ingredients for the tuile, except the butter, with a flat dough hook in the bowl of a kitchen robot. When ready, add the soft butter in small pieces and mix further, until a smooth, uniform dough is formed. Pre-heat the oven to 150 °C. Spoon the tuile mixture into a piping bag. Pipe long strips onto a baking tray and bake for 8 minutes in a warm oven. Open the oven, remove the tuiles one by one and twist them immediately around a wooden or metal cylinder, to give them a nice spiral shape. This needs to be done quickly, since the tuiles will become crisp and brittle once they cool. If necessary, return the baking tray to the oven, so that they can be kept warm or even lightly re-heated.

› Put the sugar in the water and bring to the boil. Take the pot off the heat and add the lemon grass, the hibiscus and the grated lime. Cover the pot with plastic foil and allow to stand for 5 minutes. Pass the mixture through a sieve and weigh out 100 grams of the resulting fluid. Heat this base sauce with the lemon puree, sugar and egg yolk in a pot to 85 °C (or in the thermomix on setting 5). Add the slice of gelatine, having first squeezed out any excess moisture. Remove the pot from the heat and mix briefly with a hand mixer (or in the thermomix on setting 10). Allow the resulting mixture to cool in a separate pan to 37 °C. Gradually beat in the butter a piece at a time, using a hand mixer (or in the thermomix on setting 4), so that a smooth emulsion is formed. Add the colorant. Pour this substance into a piping bag and fill a number of silicone ball moulds. Freeze these balls in the freezer. When ready to serve, remove them from the silicone moulds and allow them to thaw gradually in the fridge.

› Boil the sugar in the water for 45 minutes. Weigh out 25 grams of this sugar syrup and mix it with the raspberry puree. Add the xantana and mix thoroughly. Spoon the mixture into a siphon and keep in the fridge until ready for use.

› Heat the puree of woodland fruits in a pot. Add the cream, violet sugar and vinegar. Remove the pot from the heat and beat in the gelatine, using a whisk. Melt the chocolate slightly in a microwave or bain-marie. Pour a third of the woodland fruits mixture onto the chocolate and fold it gradually and carefully into the mixture with a spatula. Repeat this process for the second third and the final third, so that the final mixture is uniform and has a nice sheen. Carefully fold in the cream when the mixture has cooled to a temperature of 45 °C. Spoon the mousse into a mould and put it in the freezer. Remove the mousse from the mould once it is fully frozen and allow it to thaw gradually in the fridge. Use the mousse to create attractive quenelles with a spoon.

› Bring the juice and the vinegar to the boil. Add the violet sugar and bring to the boil again. Add the pectine and boil further. Remove the pot from the heat and allow to cool. Cover with plastic film and allow the jelly to rest overnight in the fridge. Mix the stiffened jelly with a hand mixer, so that it becomes a supple gel (or, alternatively, mix in the thermomix and remove the air bubbles by creating a vacuum). Spoon the gel into a siphon and keep in the fridge until ready for use.

› Beat the yoghurt, mascarpone and icing sugar into a smooth substance with a whisk. Heat the rhubarb to a minimum temperature of 30 °C and dissolve the gelatine in it, having first squeezed out any excess water. Stir two tablespoons of the yoghurt-based substance into the rhubarb juice. When smooth, add the rest of the yoghurt substance. Stir in the lime juice, then fold in the whipped cream with a spatula. Spoon the resulting mixture into a piping bag and allow to harden for at least three hours in the fridge before serving.

› Beat the yoghurt, mascarpone and icing sugar into a smooth substance with a whisk or hand mixer. Heat a quarter of the raspberry puree and dissolve the gelatine in it, having first squeezed out any excess water. Stir this into the remaining raspberry puree and then mix with the cold yoghurt-based substance, to produce a uniform mixture, light pink in colour. Fold in the whipped cream with a spatula. Spoon the final mixture into a piping bag and allow to harden for at least three hours in the fridge before serving.

› Arrange all the elements neatly on a plate and dress with woodland fruits, raspberries and basil cress.

For the quenelles of mousse with woodland fruits:

150 g woodland fruit puree
90 g cream
75 g violet sugar
3 tablespoons cabernet-sauvignon vinegar
5 g gelatine, soaked in cold water
325 g milk chocolate
350 g cream, clotted

For the violet jelly:

125 g blackberry juice
50 g cabernet-sauvignon vinegar
155 g violet sugar
15 g pectine

For the yoghurt cream:

150 g Greek yoghurt
100 g mascarpone
70 g icing sugar
20 g rhubarb juice (made with a juice centrifuge)
juice of 1 lime
150 g cream
1 slice of gelatine, soaked in cold water

For the raspberry mousse in a ball of chocolate:

140 g Greek yoghurt
140 g mascarpone
60 g icing sugar
280 g raspberry puree
2 slices of gelatine, soaked in cold water
140 g cream, whipped

For the decoration:

woodland berries
raspberries
basil cress

Presentation in 1, 2, 3

> Decorate with a sprayed strip of
> chocolate and a spiral tuile.
> Add the chocolate balls with
> raspberry mousse and the lime and
> hibiscus balls.
> Decorate with woodland fruits and
> raspberries.
> Add the quenelles of woodland fruit
> mousse.
> Pipe on the yoghurt cream.
> Decoratively position the basil cress,
> violet jelly and raspberry coulis on
> and around the completed dish.

6

1

2

3

4

5

Geert Van Hecke

∫ De Karmeliet ∖

Not all three-star chefs are ground-breaking iconoclasts. Geert Van Hecke remains faithful to the traditions of classical French and Belgian cooking. This is sometimes said as a criticism against him, but it is also the basis of his undoubted fame. The other pillars of his success are hard work and an ability to remain himself. And, above all, a love of quality products.

"La cuisine est simple comme bonheur" (cooking, like happiness, is simple)

Geert Van Hecke gives a calm, almost lazy, first impression. He is very modest, does not like to be in the spotlight and is almost apologetic when he tells you that his restaurant has three Michelin stars. But behind that misleading exterior hides a man of boundless energy and sound business sense, who knows precisely where he is going and what he wants. After finishing at secondary school, he enrolled at the Ten Duinen hotel school in Koksijde. He spent the summer months working at a small hotel in the Haute-Savoie, where he was expected to do more or less everything: washing up, cleaning, preparing vegetables. Sixteen hours a day, seven days a week, with not a single rest day. "I have never been afraid of hard work. Not then and not now," he says. Following the hotel school, he spent a short time training at 'Le Sanglier des Ardennes', but soon moved to the 'Villa Lorraine' in Brussels. When he was twenty-one, he entered the kitchen of Alain Chapel in Mionnay (near Lyon). He stayed there for two years and again worked seventeen hours a day. But this period made an indelible mark on his vision of cooking. "Chapel taught me love for the product. And for regional cooking. 'La cuisine est simple comme bonheur,' he once said. It has stayed with me ever since. I still always go in search of the very best products, and I usually find them in France. There you can still track down small producers who work with passion and are able to deliver constant quality. In French markets you can still see farmers selling tomatoes, courgettes and potatoes harvested that same morning. Usually, they are biologically grown as well, (although this is not something that the French make a big fuss about). You can't find that any more in Belgium. Here everything has become too large scale and commercial. It is up to the farmers in the first instance to grow and breed good products, but they seem to be lacking in the necessary pride. And this while top chefs and consumers are crying out for products of quality."

A light, contemporary cuisine, with a classical basis

Geert Van Hecke and his wife Mireille opened 'De Karmeliet' in the Jeruzalemstraat in Bruges in 1993, in two small houses once occupied by Carmelite sisters. They were awarded their first Michelin star just two years later. "We offered highly innovative cuisine and made the difference with the quality and originality of our products, such as mackerel, green asparagus, live scallops and aromatics such as ginger. You didn't find many of these things in the other Belgian restaurants of the day. I still work with mackerel, even though I have seen several letters from people who wrote to Michelin to say that it was a disgrace that I dare to serve such a common fish. But this has never bothered me and happily it didn't seem to bother Michelin either. What could possibly be wrong with serving such a fine-tasting fish?" Four years later came a second – and at the time unexpected – star. From then on the restaurant was full to bursting point and so Van Hecke moved

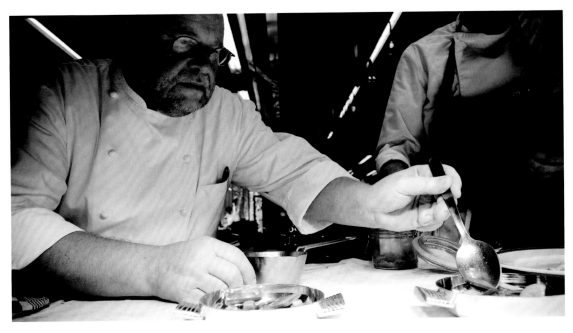

'De Karmaliet' to a beautiful new mansion house in the Langestraat, where it still is today. The third star duly arrived in 1996.

Few chefs have such a wide repertoire of recipes on which they can draw to provide constant change for their guests throughout the year. "I offer a light, contemporary cuisine, which has its roots in the traditional cuisine of both France and Belgium. And I still find inspiration in the dishes of my mentors of yesteryear and the dishes that I was already cooking in 'De Karmeliet' twenty-eight years ago. Even so, I always want add something that you will not find anywhere else. What's more, I am constantly refining my dishes and I have no need or desire to move in the direction of molecular cooking. True, I do use a number of techniques associated with molecular cuisine to make my own creation more visually appealing, but that's where it stops. A technical kind of cooking is not for me. I have great respect for Bocuse, who is very product-oriented and has been cooking wonderful dishes for almost 60 years in a typical style that he has made all his own. But this does not mean that I am averse to innovation or change. Around me I have a number of young chefs who are well versed in the new techniques. I let them experiment with my classic recipes to see what they can do with them. But I insist that they only change small details: the essence of the dish must remain the same. I don't want a different type of cuisine. In my opinion, there are too few 'molecular chefs' who make interesting food. Ferran Adrià in 'El Bulli' serves mini-dishes in which just two flavours and textures are

'La cuisine est simple comme le bonheur', Chapel once said. It has stayed with me ever since.

In a nutshell

→ **Who or what influenced your choice of profession?**
Cooking and eating at home. Also my grandfather, who was a baker.

→ **What was your first culinary experience or memory?**
When I was fourteen, working non-stop for two months as a washer-up and kitchen help in a small hotel in the Haute-Savoie.

→ **What can really make you mad in the kitchen?**
If I need to repeat the same thing five times.

→ **What is your most important personal quality?**
Having the respect of others.

→ **What would you like to have more time for?**
City trips, particular to visit fine museums and good restaurants.

→ **What other job would you like to do?**
Something artistic.

→ **For you, what is the epitome of luxury?**
Doing what you want to do.

→ **What are you best at in the kitchen?**
Stimulating variety and change.

→ **What is your favourite vegetable?**
Seasonal vegetables: peas, asparagus, porcini mushrooms, tomatoes, endives

→ **What is your favourite type or cut of meat?**
Duck.

→ **What type(s) of fish do you like to work with?**
Cod, salmon and gurnard.

→ **What are your preferred herbs for fish and meat dishes?**
Tarragon and coriander.

→ **What are you favourite aromas and smells in the kitchen?**
Coffee in the morning!

→ **What is your favourite dish?**
Steak tartar.

→ **Which small object could you not do without in the kitchen?**
My paring knife.

→ **Which chef has inspired you the most?**
Alain Chapel.

→ **What type of cuisine do you not like?**
Bad cuisine.

→ **What was the last celebrated restaurant that you visited and what was your opinion?**
'Plaza Athenée' in Paris, run by Alain Ducasse.

→ **Who is your perfect table companion?**
Any good friend.

→ **What is your favourite aperitif?**
Beer, white wine or Campari and soda.

→ **What do you most enjoy eating on your day off?**
A plate of marinated raw salmon.

→ **What are your favourite book and your favourite cooking book?**
Anything by Alain Ducasse.

combined. This results in an almost perfect taste experience. But the chefs who try to copy him often throw five or six different tastes and twenty different types of spice on a plate, so that the unity and flavour of the dish are lost. Someone who goes to dine in a restaurant wants to enjoy himself, and not just sit there thinking about the complexity of the food. It is often said that modern cuisine means more work in the kitchen. And indeed, nowadays there are more detailed elements that need to be made, and this does mean more work. But we used to work much harder in the past. Take a classic puree, for example. A good puree needs to be constantly stirred until it becomes smooth and creamy. In molecular cooking, they just put it in a piping bag and it's ready. Making brawn in the traditional manner also takes time. And good hot-pot and eel 'in the green' cannot be made à la minute. But if new techniques can simplify the preparation without changing the essence of the dish, then I am willing to use them. At Alain Chapel's we had to learn to cook with open ovens that had a constant temperature of 120 °C. That was slow cooking avant la lettre. We did the dressing on the stove itself, where there was only room for three plates, sitting on our knees, with the heat of the still open oven full in our face. Things are easier now. Take another example: pigeon. We now fry pigeon on the carcass, put it in a vacuum bag and cook it slowly for 50 minutes at 60 °C. We then put it away in the fridge until we need it. If an order comes in, you just take it out, warm it up in the vacuum bag, stick it in the 'fumoir' and finish in a little butter. This method delivers perfect cuisson and flavour – every time."

Nostalgia in the 'Refter'

In the meantime, Geert Van Hecke is also enjoying himself with a new project: Bistro 'Refter', which he opened next to 'De Karmaliet' in 2009. Here he focuses on the honest taste of honest products. Many of the dishes on the 'Refter' menu come from his first period in the old Carmelite houses. These include a royal hot-pot, with five different types of meat, shoulder of Pyrenean lamb with a rosemary persillade, T-bone steak, 'everything from a pig', rabbit slow-cooked in an oven for eight hours, candied goose liver, risotto with truffle, and a warm soufflé as dessert. "They are not dishes that you will find in a run-of-the-mill brasserie. They are dishes that I have always loved preparing, but that we no longer serve in the main restaurant – although we still make them at home. Call it a touch of nostalgia. But what's wrong with that?"

De Karmeliet
Langestraat 19, 8000 Brugge
050/33 82 59
www.dekarmeliet.be

Mechelen asparagus with king crab, soft-boiled egg and a bottarga cream

For 4 people

For the bottarga mayonnaise:
650 g grape seed oil
60 g bottarga (dried fish roe of grey mullet, tuna or swordfish)
4 g salt
2 g ground white pepper
2 eggs
1 egg yolk
50 g mustard

For the parsley coulis:
1 bunch of parsley
8 white asparagus
salt

1 claw of raw king crab (= ca. 120 g crab net)
5 g transglutaminate

For vinaigrette 1:
5 cl parsley coulis (see basic recipe above)
5 cl shellfish consommé
5 cl olive oil

For vinaigrette 2:
5 cl olive oil
2 cl white balsamic vinegar
5 cl shellfish consommé
grated peel of ¼ orange

For the bottarga cream:
10 g bottarga mayonnaise (see basic recipe above)
10 g mascarpone
10 g asparagus puree (see basic recipe above)

4 soft-boiled eggs (50 minutes at 62 °C)

For the decoration:
some sprigs of chervil
some red basil leaves
fine squares of toasted bread with squid ink (or ordinary toast)
black salt

› Mix the grape seed oil with the bottarga and finish like a classic mayonnaise.
› Blanch the parsley for 2 to 3 minutes in boiling water. Drain off the water and immerse the parsley immediately in ice-cold water. Remove and mix to a smooth consistency.
› Boil the peel and other asparagus leavings in salted water. Drain off the water and mix the cooked asparagus leavings until they form a smooth puree.
› Boil the asparagus for approximately 9 minutes in salted water. Rinse immediately in ice-cold water. Keep four whole asparagus. Cut the tips off the other four and keep them separately. Chop the remaining four asparagus stalks into a brunoise.
› Remove the king crab meat from the claw. Place it on plastic foil, sprinkle with the transglutaminate and roll into a firm sausage shape. Lightly cook the king crab for 6 minutes at 65 °C. Allow to cool. Remove the plastic foil and cut the meat into slices.
› Make a vinaigrette with the ingredients for vinaigrette 1. Do the same with the ingredients for vinaigrette 2.
› Mix all the ingredients for the bottarga cream.
› Stir the asparagus brunoise into the bottarga cream. Spoon the brunoise mixture into a kitchen ring on a plate and place one of the eggs on top of it.
› Arrange the whole asparagus on the plate. Place four slices of king crab on top of the asparagus. Spoon vinaigrette 1 around the asparagus. Spoon vinaigrette 2 on the king crab. Decorate with the chervil, red basil leaves and black salt. Serve with the toasted squares.

Presentation in 1, 2, 3

> Spoon the asparagus brunoise, mixed with the bottarga cream, into a kitchen ring.
> Place the whole asparagus around this mixture.
> Arrange the asparagus tips on the plate.
> Place four slices of king crab on the asparagus.
> Arrange the black toast and a piece of bottarga on the plate.
> Decorate with the fresh young herbs.
> Place a soft-boiled egg on top of the asparagus brunoise. Drizzle a few drops of bottarga cream over the plate. Sprinkle some black salt on the egg.
> Finish with a few drops of vinaigrettes 1 and 2.

Frog legs stuffed with snails, a chickpea cream, woodland mushrooms and smoked breast of duck

For 4 people

For the chicken and snail farce:
250 g white chicken meat
25 g egg white
1 dl cream
10 finely chopped snails
pepper and salt
pimento powder

For the mushroom foam:
1 dl chicken consommé
1 dl water
20 g mushroom leavings
1 pinch of lecithin

For the frog leg sauce:
1 finely chopped shallot
1 finely diced clove of garlic
frog leg leavings
1 sprig of thyme
1 laurel leaf
1 dl white wine
2 dl chicken stock
pepper and salt

For the chickpea cream:
100 g chickpeas
2.5 dl chicken stock
1 finely diced clove of garlic
1 sprig of thyme
1 laurel leaf
1 dl cream
5 g couscous herbs
10 pairs of frog legs
chicken and snail farce (see basic recipe above)
10 blanched lettuce leaves

30 g chanterelle mushrooms
30 g horn of plenty mushrooms
30 g shimeji mushroom
30 g enoki mushrooms
butter
1 clove of garlic
16 snails
100 g chickpea cream (see basic recipe above)
mushroom foam (see basic recipe above)
5 slices of smoked breast of duck
25 cl frog leg sauce (see basic recipe above)
4 dried leaves of bear's garlic

› Blend the chicken meat and the egg white to a fine consistency. Press the mixture through a fine sieve and beat up with the cream. Add the snails to this farce and season with pepper, salt and pimento powder.
› Stew the shallot and garlic, together with the frog leg leavings, thyme and laurel. Add the white wine and reduce by a third. Add the cream and season with salt and pepper.
› Boil the chickpeas in the stock with the garlic, thyme and laurel until they are cooked through. When ready, mix thoroughly until they form a smooth cream. Add a little cream during the mixing and season with the couscous herbs.
› Bring the consommé, water and mushroom leavings to the boil. Remove the pot from the heat and allow to 'brew' for 30 minutes. Pass through a sieve, add the lethecin and mix.
› Make small hams from the frog legs. Cut off the feet from the lower part of the legs and cut off the lower part of the legs from the upper part. Bone the upper part of the leg and stuff with the chicken and snail farce. Wrap a blanched lettuce leaf around each leg. Gently cook the frog-leg hams for 10 minutes at 70 °C.
› Cook the mushrooms with the lower parts of the legs in a little butter with some garlic.
› Also cook the snails in a little butter.
› Place some of the chickpea cream in the middle of a plate. Arrange the hams and the snails elegantly around the cream. Add the slices of smoked breast of duck in between. Do the same with the fried mushrooms and the lower parts of the legs. Decorate with a few leaves of bear's garlic.

Rib of milk calf with a black pepper crust, a green bean and Roscoff egg salad in the Liege manner and fried sugar lettuce

For the marrow beignets:
25 g flour
1/2 bottle Rodenbach (beer)
2 cl olive oil
1 beaten egg white
pepper and salt
marrow

700 g rib of milk calf
black pepper crust (5 g black pepper,
50 g finely ground black sesame
seeds)

For the sauce:
5 cl cognac
5 cl port
5 cl madeira
20 cl veal stock
10 g cold butter
10 g finely chopped shallot
10 g finely chopped chives

5 g finely chopped red onion
olive oil
20 g bints (potatoes), cut into a
brunoise and deep fried
20 g beans, blanched and cut into a
brunoise
10 g smoked ham, blanched and cut
into a brunoise
1 crop of sugar lettuce
soya sauce
12 marrow beignets (see basic recipe
above)
25 cl sauce (see basic recipe above)

› Mix together the flour, beer and olive oil. Carefully fold in the egg white. Immerse the marrow in the beignet batter and cook in a deep fryer for approximately 3 minutes at 160 °C.
› Sprinkle the black pepper onto the top of the meat and press firmly into place. Fry the meat on all sides until it is pink (rosé), remove from the pan and allow to rest.
› Add the cognac, port and madeira to the meat juices in the pan and allow to reduce. Add the veal stock and allow to reduce further. Beat in the cold butter to thicken the mixture. At the last moment, add the shallot and the chives.
› Sauté the red onion in a little oil. Add the brunoise of potato, beans and ham. Season as required.
› Cut the sugar lettuce into four equal segments. Sear them in olive oil, add a few drops of soya sauce and allow to them cook for a few moments more.
› Spoon the potato and bean brunoise into a kitchen ring on a plate. Cut the meat into thick slices and place evenly around the brunoise. Add a segment of fried sugar lettuce and three marrow beignets. Finish with a covering of sauce.

Daniel Van Lint

♪ *Le Fou est belge* ♫

When Daniel Van Lint renamed his restaurant a few years ago as 'Le Fou est belge', his decision caused quite a stir. Even the sign-writer who was asked to make the new board for the restaurant was confused. He asked Van Lint whether or not he needed to paint a whisk next to the new name! Van Lint laughed heartily, but kept the mystery of the intriguing new name to himself.

The Belgian way of eating

(*) 'Fouet' is the French word for a whisk – hence the question of the sign-writer. 'Le fou est Belge' is an obvious play on words, which means 'The madman (le fou) is a Belgian'; 'fouet' and 'fou est' are both pronounced the same.

Customers who are not familiar with the language of Molière will also miss the play on words. They keep asking which madman is a Belgian! Just like Van Lint keeps asking what exactly is the true identity of Belgian cooking. And perhaps no one is better placed to answer this question than the chef of 'Le Fou est belge' himself. According to Daniel Van Lint, our country is simply too small to be able to speak of a national cuisine – comparable, say, with French cuisine. There is certainly an identity of sorts, and this identity expresses itself in a wide diversity of local specialities, some of which are able to transcend their regional reputation. There are also dishes which undoubtedly enjoy nationwide fame and popularity. Van Lint has focused his attention on a number of these 'favourites' over the years. His shrimp croquettes, black pudding, veal brawn, eel 'in the green' (a fine herb sauce) and Liege meatballs, to name but a few, are all much-loved taste bombs on his menu card. "I am more inclined to believe in a Belgian way of eating than in a Belgian national cuisine. In much the same way, I also think that there is also an Italian way of eating and a Japanese one as well. In my own particular style, I seek to cater to this typically Belgian way of eating by trying to offer more 'refined' versions of some specifically Belgian specialities," says Daniel Van Lint. In his definition of 'the Belgian way of eating', he does not allow himself to be confined by artificial geographical boundaries: he finds much the same eating mentality in parts of Northern France and Dutch Limburg. "A Belgian is a bon-vivant with a critical nose for quality, who likes to take his time while eating recognisable products. He is mad about sauces and enjoys rich-tasting stews and casseroles.

Most of them love a grilled entrecôte, but offer them a slow-braised plat de côtes (a rib cut of beef) and they really go wild. The preparation of this last dish requires considerably more knowledge, expertise and time." Van Lint likes to combine these three qualities and seeks in this way to cater to what he sees as the eating habits of the 'typical' Belgian diner. And his focus is very close to home. The transformation of classic Belgian dishes, such as shrimp croquettes, has become his signature. "Mass production is threatening to diminish our sense of taste. If you want to know what I mean, just try a cheese croquette or a shrimp croquette that has been produced industrially. If people become used to regarding this type of food or, even worse, fast food as the norm, we are in danger of limiting ourselves to a very narrow frame of reference. It is a great pity that the number of people who are able to distinguish between things that are good, very good or even exceptional is actually decreasing rather than increasing. And I am not only talking about food. You can see the same thing happening in modern art and music, to name just two examples."

> *I am more inclined to believe in a Belgian way of eating than in a Belgian national cuisine.*

Working with top ingredients

For his shrimp croquettes, Daniel Van Lint insists on going each day to Brussels, where he can buy fresh, unpeeled shrimps. Because this, in his opinion, is where the problem starts. "If you want to produce a quality dish, you need to use quality products. In Famenne, where

> *A Belgian is a bon-vivant with a critical nose for quality, who likes to take his time while eating recognisable products.*

our restaurant is situated, you just can't find ingredients of this calibre." Van Lint doesn't think it strange that a seafood dish like shrimp croquettes should have become a star culinary attraction in the Ardennes, which is nowhere near the sea. As far as he is concerned, it is a national dish, which has no parallel anywhere else in the world. "If possible, I also like to work with local products, but only on condition that they are of excellent quality." Whilst this is not possible for shrimps, he does have a local arrangement for beef with a farmer-butcher, André Magerotte from Nassogne, who rears his own Angus cattle. "He also breeds pigs, whose meat has a far superior taste to the meat of the famed Spanish pigs. His pork is full of flavour, laced with veins of juicy fat. This is the result of years of cross-breeding with different types of pig: Landras, Piétrain and at least fifty percent Duroc. And 'porc des prairies d'Ardennes' is much calmer in temperament than its Spanish equivalent, which can be more fiery and aggressive," says Daniel Van Lint, only part tongue-in-cheek!

A personal approach

Van Lint's culinary education followed classic French lines and he began his professional career in 1982 in famous establishments such as 'Villa Lorraine' and 'L'Ecailler du Palais Royal'. But instead of sticking to his classical roots, he preferred to adopt his own personal approach to cooking – a decision he has never regretted. And he regards the fact that he was eventually awarded a Michelin star – notwithstanding his individualist style – as proof that he was right. "Some of the customers who come here for the first time are surprised when they look at the menu. You can see them thinking that some of the dishes are not what they expected to find at a star-rated restaurant. I also work with top products, such foie gras, but I incorporate these into less exotic-sounding dishes, such as Liege meatballs, where they add a touch of refinement. My black pudding is also laced with foie gras, giving it an extra smoothness which brings out the full flavour of the other ingredients. For me, there is nothing creative or challenging about working exclusively with top products. It is much more difficult to create great dishes with simple products, but with a strong and authentic identity. It gives me great pleasure when I am able to achieve this. And it gives great pleasure to my customers, too!"

Le Fou est belge
Route de Givet 24, 5377 Heure-en-Famenne
086/32 28 12
www.lefouestbelge.be

In a nutshell

→ **Who or what influenced your choice of profession?**
A passion for cooking and sheer chance.

→ **What was your first culinary experience or memory?**
The 'eel in the green' (herb sauce) that my mother used to make at Christmas.

→ **What can really make you mad in the kitchen?**
That has never happened – and hopefully it never will.

→ **What is your most important personal quality?**
A calm temperament.

→ **What would you like to have more time for?**
For my children.

→ **What other job would you like to do?**
Something with the plastic arts.

→ **For you, what is the epitome of luxury?**
A simple life, enjoyed to the full and shared with my family.

→ **What are you best at in the kitchen?**
Showing proper respect for products.

→ **What do you most enjoy doing in the kitchen?**
The washing up (sometimes); it can be relaxing.

→ **What is your favourite vegetable?**
There are so many!

→ **What are you favourite aromas and smells in the kitchen?**
The juices of slow-cooked short ribs.

→ **Which small object could you not do without in the kitchen?**
A kitchen timer.

→ **Which chef has inspired you the most?**
The great classic chefs, such as Escoffier, Gaston Clément, Prosper Montagné.

→ **Who is your perfect table companion?**
Someone Someone who's mouth waters at the prospect of good food.

→ **What is your favourite aperitif?**
Champagne.

→ **What do you most enjoy eating on your day off?**
What my wife and children want to eat.

→ **What are your favourite book and your favourite cooking book?**
I don't read very much: my passion for cooking doesn't leave me much time. I'll have to catch up later...

→ **Which famous customer would you one day like to welcome, and why?**
Toots Thielemans. I met him once at a gala dinner back in the 1980s. We talked for just a few minutes, but it is clear that he is an immensely impassioned man.

Crispy seasonal salad with marinated young 'rolmops' (rolled herring)

For 4 people

4 young herring
2 two tablespoons of finely chopped, conserved shallot

For the marinade:
2 dl dry white wine
2 dl water
3 tablespoons white wine vinegar
ground pepper
4 juniper berries
1 clove
dill
thyme
laurel
juice of 1/2 lemon

crisp mixed salad, in season
vinaigrette of your choice

› Remove the bones from the herring. Stuff them with the conserved shallot and roll them up. Mix together all the ingredients for the marinade. Heat in a pan and allow to boil gently for a couple of minutes. Pour the warm liquid over the rolled herrings. Allow to stand for at least 12 hours in the fridge. Serve the 'rolmops' on a bed of crispy mixed salad, with a vinaigrette of your choice.

Black pudding with foie gras, caramelised apples, a raisin sauce and a vegetable puree

For 4 people

500 g black pudding with foie gras (or without foie gras, if preferred)
3 tablespoons of cleared butter
400 g vegetable puree on a basis of 1/3 potato and 2/3 vegetables (red beetroot, pumpkin, celeriac, etc.)

For the sauce:
caramel of 20 g sugar and a half glass of sweet white wine
1 dl veal stock or poultry stock
20 g dried raisins (sultanas)
20 g butter at fridge temperature

2 apples (Jonagold or Cox's Orange), cut into 10 segments
1 pinch of fine, white sugar
50 g dried raisins (sultanas or Corinthian raisins)

› Cut the black pudding into four pieces and colour these in a pan with the cleared butter. Depending on the thickness, place these in a warm oven at 200 °C for 12 to 18 minutes. Test with a needle to see when they are cooked. In the meantime, heat up the vegetable puree.
› Make the sauce by de-glazing the caramel with the stock. Add the raisins and beat in the butter to bind the mixture.
› Bake the apples at high temperature. Add the sugar and allow the apples to colour gently for 2 to 3 minutes in cleared butter.
› Place the black pudding onto a warm plate. Make two quenelles of vegetable puree for each plate. Serve with the apple on the black pudding and dress with the sauce.

'Pain perdu' (French toast) with caramelised apples

For 4 people

2 egg yolks
60 g white sugar (S2)
2 dl fresh cream
4 slices of white bread, 2 cm thick and
6 by 7 cm square
50 g cleared butter
2 apples (Jonagold), peeled and cut
into 10 segments
4 tablespoons of fresh cream
16 soft caramels
8 tablespoons of confectioner's cream
4 scoops of vanilla ice-cream

› Beat the egg yolks, add first the sugar and then the fresh cream. Cut slices from the bread and soak them in this mixture for 15 minutes, turning regularly.
› Caramelise the apple segments in a pan. When the apples are half cooked, fry the bread slices in a second pan.
› Warm the cream and melt the soft caramels in it. When the toasted bread is golden brown, put a stripe of confectioner's cream on each plate.
› Add a slice of toast, topped with the apples.
› Coat with the sauce and finish with a ball of vanilla ice-cream.

The preparation in 1, 2, 3

Peel the apples.

Slice the bread and remove the crusts.

Fold the sugar into the egg yolks.

Add the cream to this mixture.

Fry the apples with some sugar in a pan.

Remove the bread slices from the batter mixture and fry until golden brown.

Melt the soft caramel in the warm cream.

Spread the confectioner's cream on a plate and add a slice of browned toast, topped with apples. Coat with the caramel sauce and finish with a ball of vanilla ice-cream.

Franky Vanderhaeghe

Hostellerie St.-Nicolas

Franky Vanderhaeghe is not exactly the most well-known chef in our country. Nevertheless, this self-made man has been slowly building a reputation during the past twenty years at his restaurant in Elverdinge, which stands comparison with the very best. With his refined signature style, this quiet and reserved man mainly attracts customers from his home province of West Flanders. And the acquisition of a two-star rating in the Michelin Guide has also ensured that an increasing number of gastronomes are finding their way across the nearby border with northern France.

Every week to the early market

Following his initial training as a carpenter and woodworker, he took his first steps in the restaurant world as a washer-up. Like Ferran Adrià, it was from these humble beginnings that he began to develop his interest in real kitchen work. He quickly traded in his place at the sink for a place at the stove. He started in the kitchen of Robert Van Duuren in Brussels and went on to work in a number of other quality restaurants. Periods with Eddie Van Maele and Lucas Carton in Paris honed his technical skills. Further foreign adventures at (amongst others) Pierre Troisgros and Pierre Gagnaire added refinement and depth to his culinary vision. In 1991, at the tender age of 23, he took over the Hostellerie 'St. Nicolas' in Elverdinge. As the new century dawned, so his fame quickly began to grow. He was awarded his first Michelin star in 2003, followed by a second one just two years later. "My approach to classic cuisine is largely based on my first period with Eddie Van Maele. As far as creativity is concerned, Pierre Gagnaire has always been an important source of inspiration. Together, they helped to make me what I have become today. Once you become familiar and comfortable with a particular style as a chef, you need to focus your attention on the quality of your products. To a large extent, this determines the success or failure of the end result on the plate. This is why I still like to go every Thursday

I have always just tried to be myself and I still enjoy my work as much as on the very first day I started here.

to the early market in Brussels. I drive there after the evening service has been completed at about a quarter past eleven, arriving at the market around half past midnight. Nowadays, they open up a little earlier for people who have to travel a good distance. The big advantage is that you build up and keep a personal relationship with your suppliers. They know that I am going to be there every week, come rain or shine, and so they reserve their best products for me. This allows me to build certain guarantees into my cooking. It is also interesting from a price point of view, although you need to buy in sufficient quantities to make the drive worthwhile. Even so, I have always been prepared – and still am – to invest the time and energy necessary to ensure that my products can live up to my own high expectations. I buy my ingredients on the basis of what I see and the things that are specially recommended to me. This is a very different way of working than deciding in advance what you want, and then just sending off an e-mail with your list of requirements. I am usually back in Elverdinge by about four o'clock in the morning, so that I can grab a few hours of sleep before we begin the next day's preparations. My kitchen staff begin to arrive around eight o'clock and I join them an hour or so later. It's tough, but really worth the effort – and I wouldn't miss it for the world! My Thursday drive to Brussels has become something of a ritual. Fortunately, I can usually rely on my father to act as chauffeur! But it's a real pity that I meet fewer and fewer of my fellow-chefs there. But I still regularly bump into Lionel Rigolet of 'Comme Chez Soi' – and that's always fun."

In a nutshell

→ **Who or what influenced your choice of profession?**
My dad. He found a holiday job for me in catering.

→ **What was your first culinary experience or memory?**
The farmer's where we used to go and harvest tobacco. There they used to make everything for themselves, from bread to black pudding. I can also remember their pig's trotters and even pig's ears. Nothing went to waste.

→ **What can really make you mad in the kitchen?**
If my team are not ready on time.

→ **What is your most important personal quality?**
I am always ready to help someone (but am careful to make sure that I am not being used).

→ **What would you like to have more time for?**
My family and friends.

→ **What other job would you like to do?**
None!

→ **For you, what is the epitome of luxury?**
Good health.

→ **What do you most enjoy doing in the kitchen?**
Making sauces.

→ **What is your favourite vegetable?**
Asparagus.

→ **What is your favourite type or cut of meat?**
Entrecôte of beef (prime rib).

→ **What type(s) of fish do you like to work with?**
Scallops, langoustines and sea bass.

→ **What are your preferred herbs for fish and meat dishes?**
Tarragon and thyme.

→ **What is your favourite dish?**
Entrecôte with Béarnaise sauce and freshly-made chips.

→ **Which small object could you not do without in the kitchen?**
Tweezers.

→ **Which chef has inspired you the most?**
Pierre Gagnaire.

→ **What was the last celebrated restaurant that you visited and what was your opinion?**
Hostellerie 'Le Fox', very good.

→ **What is your worst ever culinary experience?**
Sweetbreads larded with truffle that had gone off.

→ **Who is your perfect table companion?**
My wife.

→ **What is your favourite aperitif?**
Hommel (hop) beer or St. Bernardus Tripel (a blond Trappist beer).

→ **What do you most enjoy eating on your day off?**
Asparagus à la flamande (in the Flemish manner).

→ **What are your favourite book and your favourite cooking book?**
I have so many books that it is impossible to make a choice.

→ **For whom would you one day like to cook, and why?**
Philippe Geubels, for his humour.

→ **Which famous customer would you one day like to welcome, and why?**
Tina Turner, for her fantastic music.

→ **Which famous person from the past would you like to have welcomed as a customer?**
Princess Diana.

→ **In which city would you like to live and work?**
I am very happy where I am, here in our village of Elverdinge. We are certainly going to stay here, when I retire.

Collaboration with passionete local supplies

"For the rest, I like to work with local produce, delivered fresh from the farm. This has become easier to arrange in recent years, thanks in part to a clever initiative suggested by my colleague chef Kobe Desramaults. Products are picked up from different farms by a single collection service and then delivered directly to various restaurants in the area. Good contacts with specialised and quality-driven suppliers are vital. For fish, I know I can always count on a small fishmonger's in Koksijde. Reginalt provides fish so fresh that sometimes it is still moving! This is the kind of passionate professional that I like to work with. It's exactly the same with my cheese supplier, Michel Van Tricht. I can rely on a connoisseur like Michel to tell me at their best at any given time which cheeses reach maturity at different times of the year. This means that I can always offer a seasonal selection of cheeses that is refined, complimentary and full of flavour, but with enough variety to satisfy even the most choosy cheese buffs. It is essential that suppliers understand what chefs need. My supplier of foie gras understands perfectly when I need goose liver for frying, for conserving or for making a terrine. There are different types of goose liver on the market for each of these preparations and I expect him to deliver the right type according to my requirements. If you want to run a restaurant based on quality and taste, collaboration with suppliers who are just as passionate about these values is a 'must'. Without them, it is impossible to raise the bar of your ambitions to new heights."

One star after the other

"Perhaps the location of my restaurant is a little remote, but this has an advantage: it's easier to get hold of typical farm products. My cuisine is certainly not 'rustic', but I try to take full advantage of the possibilities offered by the numerous local farmers who are growing flavour-packed agricultural produce more or less in my own backyard. I believe that this type of situation helps to determine the style and signature of a kitchen. When I first began here, I never thought that a self-made man like me would ever get a single Michelin star, let alone a second one just a few years later. I never consciously worked towards this as a specific objective, but when they came I realised that this kind of recognition requires more than just ordinary daily commitment. Fortunately, I already had this kind of commitment, so the stars have never really added any extra pressure. I have always just tried to be myself and I still enjoy my work as much as on the very first day I started here.

Once you become familiar and comfortable with a particular style as a chef, you need to focus your attention on the quality of your products.

Hostellerie St.-Nicolas
Veurnseweg 532, 8906 Elverdinge
057/20 06 22
www.hostellerie-stnicolas.com

Milk chocolate duo with avocado mousse and a rhubarb consommé

For the milk chocolate ice-cream:
1 litre milk
2 g stabiliser
12 egg yolks
150 g fine sugar
300 g milk chocolate
3 slices gelatine
50 g pro-cream (Sosa)

For the milk chocolate brownie:
450 g butter
550 g milk chocolate
10 egg yolks
800 fine sugar
8 g salt
200 g sieved flour

For the cacao meringue:
250 g egg white
40 g icing sugar
1.5 g xantana
8 g cacao
1 pinch of gold leaf foil

For the avocado mousse:
100 g sugar water
2 g mace
50 g sugar
8 slices gelatine
400 g avocado
juice of 1 lemon
125 g cream, clotted

For the rhubarb consommé:
1 litre sugar water

300 g water
500 g rhubarb
juice of 1½ lemons
per litre of consommé: 1 g malic acid
and 3 drops of rhubarb extract (Sosa)

For the rhubarb coulis:
1 kg rhubarb puree (Boiron)
100 g sugar
100 g water
10 g agaragar

For the dressing and decoration:
atsina cress
rhubarb brunoise, marinated in sugar
water with extract
rhubarb cookies, dried with sugar water,
extract and red colorant

› Boil the milk with the stabiliser. Beat the egg yolks with the fine sugar to create a light, fluffy mass (ruban). Stir the milk gradually into the ruban, without the mixture coming to the boil, and allow to simmer until a crème anglaise is formed. Add the milk chocolate and the gelatine, and allow to cool. Stir in the pro-cream. Use the resulting mixture to make ice-cream in the ice-cream machine.

› Heat the butter for the brownie and melt the chocolate in it. Beat the egg yolks with the fine sugar to create a light, fluffy mass (ruban). Add the melted chocolate to the ruban. Fold in the salt and the flour. Pour the mixture into brownie moulds and bake in the oven for 25 minutes at 180 °C.

› Beat up the egg whites. Add the icing sugar, xantana and cacao. Mix well, spoon into a piping bag and pipe out the meringue shapes. Allow to dry for 24 hours at 45 °C in a drying oven. Sprinkle with the gold leaf foil and allow to dry further.

› Bring the sugar water, mace and sugar to the boil. Stir in the gelatine and then allow to cool. Blend the avocado with the lemon juice into a puree. Add the sugar water and blend again. Finally, add the cream.

› For the rhubarb consommé, stir together the sugar water, water, rhubarb and lemon juice and place the mixture in the roner for 4 hours at 64 °C. Add the malic acid and the rhubarb extract.

› Boil the rhubarb puree with the sugar and water. Add the agaragar and allow to cook for a few minutes more.

Ceviche of yellowfin tuna with a garden cress cream, asparagus and radish

For the marinade:
100 g fresh ginger, finely chopped
1 shallot, finely chopped
2 stalks lemon grass, finely chopped
1 clove garlic, finely chopped
1 tablespoon coriander
1 tablespoon lemon verbena
1 dl sushi vinegar
juice of 2 limes
zest of 1 lime, finely grated
4 dl olive oil
pepper and salt

160 g yellowfin tuna
pepper and salt

For the garden cress cream:
250 g mayonnaise
75 g garden cress
sushi vinegar (according to preference)
1 tablespoon lemon juice
pepper and salt

For the lemon coulis:
300 g lemon juice
100 g crystal sugar
6 g agaragar
100 g water
1 g citras

4 asparagus, 2 raw and 2 cooked

For the decoration:
crispy pieces of toast
olives
some stalks of cress
slices of radish

› Mix together all the ingredients for the marinade and allow them to stand for 24 hours. Pass the marinade through a sieve.
› Cut the tuna into long strips. Season with pepper and salt. Roll up the strips tightly. Place the rolls in the marinade for 5 minutes.
› Mix the mayonnaise with the garden cress and flavour with the sushi vinegar, lemon juice, pepper and salt.
› Bring all the ingredients for the lemon coulis to the boil and keep them at boiling point for a few minutes. Allow to cool in the fridge and then mix as finely as possible.
› Dress the plate with raw asparagus, cut finely and layered on top of each other, like tiles on a roof. Arrange the marinated tuna rolls neatly on each other and add the cooked asparagus and the asparagus tips. Decorate with crisp pieces of toast, olives, the garden cress cream, the lemon coulis, some water cress and a few slices of radish.

The presentation in 1, 2, 3

> Cut the raw asparagus finely; layer the slices on top of each other, like tiles on a roof.
> Arrange the tuna rolls neatly on top of each other.
> Add the cooked asparagus and the asparagus tips.
> Add some slices of radish.
> Add some olives.
> Further dress the plate with the garden cress mayonnaise.
> Add some watercress shoots.
> Garnish with some pieces of crisp toast.
> Drizzle some drops of the lemon coulis over the finished dish.

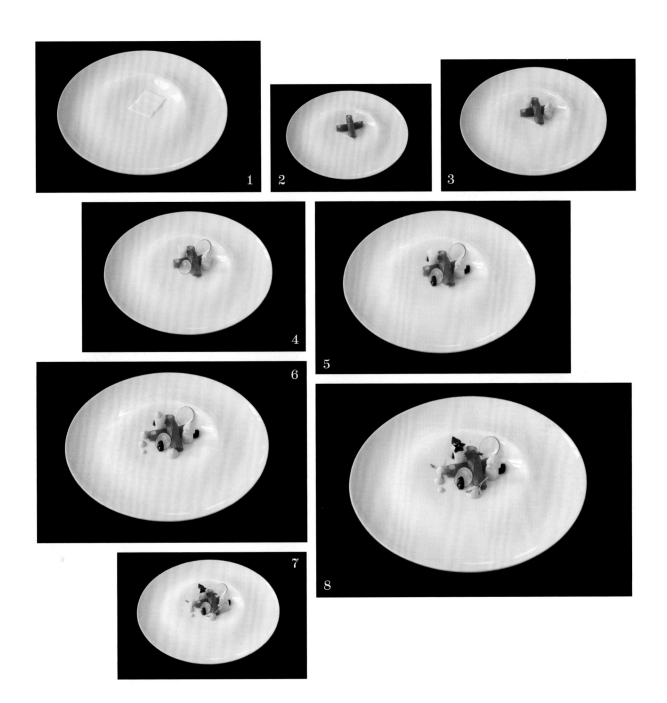

Steenvoorde pigeons with calf's tail, foie gras and peas

For 4 people

4 pigeons
2 onions
2 shallots
1 carrot
2.5 dl red port
1 dl tarragon vinegar
2 litres of calf's tail juices
butter

For the calf's tail:
2 kg calf's tail
1 onion
1 carrot

2 stalks celery
1 clove garlic
4 tablespoons tomato puree
thyme
laurel

For the potato and carrot lasagne:
6 carrots
12 potatoes
50 g cleared butter

For the kohlrabi puree:
1 kg kohlrabi (cabbage turnip)
150 g cream
pepper and salt

For the ravioli of conserved pigeon leg:
8 conserved pigeon legs
goose fat
1 shallot, finely chopped
4 pigeon livers
100 g foie gras
16 wonton skins

For the dressing:
fried mini-shiitake's
a few dots of pea puree

› Clean the pigeons. Remove the innards and keep the livers separately. Cut off the legs and the breast fillets from the carcass. Colour the carcass in the oven with the onion, shallot and carrot. Dilute with port, tarragon vinegar and the calf's tail juices. Reduce this mixture, pass it through a sieve and add some cooled butter as a thickener.
› Cut the calf's tail into pieces and colour them in the oven. In a separate pot, heat up the onion, carrot, celery and garlic. Add the tomato puree and dilute with water. Add the thyme and laurel. Cook gently for a further 2 hours. Allow to cool. Remove all the meat from the calf's tail and keep it warm.
› Cut the potatoes and carrots for the lasagne into slices with a mandolin. Cook the slices lightly in the cleared butter. Use the slices to make a lasagne 8 centimetres in height. Place in a vacuum bag and cook for a further 1 hour at 80 °C in the roner. Allow to cool and then cut to the desired thickness.
› Boil the kohlrabi in water until cooked through. Make a puree and add the cream. Season with salt and pepper.
› Conserve the pigeon legs by slow cooking them in goose fat for 1½ hours at 110 °C. Remove the meat from the legs and chop it finely. Brown the shallot, add the finely chopped pigeon livers and cook these together with the meat from the conserved legs. Remove from the heat and add the raw foie gras. Stir thoroughly and place a small amount of the mixture in the middle of a wonton skin. Moisten the edges of the skin and press on a second skin to form a sealed envelope. Use a circular cutter to make round ravioli.
› Colour the breast fillets on both sides in a pan and then cook a further 10 minutes in the oven at 160 °C. Allow the fillets to rest for 3 minutes, but keep them warm. Serve with the calf's tail, ravioli, sauce and lasagne. Dress with the mini-shiitake's and the pea puree.

INDEX

www.lannoo.com
Register on our website and we will send you a regular newsletter with information about new books
and interesting, exclusive offers.

Text: Willem Asaert and Marc Declercq
Translation: Ian Connerty
Photography: Andrew Verschetze and Kris Vlegels, photo Yves Mattagne: Jo Exelmans
Layout & design: Studio Lannoo

If you have any comments or questions, please feel free to contact our editorial team:
redactielifestyle@lannoo.com

©Uitgeverij Lannoo nv, 2013
D/2013/45/498 - NUR 440
ISBN: 978 90 209 0555 7